Security, Citizenship and Human Rights

Palgrave Politics of Identity and Citizenship Series
Series Editors: **Varun Uberoi**, University of Oxford; **Nasar Meer**, University of Southampton and **Tariq Modood**, University of Bristol

The politics of identity and citizenship has assumed increasing importance as our polities have become significantly more culturally, ethnically and religiously diverse. Different types of scholars, including philosophers, sociologists, political scientists and historians make contributions to this field and this series show-cases a variety of innovative contributions to it. Focusing on a range of differ-ent countries, and utilizing the insights of different disciplines, the series helps to illuminate an increasingly controversial area of research and titles in it will be of interest to a number of audiences including scholars, students and other interested individuals.

Titles include:
Derek McGhee
SECURITY, CITIZENSHIP AND HUMAN RIGHTS
Shared Values in Uncertain Times

Nasar Meer
CITIZENSHIP, IDENTITY AND THE POLITICS OF MULTICULTURALISM
The Rise of Muslim Consciousness

Michel Seymour (*editor*)
THE PLURAL STATES OF RECOGNITION

Palgrave Politics of Identity and Citizenship Series
Series Standing Order ISBN 978-0-230-24901-1 (hardback)
(*outside North America only*)

You can receive future titles in this series as they are published by placing a standing order. Please contact your bookseller or, in case of difficulty, write to us at the address below with your name and address, the title of the series and the ISBN quoted above.

Customer Services Department, Macmillan Distribution Ltd, Houndmills, Basingstoke, Hampshire RG21 6XS, England

Security, Citizenship and Human Rights

Shared Values in Uncertain Times

Derek McGhee
Professor of Sociology, University of Southampton, UK

palgrave
macmillan

First published 2010 by
PALGRAVE MACMILLAN

Palgrave Macmillan in the UK is an imprint of Macmillan Publishers Limited,
registered in England, company number 785998, of Houndmills,
Basingstoke, Hampshire RG21 6XS.

Palgrave Macmillan in the US is a division of St Martin's Press LLC,
175 Fifth Avenue, New York, NY 10010.

Palgrave Macmillan is the global academic imprint of the above companies
and has companies and representatives throughout the world.

Palgrave® and Macmillan® are registered trademarks in the United States,
the United Kingdom, Europe and other countries.

ISBN 978–0–230–24153–4 hardback

This book is printed on paper suitable for recycling and made from fully
managed and sustained forest sources. Logging, pulping and manufacturing
processes are expected to conform to the environmental regulations of the
country of origin.

A catalogue record for this book is available from the British Library.

A catalog record for this book is available from the Library of Congress.

10 9 8 7 6 5 4 3 2 1
19 18 17 16 15 14 13 12 11 10

Printed and bound in Great Britain by
CPI Antony Rowe, Chippenham and Eastbourne

In memory of Hector

Contents

Acknowledgements

There are numerous people I would like to thank with regard to their support in the writing of this book. I would like to thank my fellow presenters and the members of the audience for their insightful comments on the papers (parts of which have been included in the chapters of this book) I presented at a number of international conferences between 2007 and 2009 (for example, the European Association conferences in 2007 and 2009, The American Sociological Conference in 2008 and the International Sociological Association Congress in 2008). Furthermore the comments I received from other participants and the members of the audiences on the occasions when I have been asked to present papers at seminars, symposia and small conferences have also been very helpful in developing the ideas included in this book. For example, parts of a paper I presented on the Bill of Rights at the Runnymede Trust in 2009 are included in Chapter 5 of this book; I also presented aspects of Chapters 3 and 5 at The Politics of Social Cohesion Conference, hosted by the Centre for the Study of Equality and Multiculturalism at the University of Copenhagen in 2009. I was also invited by Prof. Tariq Modood, director of the Centre for the Study Ethnicity and Citizenship at Bristol University to present a paper (parts of which is included in Chapter 3). In 2008 I presented a paper (based on parts of Chapter 1) at the AHRC/ESRC-funded Religion and Community Cohesion workshop hosted by the Centre for Global and Transnational Politics at Royal Holloway. Also in 2008 I was invited to present a paper at a one-day seminar on War on Terror: Policy and Legislative Responses held at the Bristol Institute of Public Affairs, Bristol University, which included parts of Chapter 2. In terms of publications, an early version of Chapter 3 was published in *Patterns of Prejudice* under the title 'The Paths to Citizenship: A Critical Examination of Immigration Policy in Britain Since 2001', volume 43 (1), pp. 41–64. I would like to thank the editor and the anonymous reviewers for their very helpful comments on this article. I owe the proposal reviewer and manuscript reviewer (in this case the same person) selected by Palgrave Macmillan a great deal of thanks for their insightful comments and suggestions for improving the overall presentation of the book.

As well as the above I would like to thank a number of academics who have in various ways offered advice, support and suggestions in conversations, in responding to papers and in the reading draft chapters: Andrew Mason, David Owen, Neil Chakraborti, Varun Uberoi, Nasar Meer, Gabe Mythen, Dave Whyte, Basia Spalek, Frank Gregory, Tariq Modood, Tony McGrew, Tony Breslin, Liz Fekete and Ellie Vasta.

I would also like to thank friends (you know who you are) and family, especially, Andy and the Cullis family and my parents, Jeanette and John, for all of their support in the writing of this book.

Preface

The idea of writing this book emerged out of the final chapter of my previous book *The End of Multiculturalism? Terrorism, Integration and Human Rights* (Open University Press) in which I briefly speculated on some of the discourses, policies and proposals that emerged in the first few months of Gordon Brown's premiership. By the time I submitted *The End of Multiculturalism?* for publication in the autumn of 2007, Gordon Brown had only been in office for a few months. At this time, the Prevent (counter-terrorism community policing) strategy had just been introduced and the managed migration points system which was introduced in the Immigration, Asylum and Nationality Act 2006 had not come into force yet (it came into force in March 2008). Furthermore the proposals for the creation of a Statement of British Values and a potential Bill of Rights and Duties had been introduced in *The Governance of Britain* Green Paper just a few months before in July 2007. The purpose of writing this book, *Security, Citizenship and Human Rights: Shared Values in Uncertain Times*, is to follow-up on these and other areas of public policy under Gordon Brown. However, in a number of chapters of this book I compare and contrast the differences, similarities, continuities and discontinuities in the approaches adopted by Blair and Brown to a range of areas of public policy, for example, counter-terrorism, immigration, integration, citizenship and human rights.

Security, Citizenship and Human Rights: Shared Values in Uncertain Times includes chapters that take on critical and sometimes normative perspective with regard to some of the most high-profile aspects of Britain's public policy arena: counter-terrorism, immigration, citizenship, human rights and even the 'equalities' agenda in the context of the economic downturn. The chapters in the book also offer an examination of the shifting discourses of 'shared values' and human rights in contemporary Britain.

One of the arguments at the centre of the book is that citizenship is being remade and remoulded around public security in the context of a culture of fear in contemporary Britain. The major question posed in this book is do policy and legislation driven and legitimized by fear strengthen or weaken 'our' sense of citizenship, shared values and commitment to human rights? A further argument is made in the book concerning the 'politics of fear', that is, it not only leads to 'value trouble' it also leads to what Parekh calls hierarchical thinking with regard to deciding whose human rights come first. As well as including chapters that explore 'fear'-driven policy making with regard to counter-terrorism, immigration, citizenship and human rights, this book also contains chapters that examine evidence of examples of what will be tentatively called here 'the politics of hope' in the arena of British public policy dedicated to promoting procedural fairness and greater equalities. It will be suggested in these chapters that glimmers of a politics of hope are evident in debates with regard to the extension of human rights protections and the developments with regard to the new 'equalities' legislation in the UK. It will be argued here that rather than the authoritarian deployment of the discourse of 'British shared values' and the hierarchical, rebalancing discourses with regard to human rights proffered by politicians in the name of public security, the politics of hope is associated with encouraging debates on what 'our' shared values actually are and should be and the formal role these values ought to play in 'our' constitutional framework, including underwriting a potential Bill of Rights in the UK.

Introduction: Value Trouble

> A community's dominant values and ideals are never transparent and unambiguous. They are precipitates of different historical experiences and its members' attempts to make sense of them, and are not and cannot be a matter of simple discovery.
>
> *Parekh 2008: 60*

The chapters contained in this book are an exploration of 'the politics' of security, citizenship and human rights in contemporary Britain. 'Politics' here is being used to express in shorthand a world of political debate, government and parliamentary discourses and government and parliamentary artefacts in the form of Green Papers, White Papers, Select and other Committee Reports and Parliamentary debates. Each chapter in this book will analyse and explore these policy regimes, for example, on 'security', extremism, citizenship, integration, immigration, as well as, later in the book, on questions of national identity with regard to who 'we' are and what 'we' stand for. At the same time, in each chapter I will explore the relationship between these policy regimes and human rights in the context of an overarching discourse of 'shared values'.

The book is an exploration of both a 'politics of fear' and a 'politics of hope' (and the tensions that exist between them); as such the book presents what to some might be an uneasy crossover between the critical examination of policy and policy developments in the areas of public policy mentioned earlier, yet also includes chapters that are less critical than speculative, in that they attempt to speculate in these uncertain times what might happen in the future. I describe this combination of approaches as an uneasy crossover because they contain both a critical analysis of public policy (see Chapters 1, 2, 3 and 4) and elements of normative political philosophy (see Chapter 5 and 6). The first four chapters of the book contain chapters that are dedicated to exploring the new politics of security, control and vigilance associated with a number of high-profile policy developments in recent years, for example, preventative and pre-emptive counter-terrorism, managed migration and new border controls. I refer to these as examples of a politics of fear. In contrast the last three chapters tease out some alternative discourses, policy developments and proposals which could lead Britain out of the grip of the politics of fear. The latter is associated with attempts (1) to mobilize the country around a Bill of Rights; (2) to promote a sense of belonging to an evolving and inclusive polity; and (3) to extend the human rights protections in the name of greater equality. I describe these as evidence of a precarious politics of hope.

As noted earlier, there are a number of recurrent themes (and tensions) that will emerge in the chapters contained in this book with regard to 'security', safety, human rights and 'shared values'. For example, in Chapters 2 and 4, I explore proposals whereby human rights are to be rebalanced in order to ensure that the rights of the law abiding majority come first; while in Chapter 6, I examine debates with regard to extending 'equalities' policies (which also includes debates on the rebalancing of human rights in terms of giving greater priority to social and economic rights). With regard to 'shared values' this collection of norms, principles, virtues, aspirations and in some cases rights, seems to shift and change and is dependent on who (in terms of politicians) is attempting to articulate them and for what purpose. In a number of chapters in the book it will be noted that when these 'shared values' (especially when they are described as 'British shared values') are being invoked it is usually for the purpose of encouraging a sense of enmity rather than amity especially when they are invoked to make 'us' see what is at stake and what is threatening to 'us'. That is, these, not particularly British, universal and abstract values[1] are often deployed for particular purposes with regard to shoring up our sense of security and protection. For example, they give 'us' security, yet at the same time they are presented as being vulnerable in the face of new threats (Chapter 2); furthermore, they are also presented as giving 'us' an identity in that they, according to politicians, tell 'us' who 'we' are and what 'we' stand for (Chapter 5); they are also presented in authoritarian terms as the yardstick for measuring the degree of commitment in the applicants for British citizenship (Fekete 2008: 15) and as a measure of the 'integration' of established communities of immigration in Britain (see Chapters 3 and 4). The 'shared values' discourse is polyvalent in its applicability, it has multiple uses and it has become 'strategic' in a number of intersecting policy areas. Therefore, one of the central arguments that connects the chapters contained in this book is that just as citizenship is being remade and remoulded around, for example, public security (see Chapter 2); what Gordon Brown calls 'our' historically enduring and institutionalized 'British shared values' are also being remade and remoulded to fit the uncertain times 'we' live in. The multiple uses of the discourse of 'shared values' is evident in Gordon Brown's introduction to the book *Being British: The Search for Values that Bind the Nation*. For example:

> With a clearer sense of who we are and of the values we share, we are far better equipped as a country to manage constitutional change, citizenship and security, and – with a clearer sense of our common national purpose – to address the challenges that Britain faces in a rapidly changing world.
>
> (Brown 2009a: 34)

'Shared values' therefore become the bulwark, the yardstick, the life raft and 'our' ultimate security in the face of what are presented as 'new' and unpredictable threats (see Chapters 1, 2 and 3), they are what unites 'us' and they are also supposed to provide us with a place of commonality, identity and belonging in multicultural societies among all of 'our' diversity and multiplicity in a fast-changing and turbulent world (see Chapter 5). Furthermore politicians tell us that these shared values are institutionalized and expressed through 'our' historically and enduring British institutions (also Chapter 5) yet, these same values are also talked of in exploratory terms, as needing to be discovered, debated, agreed upon and ultimately written down and hence constitutionalized (see Chapters 4 and 6). With regard to the latter, what I am referring to is the proposal to launch a national debate on shared values (in terms of discovering *the* 'values' the 'British public' deem to be 'their' 'fundamental' values). It is proposed that these 'shared values' will then be included in a statement of shared values in the preamble to a potential British Bill of Rights (see Chapters 4 and 6). In this sense 'our' 'British shared values' are a concoction of certainty and uncertainty, deployed in the politics of fear (associated with security, exclusion, restriction and defensiveness in the face of 'threats') and in the politics of hope (associated with finding common ground and giving clarity and legislative force to 'our' collective living together through playing a crucial role in underwriting a future Bill of Rights). It is for this reason that my approach to examining the different uses of the discourse of shared values is diverse and necessarily multidisciplinary. Yet more than this, in order to explore the multiplicity of the deployment of the discourse of shared values across numerous examples of public policies I have indulged in both critical and normative analyses. This has in turn led to the creation of a tension in the book between scepticism and optimism with regard to the place and role of shared values in contemporary Britain. That is, scepticism with regard to how the discourse of 'British' shared values is and has been articulated by politicians in security, citizenship and integration discourses (see Chapters 1, 2, 3 and 4). Yet at the same time, I indulge in a degree of optimism with regard to the potential role that core values could play in the processes suggested for generating a statement of British values that would form the preamble to a potential Bill of Rights in the UK (see Chapters 5 and 6). This tension between my scepticism and optimism with regard to shared values unfolds in the context of considerable 'value trouble'. I fully endorse Bhikhu Parekh's statement (see the opening quotation of this chapter) with regard to 'a community's dominant values'. For Parekh, these values are never transparent and unambiguous, they cannot just be discovered or worse used (in contradictory ways) for political short-term gain, without consequences.

In many ways the 'troubled' nature of the emergent discourse of human rights and 'shared values' in contemporary Britain alluded to in the title of this Introduction, is a wider problem facing the West in the form of what van den Brink calls the 'crisis in integrity' (2007: 351). This crisis of integrity is associated with Fekete's injunction that 'western values' are often only observed 'in their breach' (2009: ix). There is, and this will be explored in Chapter 4, a conflict between the rights of citizens and the rights of Others in contemporary Britain. This is usually expressed in terms of what Parekh calls a 'hierarchical view of rights' (2006: 22) associated with debates on whose rights should come first and how the application of human rights legislation in the courts should reflect this (see Chapter 2). In other chapters I will explore the breach of the universality principle of human rights when politicians such as Jack Straw promote a conditional relationship between responsibilities and rights in the debates on the Bill of Rights (see Chapter 4). Furthermore, in Chapter 1 I will examine the ignoble practices associated with deterring and preventing those seeking asylum from reaching the UK in the context of our international obligations as signatories of the 1951 Geneva Convention relating to refugees. In these instances 'our' shared values of, for example, tolerance, equality, the respect for the rule of law, human rights, fair play and anti-discrimination become troubled by political leaders and troublesome for them. These 'shared values' are invoked and breached, in some cases, simultaneously. Human rights, shared values and the inclusive and exclusive boundaries of British citizenship and belonging are the main themes to be explored in this book in the context of a wider 'security, safety and protection' *dispositif*.[2] It is by adding the prefix 'public' to these already loaded words, in the form of 'public security', 'public safety' and 'public protection' that politicians can be observed in attempting to 'stabilize by attachment' their interrelated 'security' strategies, policies and programmes (Baker, Graham and Scott 2009: xvii). Thus 'security' in this *dispositif* is co-opted by moral reasoning through attachment to the word 'public' which in turn enlists other moral vocabularies such as 'duty' and 'responsibility'; it is in this process that 'moral terms gain their interpretative weight' (Baker, Graham and Scott 2009: xvii). It is through the shifting effects of these moralizing co-options in the context of the attempt to control 'our' uncertain future that the pre-emptive turn can be observed. The first three chapters of the book can be described as an elaboration on the dangers associated with a pre-emptive politics of protection. This variety of politics with all its 'public security' and 'public reassurance' rhetoric has a tendency to undermine the very values and institutions they claim to be protecting and securing. The much mentioned 'British shared values' of equality, tolerance, fair play, anti-discrimination, respect for the rule of law and human rights which will be presented by a number of politicians throughout the chapters included in this book are precisely the values, norms, virtues, rights and principles that come under fire in the pre-emptive politics associated with the strategies of increasing public security (see Chapters 2 and 4) and of reassuring the public through evermore restrictive asylum, immigration and naturalization policies (see Chapters 1 and 3).

It is for this reason that in the more normative and 'philosophical' chapters contained in the book (see Chapters 5 and 6) I attempt to promote what I consider to be the appropriate place, role and articulation of shared values in conjunction with human rights in Britain. Thus, this book is not just given over to the exploration of the pre-emptive politics of fear, it also attempts to explore glimpses of what I tentatively call a politics of hope with regard to the deployment of the discourse of 'shared values' and in proposals with regard to Britain's evolving human rights policy. It is through exploring the occasions where examples of 'value trouble' are exposed, challenged and corrected by, for example, powerful parliamentary select committees such as the Joint Committee on Human Rights (see Chapters 4 and 6) that proposals which could lead to alternative human rights cultures are observable. In these instances 'shared values' are to be forged through a national debate on what 'our' values are and how they should be used (see Chapters 4 and 6). By institutionalizing shared values in an explicit way, for example, in the preamble to a Bill of Rights, a proper culture of human rights which could be underwritten by an explicit set of truly shared values[3] might emerge.

In many ways this book offers an account of how the concepts of 'security' and 'citizenship' are intricately related. What I mean by this is that it is through the lens of 'security', or more accurately 'public security', that one can observe the processes through which citizenship is being remade and remoulded in contemporary Britain. In a number of chapters I critically engage with particular strategies and policies associated with addressing what is viewed as a weak sense of citizenship in Britain and how these concerns are projected onto newcomer and established communities of immigration in Britain.

Ted Cantle notes (without acknowledging the part he has played in this, see Chapter 3) that in the last few years British citizenship has become 'value-laden', it has become overtaken by the necessity of 'social responsibility' and upholding 'common values' (Cantle 2008: 129). I must agree that citizenship in Britain and the processes of naturalization that have been introduced in recent years are associated more with a discourse of 'lack' and of 'weakness' than with a celebration of what it means to be a British citizen. Furthermore, the often authoritarian discourse of Britishness that has emerged in recent years has added to this assumption of 'lack' and 'absence' in particular communities in Britain (see Chapter 5). This has resulted in the extension of the requirements of naturalization and the proposals for extending these even further (see Chapter 3). In this regard citizenship in the context of the requirement that new and established communities of immigration 'accept and share' British values (Chapters 3 and 4) has become a stick to beat particular communities with. In the last two chapters of the book, I explore alternative ways of belonging, which bypass the emphasis on 'belonging together' and the promotion of overarching national identities found in, for example, liberal and ethnic nationalisms. It will be suggested in these chapters that these alternative ways of belonging also have the potential to extend the parameters of the various civic nationalist (associated with Gordon Brown, see Chapter 5) and civic integration and civic identity projects (associated with David Blunkett, see Chapter 3) to instead explore the potential for what Habermas calls an ethical solidarity through a consensus, not on 'shared values' but on 'procedural fairness'. It is therefore through the opportunities for forging a variant of constitutional patriotism through the process of creating a Bill of Rights and Freedoms in Britain that I will explore the potential for the facilitation of new ways of being British which is associated with new ways of belonging to an evolving polity which is symbolized by a Bill of Rights (see Chapters 5 and 6).

Organization of the book

Chapter 1

This chapter is an exploration of the pre-emptive politics associated with the new offshore border controls and the UK's recent 'preventative' counter-terrorism strategies focusing on local Muslim communities. I decided to locate this chapter at the beginning of the book as it brings together two very different (yet similar) programmes dedicated to enhancing 'public security' in the UK. The programmes under examination in this chapter therefore ground my analysis of the intersecting policy regimes (of, for example, counter-terrorism, immigration and citizenship) with 'real' repercussions for particular communities and individuals. In the chapter I will suggest that both the new border controls and the preventative counter-terrorism strategies are pre-emptive in terms of their proactive attempts to identify 'risky' or 'at risk' individuals in order to prevent them from coming to the UK (in a 'security continuum' which includes extremists, illegal immigrants and asylum seekers) or preventing individuals (mostly young Muslims) from engaging in extremist violence. These external and internal 'security' programmes are dedicated to the identification of certain individuals in a particular 'politics of harm' which encourages heightened vigilance in society. 'The risky' and the 'at-risk' are to be identified under these strategies through 'high-technology' (for example, biometrics) and 'low-technology' (for example, internal community surveillance) dataveillance and surveillance techniques in the context of an emergent 'knowledge economy' in which 'the State' is both rolled back and rolled forward as 'the border' is exported to new 'European frontiers' and new internal borders of surveillance which are relocated through the enrolment of local Muslim communities, families and neighbours in the new requirements of vigilance in which they are implicated in the search for the signs of 'enmity' among their own in the name of 'public security'. In this chapter I analyse the place of 'shared values' in the moralizing discourse of fighting 'the good fight' against extremism in the context of the Prevent strategy. However, in this chapter I also explore the 'value' trouble that the 'security continuum' (Bigo 1994) introduces in the UK with regard to the plight of asylum seekers and 'our' obligations under the 1951 Geneva Convention on Refugees.

Chapter 2

In this chapter attention shifts away from the pre-emptive policies of 'security' in the form of the new border controls and preventative counter-terrorism strategies to focus directly on the shifting definitions of 'security' in politicians' discourse and in the academic field of Politics and International Relations. This chapter will explore a number of theoretical and conceptual developments in and through the expression of academic debates and developments in UK 'security' policy terms. The focus of the chapter is on the different ways recent Prime Ministers (Blair and Brown) and senior members of their cabinets have attempted to 'achieve' a consensus on counter-terrorism legislation. In this chapter I employ both securitization and desecuritization theory and the widening, broadening and dedifferentiating definitions of 'security' in International Relations debates as the context from whence to explore the different attempts at achieving consensus on counter-terrorism in recent labour governments. The central argument made in this chapter is that the National Security Strategy introduced by Gordon Brown has had the effect of personalizing and humanizing 'security' (thus mirroring the debates in International Relations) and by so doing has opened up the possibility for linking counter-terrorism legislation to what has become the ultimate shared or core value in the UK, namely, personal safety through the promise of 'public security'. In this chapter I suggest that the knock-on effect related to the emergence of public security and thus personal safety as the ultimate value in the face of what are described as unprecedented threats is that the application of human rights could be rebalanced to reflect these ultimate 'values'.

Chapter 3

This chapter takes observations with regard to the biopolitics of 'public' safety and security in Chapters 1 and 2 further in the analysis of Britain's managed migration strategy. It explores the combination of the management migration points system with Gordon Brown's proposals for introducing yet another layer of citizenship tests to ensure that naturalizing citizens of the future 'earn' their British citizenship. It is Brown's intention to make sure that the highly selective managed migration points system works in tandem with the new tougher citizenship-testing regime. It will be suggested in this chapter that in order to fully understand the extent and potential impact of these combined strategies we have to employ concepts that capture the complexity of these developments. In the chapter I suggest that institutional racialization, rather than institutional racism, can help us grasp the multiple layers of exclusions and restrictions associated with these new immigration and naturalization policies. It will be suggested in this chapter that in this context institutional racialization can be observed in the calibration of the desirability and undesirability of would be immigrants in geographical, cultural and economic terms. It will be suggested here that Gordon Brown's proposals that his 'shared values'-centric, new 'earned' British citizenship tests should work in tandem with the managed migration strategy is an example of a preemptive neo-biopolitics dedicated to ensuring 'public security' against future episodes of disorder (for example, disturbances such as 'race riots' and 'home grown' extremism) and ensuring the prosperity of 'the nation' against the further importation of low-skilled, non-European Economic Area (EEA) immigrants who might fail to integrate sufficiently in economic, cultural and social terms. It will also be suggested in this chapter that these proposals are also the site for the emergence of heterogeneous and indiscrete regimes of power – biopower, but also governmental and sovereign power.

Chapter 4

In this chapter I explore the government's (under Blair and Brown) relationship with the Human Rights Act (this act introduced many aspects of the European Convention on Human Rights (ECHR) into British law in 1998). I will examine the tension that has arisen between what will be called here the politics of civic citizenship and the universality of human rights. As well as tracing the governments' on and off relationship with the Human Rights Act I will also examine the place of the Human Rights Act in Britain's evolving human rights culture, especially the creation of a British Bill of Rights (as proposed by the late Labour leader John Smith). This chapter explores the governments' (and David Cameron's) proposals for increasing 'security', responsibility and a sense of Britishness and citizenship with regard to the creation of the potential British Bill of Rights and Responsibilities. At the same time I will explore Liberty's and the Joint Committee on Human Rights' responses to the governments' (and David Cameron's) proposals for enhancing 'public security', social responsibility and strengthening citizenship through a potential Bill of Rights. In each case Liberty and the Joint Committee on Human Rights found that the governments' actions with regard to the Human Rights Act and their proposals for a British Bill Of Rights and Responsibilities colludes with rather than challenges the tabloid hostility to human rights in Britain. This chapter can be described as being a bridge between the normative analysis of the final two chapters of the book which explore, among other things such questions as who 'we' are, and what 'we' stand for and the first three chapters of the book which critically examine the pre-emptive policies and strategies with regard to asylum seekers, extremism and immigration (and the consequences of immigration). This chapter explores further the governments' attempted modification of the application of human rights in favour of who they perceived to be the deserving recipients of these rights, namely, the responsible, law abiding citizens who accept and share British values.

Chapter 5

In this chapter I will examine recent debates on Britishness, 'British shared values' and multicultural, multiracial and multiethnic identities in the UK. I will also examine the discourses associated with determining who 'we' are and what 'we' stand for. In order to do this I explore these questions by critically examining the relationship between Britishness, British citizenship and the 'shared British values' discourse found in Tony Blair and Gordon Brown's archive of speeches and through examining two theoretical traditions: (a) liberal nationalism with its emphasis on national identity and 'belonging together' and (b) Andrew Mason and Bhikhu Parekh's emphasis on 'belonging to the polity'. In this chapter I take Mason and Parekh's observations with regard to the latter further through employing Charles Taylor's concept of deep diversity, in which different groups of people living in multicultural societies belong to the polity in diverse ways. It might appear strange to some readers that this review of these literatures should appear in the penultimate chapter contained in this book. However, in this chapter I present this literature review (that is, Mason and Parekh's work on belonging to the polity and Taylor's theory with regard to the multiple ways people belong to a polity) for the purpose of contextualizing the debates surrounding the creation of a Bill of Rights in the UK. In order to do this I also explore Jurgen Habermas' writings on constitutional patriotism for teasing out some of the potential with regard to the creation of new ways of belonging to an evolving polity symbolized by a Bill of Rights. That is a Bill of Rights that has been sanitized of the government's intended exclusivity (as a British Bill of Rights for British citizens) and conditionality (that rights are conditional on responsibilities).

Chapter 6

In this chapter I further explore the creation of a Bill of Rights as a vehicle for promoting new ways of belonging to the polity in the UK. Furthermore this chapter provides an opportunity, in a different set of public policy arenas, for considering the questions of security, citizenship, shared values and human rights that are central to the other chapters included in this book. In this chapter I delve a little deeper into Habermas' political philosophy of constitutional patriotism, especially with regard to the 'ethical solidarity' that is made possible through procedural fairness. I describe the variant of constitutional patriotism made possible through the creation of a Bill of Rights as being procedurally 'thin' in terms of generating 'ethical solidarity' but also potentially 'thick' with regard to emotional and patriotic attachments. Particular 'values' and principles are explored in this chapter, namely fairness and equality. Fairness and equality are explored here not just as abstract and neutral values and principles. In this chapter I examine an unfolding 'politics of equality' in the UK associated with the recent Equalities Review, Discrimination Law Review and with regard to the debates on the introduction of ECHR + social and economic rights in a potential Bill of Rights. This chapter explores the debates on equalities, discrimination and especially social and economic rights in the context of the tensions that exist in actualizing these rights with regard to concerns over the sovereignty of parliament, the power of the judiciary and the statutory/constitutional split with regard to discrimination legislation. In this chapter I suggest that the simplification of discrimination law and the incorporation of an interpretative clause with regard to equality and fairness in the preamble of a potential Bill of Rights could usher in a new, fairer, more equal Britain.

1

Pre-Emptive Securities – Border Controls and Preventative Counter-Terrorism

1.1 Introduction

This is the first of two chapters that focus on emergent 'security' rhetoric and practices in contemporary Britain, namely, security through recourse to the discourse of 'public security'. In this chapter and the next, these political discourses will be connected to policies, strategies and real effects on particular targeted communities, especially asylum seekers, illegal migrants and Muslims in Britain. In the next chapter I will focus on the theoretical developments in political and academic discourses on 'security' and how this has had an impact on the application of human rights in the UK. Prior to that, in this chapter I will examine some of the social and political effects with regard to 'high-technology' surveillance practices and border controls (in section 1.2) and also 'low-technology' community-focused counter-terrorism activities under the Prevent strategy (in section 1.3). Both of these developments will be presented here in terms of what Louise Amoore calls an emergent politics of 'watchfulness' in the form of a vigilant visuality (2007: 215) in contemporary Britain.

Many commentators have suggested that it is in the arena of surveillance technologies that the imbalance between civil liberties and security techniques is most marked. In this chapter I will explore the underlying motivations and context behind the developments with regard to surveillance, dataveillance and biometric documentation in the new border controls and I will suggest that similar motivations can be detected in the developments in British counter-terrorism policing in local areas under Prevent. It will be suggested here that both the high-technology border controls and the low-technology responsibilization processes associated with internal-community surveillance in Muslim communities in the UK under Prevent are pre-emptive security strategies. These strategies are associated with the task of proactively identifying or recognizing a range of targeted individuals, for example, 'unsafe' travellers, failed asylum seekers and (in the Prevent strategy) individuals at risk of becoming extremists in Britain, for the purpose of early intervention in the name of 'traveller' and 'public security'.

The new border controls have been introduced to try to keep 'dangerous' individuals out of the UK (and off transportation vehicles, especially air travel) through offshore border controls informed by transnational dataveillance systems, in what Bigo calls the ban-opticon *dispositif* (2006a: 16). On the other hand, the Prevent strategy is dedicated to identifying those already in the UK who are suspected of being extremists or those thought to be at risk of becoming extremists, in order to interrupt their potential future violent extremist activities. I will suggest in the chapter that these two examples of pre-emptive and proactive interventions can be described as highly visual, surveillant practices associated with a new politics of vigilance (Amoore 2007). I will argue here that these activities are also evidence of an unfolding politics of harm (section 1.2) and vulnerability (section 1.3) in the context of the powerful discourse of 'public security' in the UK. The purpose of this chapter is to explore concrete examples with regard to developments in public policy (border controls and preventative counter-terrorism) with the intention of contextualizing the argument that I will make in the next chapter, namely, that 'public security' is becoming the ultimate value in an emergent hierarchy of values in contemporary Britain.

It is undeniable that all of the profiling, surveillance and dataveillance in these new border controls amount to what Judith Butler calls an 'amorphous racism' (2006: 39) associated with a heightened post-9/11 surveillance of what she calls 'Arab peoples' and 'anyone who looks vaguely Arab according to the dominant racial imaginary' (Butler 2006: 39). However, it will be suggested here that the internal community surveillance associated with the local policing strategies under the Prevent strategy are more complex than the amorphous racism associated with, for example the profiling of 'safe' and 'unsafe' travellers which will be examined in section 1.2. The Prevent strategy, in the end, evokes myriad emotions and feelings (fear, love and loyalty) and various ambivalent subject positions in which various actors (Muslims in particular) are cast, for example, as responsible citizens, the members of a suspect community and perhaps even the relatives and neighbours of someone deemed to be an 'extremist' or who is suspected of being 'at risk' of becoming an extremist.

In summary, therefore, section 1.2 is an exploration of the political pursuit of certainty symbolized by the faith in biometric documentation and registration for keeping 'external' danger and harm at bay; and section 1.3 is an exploration of the limits of certainty and technology associated with the insecurity and unknowability of 'inner' home-grown threats. By bringing these two different 'security' threats and interventions together I trouble the assumptions that the new technologies of surveillance and control are associated with a neoliberal rolling back of the state (Monahan 2006; Lyon 2006). In this chapter I demonstrate that they are and they are not. The new border control strategies across the European Union (EU) are prime examples of the rolled back state and rolled back borders, that is, dissolving internal borders and (re)territorialized external borders/frontiers made possible through technological and political co-ordination. However, at the same time, the new border control measures such as e-borders, identity cards and associated databases and the Prevent policing strategies can be described as the state (in the form of numerous agencies and government departments) rolling ever forward and ever deeper into the lives of, for example, non-EEA nationals and asylum seekers (with regard to biometric technologies) and into the lives of particular Muslim communities in the name of public safety and early intervention (with regard to Prevent strategies).

1.2 Border control – the vigilant visuality of the dangerous/undesirable other

In Europe, according to Fekete (2004), there were two options for EU member states with regard to the incorporation of the EU Common Position and Framework Decision issued by the European Commission (EC) after 9/11. Some, the UK in particular, introduced state of emergency legislation and new anti-terrorist laws, while other EU member states, for example Spain, amended existing public order, criminal justice and aliens' legislation and extended police powers (Fekete 2004: 6). As a result of the special legislation that the UK has introduced, the UK comprises of an appropriate case to explore the question of the balance between civil liberties and national security which will be elaborated on in different chapters of this book (see especially in Chapters 2 and 4). For example, the UK has already acted upon tensions that have arisen between national security and international law and conventions by adopting particular policies. For example, the UK is the only EU member state to have derogated from Article 5 (right to liberty) of the European Convention on Human Rights and Fundamental Freedoms in order to introduce indefinite detention without charge for foreign national terror suspects under part 4 of the Anti-Terrorism, Crime and Security Act

2001 (McGhee 2008a, 2008b). The UK has also introduced mechanisms under which they can contravene the principle of non-refoulement established in Article 33 (1) of the 1951 Geneva Convention Relating to the Status of Refugees that prohibits contracting states to expel or return a refugee to the frontiers of territories where their life and freedom would be threatened (Fekete 2005). Section 54 of the Immigration, Asylum and Nationality Act 2006 allows the Home Secretary to automatically refuse asylum in Britain to those suspected of being involved in terrorist activities (McGhee 2008a, 2008b).

Rather than examining counter-terrorism legislation directly[1] this section will take a rather more indirect route to exploring a related aspect of Britain's new 'security' arsenal, namely border control. In this section the emphasis will be on the particular effects the UK's new border control measures will have in the context of free movement within the EU in terms of separating out 'safe' from 'unsafe travellers' but also the wider effects on those attempting to claim asylum in the UK. As will also be noted in the next chapter, when it comes to the threat from terrorism, especially with regard to public transport and air travel there is a great deal of public acceptance of the routines of surveillance (Bigo 2006b: 47). A number of authors have given us some pause for thought with regard to the price that 'our' personal safety as air travellers comes with, especially for others. Behind the convenience, albeit in the context of increasingly surveilled air travel, there is a burgeoning transnational bureaucracy of exclusion and restriction which begins before a passenger has even boarded a plane destined for the UK. On the whole, passengers are pleased to be the object of ubiquitous forms of mostly unobtrusive but nonetheless all-pervasive tracking and surveillance practices (van der Ploeg 2006), if it means they have protection against danger (Bigo 2006b). However, behind this veneer of personal safety (through faith in surveillant and dataveillant technologies) is a globalized acceptance of what Lyon (2003b, 2006) describes as 'surveillant sorting' practices. What is clear is that these developments have divergent effects on different types of 'travellers'. The result of this is that there is evidence of a speeding up of the mobility of the privileged few and the slowing down or restricted mobility of those deemed less desirable (Lyon 2006: 196). Thus, 'our' personal safety when travelling by air comes with a certain indifference to the plight of 'undesirable travellers' (e.g. asylum seekers) and also those individuals identified as terrorist suspects through ignoble and perhaps inaccurate and illegal intelligence-gathering techniques operational during the war on terror. Bauman's sound bite 'divided we move' (1998: 85) captures the emergent stratification of mobility through the parallel processes of stratifying dangerousness (Huysmans 2006: 97) between the cosmopolitan first world and the often surreptitious and dangerous journeys made by second world travellers (Bauman 1998: 89).

Technology, identity and safety

Gordon Brown taps into what Guild et al. describe as the establishment of the antithetical values, namely 'freedom' and 'security' in political discourses associated with contemporary border control systems (in Vaughan-Williams 2008: 66). In his foreword to the Cabinet Office's *Security in a Global Hub* report of 2007 Gordon Brown justified the restructuring of the UK's border agencies, thus: 'The United Kingdom's border controls need to protect us against terrorism and crime, while encouraging the flows of people and trade on which our future as a global hub depends' (Brown, in Cabinet Office 2007a: Foreword). Taking the theme of the balance between freedom and security further, Huysmans suggests that the practical realization of free movement in the EU is a matter of 'the governing of the conduct of freedom through objectifying and controlling dangers' (2006: 97). 'Freedom' in this context, or more accurately what Nikolas Rose refers to as 'the exercise of freedom' requires 'proof of legitimate identity' (in Lyon 2008: 36). The twin desires to objectify and control dangers in the context of unprecedented mobility has resulted in technocratic and technological advancements in border controls, which will be the focus of this section. In practice what the freedom/security balance at 'the border' comes down to is a marked bifurcation in that 'borders can be barriers for some but gateways for others' and they 'serve as either opportunity for or restriction on mobility depending on who you are' (Rumford 2008: 2). For Bauman, these developments are evidence of what he calls 'the ambivalence of identity' associated with the imposition of the twin poles of 'oppression and liberation' (2004: 8). With regard to travel and mobility, van der Ploeg refers to these developments as heralding 'the politics of technological identification' (2006: 179) in which questions of identity and identification have become increasingly central to citizenship and indeed the ordinary everyday life in today's society (Lyon 2008: 35).

Politicians, including Gordon Brown, have put enormous faith (and resources) into new technological solutions with regard to objectifying and controlling dangers. According to Brown, in the new world of new threats 'the government must work out how it best discharges its duty to protect people. New technology is giving us the modern means by which we can discharge these duties' (2008a: 1). Brown is also correct when he says that 'we need to employ these modern means to protect people from new threats, we must at the same time do more to guarantee our liberties' (2008: 1).

In many ways, Bigo is right when he says that the emergent politics of national and internal security both molilizes and plays upon fear and unease to legitimize itself (Bigo, in Walters 2004: 141). Particular developments since 2007 are evidence of the UK's increasing involvement in what van der Ploeg describes as the intensification in external border-securing policies which increasingly use new technologies to profile 'at risk' individuals (2006: 180); for example, the Cabinet Office's (2007a) report *Security in a Global Hub*, the Home Office's (2007) report *Securing the UK Border*, and the House of Lords' European Union Committee (2008) report of evidence on *Frontext: The EU External Borders Agency*. Many of these developments are associated with the establishment of the UK's 'new border arrangements', including offshore borders designed to prevent particular individuals from travelling to the UK (Huysmans 2006; Rumford 2008; Vaughan-Williams 2008). It has been suggested that these supra-national and often globalized networks of surveillance are more or less immune from democratic control and are often out with the jurisdictions of privacy and data protection regimes (van der Ploeg 2006: 179). In many ways, the technological developments with regard to the new border control arrangements, which I will elaborate on later, have resulted in new unprecedented security regimes associated with what Bigo (2002) calls the convergence between the meaning of international and national security. This has come about, as noted by van der Ploeg (2006), through the development of increasingly international (in terms of increasing harmonization, integration and convergence) exchanges between bureaucratic technologies of surveillance, dataveillance and control (Bigo 2006a, 2006b).

The management of identity – the 'politics of harm'

Walters informs us that 'borders are not what or where they used to be' (2004: 251). The Schengen Convention, which came into effect in 1996, paved the way for new forms of cooperation in policing, immigration and asylum policy across the EU (Walters 2004: 252; van der Ploeg 2006: 178). Thus the balance between freedom and security and the objectification and control of danger as alluded to earlier, should be contextualized in the fact of the increasing erosion of internal borders between EU member states, and the security deficit this has created which has resulted in the invention of a new border or 'external frontier' to protect member states (Walters 2004: 252). In recent years a number of commentators (e.g. Balibar 2002, 2003, 2004;

Guild 2003; Walters 2002, 2004; Rumford 2006, 2007) have examined the de-bordering and re-bordering of European nation states and the EEA. These de-bordering and re-bordering developments have crystallized into the pan-European model of integrated security called Frontex (Vaughan-Williams 2008: 65).[2] The UK occupies an unusual position with regard to the Schengen *Acquis*[3] and Frontext, in that the UK is not a full Schengen state and therefore is not a full Frontext state either (House of Lords European Union Committee 2008: 23). Nevertheless the UK, despite being unable to play a full role in Frontex, is participating effectively in the operation of Frontex in the EEA (House of Lords European Union Committee 2008: 24). It is in the context of development of cooperation, co-ordination and a new external border in the EEA that the UK has been forging ahead with the restructuring and reshaping of its border controls. The Cabinet Office lists the four primary developments with regard to border controls in the UK. As noted earlier, the government has been in the process of 'exporting the border' through moving a greater proportion of UK border controls overseas; improving document integrity through the use of biometrics (through the biometric identity scheme); improving the use of data (through the e-borders programme) and enhancing risk-profiling technologies and improving protection against particular threats (Cabinet Office 2007a: 7). In many ways the process of 'exporting the border' is an example of what Lahav and Guiraudon call 'remote control' in which a range of local, transnational and private actors outside the central state apparatus become enmeshed in the process of forestalling and restricting unwanted, illegal and 'risky' migrants 'at the source' (in Rumford 2008: 6). Liam Byrne, the Minister of state for Borders and Immigration, has been particularly transparent in his statements with regard to why the government has restructured and developed these border control strategies and what they are for. In a speech titled 'Border Security and Immigration: Our deal for Delivery' made in January 2008, Byrne justified the new border controls by informing us that 'the public wants stronger borders. The public want us to prevent illegal immigration by attacking its causes'. Byrne announced in this speech that 'we got the message'; he goes on to inform his audience that 'over the last 12 months we have drawn up plans for the biggest ever shake up of Britain's border security' (Byrne 2008: 4–5). In a previous speech, Byrne suggested that the new biometric visa programme would introduce 'tougher checks abroad' which would 'mean we keep risky people out' (Byrne 2007: 1). According to Huysmans, political security discourse such as these, are beyond mere rhetoric, they have become embedded within powerful technological processes that govern everyday practices through technological devises such as the visa (2006: 96).

The border, or more accurately, the e-border becomes what Walters describes as a 'privileged institutional site' not only with regard to restrictions and the oppression of unwanted or risky travellers, but also in relation to acquiring biopolitical knowledge about populations (2002: 572). The Home Office in their *Securing the UK Border* report gives weight to Walter's thesis that the border has become a site of biopolitical knowledge accumulation when it was stated that 'our aim is to build up as rich a knowledge of the travelling public as possible'; however, the Home Office, qualifies this statement with the following which describes their intention: 'to use this information to stop those who could cause harm to the UK from coming here' (Home Office 2007: 16). In the report *Securing the UK Border* the Home Office employed the discourse of 'harm reduction' to legitimize their introduction of pre-emptive border controls in a number of passages, for example, 'we are putting in place a border security system which makes life easier for legitimate travellers but stops those who cause harm' (Home Office 2008: 3). The vague reference to 'harm' here and the loaded label 'legitimate traveller' acts to de-legitimize and, as we shall see later, criminalize a growing range of 'travellers' to the UK in a continuum which includes those suspected of being capable of (or planning to perpetrate) extremist violence to those individuals at the other end of the continuum, for example, who are intending to make an application for asylum.

'Harm' reduction through border controls, for the Home Office, is a matter of 'managing identity' (2008: 3), through employing biometric technologies that make it possible to 'permanently link people to a unique identity' (Home Office 2008: 3). This amounts to the biopolitical dream of being able 'to fix people's identities at the earliest point practicable' (Home Office 2008: 3) through offshore, pre-inspection facilities for the presentation of biometric visas (Home Office 2008: 4). Furthermore, the offshore prevention of 'harmful', 'illegitimate' and 'risky' individuals from boarding the vehicle that would transport them to the UK is to be complemented, according to the Home Office, by the 'in-country' 'commitment to a unique, secure ID for all non-EEA nationals by 2011' (Home Office 2008: 4). This integrated approach was devised in the *Controlling Our Borders* White Paper in 2005 where a 'fully integrated pre-entry, border and in-country control' was proposed that would include pre-boarding biometric electronic checks and the requirement that 'all foreign migrants staying in the UK for more than three months to have an ID card' (Home Office 2005a: 10). The 'in-country' harm reduction function that the ID cards were supposed to perform, according to former Home Secretary Charles Clarke (in the foreword to the White Paper) was wide ranging:

> ID cards will provide a simple and secure way of verifying identity, helping us to tackle illegal working, organized crime, terrorist activity, identity theft, and fraudulent access to public services.
>
> (Clarke, in Home Office 2005: Foreword)

The genesis of what was to become the Identity Card Act 2006[4] can be found even further back in the *Secure Borders Safe Haven* White Paper of 2002 in the form of proposals for the introduction of 'an entitlement card' (Crossman 2007: 52). This was initially to be a voluntary scheme which would make access to public services easier. However, the government in subsequent drafts of the ID Card Bill began to propose, to considerable Conservative, Liberal-Democrat and Labour Back-Bench opposition, a compulsory scheme for everyone in the UK (Crossman 2007: 52). Furthermore, the identity card scheme was to be introduced in the context of the development of a National Identity Register. The National Identity Register was to have two specific purposes: to create the means for people to establish their identity and to allow a means for that identity to be checked when necessary 'in the public interest' (Crossman 2007: 53). What constitutes 'in the public interest' (like 'causing the UK harm') is rather broad. Crossman lists the following as being in the public interest (from the government's perspective): national security, prevention or detection of crime, immigration, employment prohibition and provisions of public services (2007: 54). As a result of the considerable public and parliamentary opposition to the universal introduction of ID cards in the UK, the government (the Home Secretary was granted the power of designation in the Identity Card Act) decided to introduce compulsory registration for initial groups, namely asylum seekers and non-EEA nationals living in the UK for more than three months (Crossman 2007: 56).[5] According to the Home Office:

> [T]he fixing of all non-EEA identities by 2011 will provide a robust defence against many existing patterns of immigration abuse as well as playing an important role in the national security and the fight against criminality from overseas.
>
> (Home Office 2007: 19)

Without declaring it, the UK seems to be at war with particular social groups. The groups in question are certain foreign nationals who are trying to enter the UK and those foreign nationals who are already here in the UK. The 'amorphous racism' that Judith Butler talked about with regard to the war on terrorism becomes, in this context, a variety of what Sivanandan calls xenoracism. According to Sivanandan, xeno-racism combines racist prejudice with xenophobia: 'the (natural) fear of strangers' (Sivanandan 2001: 2). Xenoracism is associated not only with fear and/or hatred of strangers but is also concerned with counter-modern defensiveness (Beck 1997) in which 'host' people attempt to preserve their way of life, standard of living and/or identity (Sivana-ndan 2001: 2). The UK appears to be in the grip of a quite war, under the fanfare of the war on terrorism (and its continuing legacy).[6] The xeno-racist and asylophobic tones of the non-EEA and asylum seeker designa-tion illuminates 'implicit battlefronts' (Morton and Bygrave 2008: 1) for our observation. The political effects associated with these strategizing techniques which evoke implicit battlefronts through their terminology of 'immigration abuse', 'harm' and 'in the public interest' is that 'power recruits and utilises life', that is, the lives in the form of the prosperity and safety of the citizenry. Thus, concerns about 'species life', in bio-political terms, 'is put to work' (Morton and Bygrave 2008: 3) in these strategies. Who can argue with a strategy that attempts to prevent abuse, criminality and potentially extremist violence in the name of public safety and national prosperity? However, as alluded to earlier, what Amoore describes as 'the allure of biometrics' associated with 'risk management technologies' that present 'the body' as a source of 'absolute identification' (2006: 342) must be contextualized in the often shadowy world of integrated databases.

Yes, the body is a possible source of absolute identification, however, linking biometrics to integrated databases (and thus 'fixing identities' in Home Office speak) appears to make the identification of a person 'beyond question' (Amoore 2006: 343). Thus, the linking of biometrics to integrated databases apparently lends authenticity and credibility to all the data that has come through numerous processes, both legitimate and illegitimate,[7] to be connected to that identity (Amoore 2006: 343). Thus the certainty of the comprehensive identity management systems (at the borders and internally through ID cards) must be linked to the uncertainty of the providence of the datum that particular identities could be connected to. This is not just a matter of the potential per-sonal catastrophic effect of an erroneous connection of an 'innocent' individual to a high risk or excluded profile but is also a fundamental issue with regard to the infringement of human rights standards and the democratic values of states who have bought into what Lyon and Bennett call the 'card cartels' involved in the production of identity card systems (2008: 4).

The transference of illegitimacy in the security continuum

There is one further issue to consider here, that is, what Bigo calls the 'transference of illegitimacy' (1994: 166) across groups in these practices. This transfer of illegitimacy can be described as a political sleight of hand in which terrorism and asylum have become increasingly interdependent in what Bigo describes as 'the security continuum' (1994: 164). According to Bigo, the 'security continuum' often links separate activities, for example, extremism, drug-smuggling, football hooliganism, organized crime and clandestine immigration to one another (1994: 164). The result being that the security continuum can lead to the development of new paradigms, procedures and conceptualizations of previously unrelated 'social problems'. The social and political effect of all of this is that issues such as asylum become displaced from the way they have been previously administered, for example, as a human rights issue or an economic or social issue linked to wider immigration policies. The inclusion of asylum and, for example, non-EEA migration, in the security continuum with its associated transfer of illegitimacy results in asylum becoming a 'security-led' issue (Bigo 1994: 164). Terrorism, immigration and asylum have in the post-9/11 world become what Tsoukala calls 'the terrorism-immigration-asylum nexus' in which immigrants and especially asylum seekers (2008: 66) became accused of 'playing a "fifth column" role on behalf of the global terrorist network' (Bauman, in Tsoukala 2008: 66). In the UK in particular, this nexus resulted in the extension of the accusations with regard to 'bogus' asylum seekers abusing the UK's generous welfare system to a more pronounced discourse of 'abuse' presented in the form of a particularly evocative discourse of hospitality abuse. Judith Butler describes speech acts, such as those uttered by David Blunkett (see below) as an example of the exercise of sovereign power; in speech acts such as these, according to Butler, 'sovereign power extends itself' (2006: 80). For Butler, there is a reciprocal relationship between the extent of the equivocation the speech act can produce and the augmentation of this variety of sovereign power 'in the apparent service of justice' (Butler 2006: 80). An example of the attempt to extend 'sovereign power' through a speech act can be found in the aftermath of 9/11 when the former Home Secretary

David Blunkett blatantly linked asylum, terrorism and the abuse of hospitality, for example:

> This is our home. It's our country. We have a right to say that if people are abusing the right to and seek to abuse rights of asylum in order to plan or promote terrorism we must take steps to do something.
> (Blunkett, in Tsoukala 2008: 67)

It is in this context, according to Fekete, that the EU Common Positions on combating terrorism instructs all member states to vet all asylum seekers to determine whether they have any connection to terrorism 'including that notorious catch all "passive" support for it' (2009: 49). I have previously described the emergence of 'the politics of deterrence' associated with strategies designed to prevent certain asylum seekers coming to the UK under the accusation of benefit shopping (McGhee 2005) which amounted in practice to restructuring the system including the introduction of 'food' and other vouchers, the dispersal policy and fast tracking asylum claims (in order to better identify and separate out 'the genuine' from 'the bogus' claimants). However, what has emerged in recent years is an explicit and deliberate attempt to prevent asylum seekers from entering the country in the first place. It is as if the UK has taken the decision that all asylum seekers, irrespective of the persecution they have suffered and the well-foundedness of their application are undeserving of the asylum the UK has promised to grant them as signatories of the 1951 Geneva Convention. According to Gibney, there now exists a paradox in the West in that Western states recognize the rights of refugees but have simultaneously criminalized their search for asylum through 'non-arrival measures' (2006: 14 and 143) through closing down all 'the legal avenues by which legitimate refugees might enter the UK' (Gibney 2006: 153). For Gibney this raises the moral question: can a state evade moral responsibility for refugees simply by preventing their arrival? (2006: 155). In many ways, this question is answered by Fekete who supports some of my observations with regard to the discourses of 'public safety', 'abuse' and 'harm' reduction with regard to asylum seekers. According to Fekete (2009: 30), these new asylum strategies are 'not designed to protect their human rights but to protect the public from them'. These new regimes are not just a matter of preventing would be asylum seekers from boarding vehicles to come to the UK at the sites of new offshore borders. The UK is also implicated through 'participating' in Frontex in interception and interdiction activities targeting asylum seekers attempting to enter into Europe. According to

Magner, the interception and interdiction policies of contracting states which 'reach beyond its territory to seize and return refugees' would have been 'unimaginable' at the time the international legal regime (that is, the 1951 Geneva Convention) for refugee protection was drafted (in Weber 2006: 29). The interdiction policies and practices adopted by many states, including Frontex activities, for example Hera I and Hera II[8] are located above and beyond the reach of law, they exist in 'a unique realm exploited by states to exert an unprecedented level of immigration control' (Weber 2006: 27).

In the next section the focus and context will shift from the examination of high-technology border controls and their myriad effects on particular targeted populations to focus instead on the low-technology strategies being devised in Britain for penetrating ever deeper into 'the hard to reach' recesses of Muslim communities in yet another example of a pre-emptive identification technique (Amoore 2008: 24) in the name of public safety.

1.3 Prevent, CONTEST and the policing of Muslim communities

There are a number of similarities between the new border controls explored in section 1.2 of this chapter and the new (since the second half of 2007) emphasis on preventative counter-terrorism in the UK. Both sets of policies are (1) 'knowledge systems' driven by 'intelligence'; (2) both involve the targeting or designation of priority or high-risk groups; (3) both, in different ways, attempt to penetrate the depths of the knowable whether through faith in biometric identification and connection to extensive databases or in the form of 'reaching deep' into the 'hard to reach' groups within Muslim communities; and finally (4) both are associated with the strategies of governing at a distance and responsibilization processes with regard to, for example, the co-ordination of collective external frontiers (at the borders of the EEA and beyond) or in terms of the connection between the central governments' national security strategy and the targeted governance of local Muslim communities. There are, however, a number of differences between the two groups of policies. Whereas the new border control measures can be described as being at the 'hard edge' of the assertion of sovereign power (Butler 2006) evident in the emphasis on exclusion, restriction and expulsion, the preventative counter-terrorism strategies that will be examined later invoke the governmental language of 'engagement' and 'partnership' and the therapeutic discourses of 'early intervention' and 'treatment' in the pursuit of building 'community resilience' against extremism.

In this section I will first examine the context from whence the Prevent strategy emerged. I will then explore what the Prevent strategy is supposed to achieve before examining what the implications of this strategy are for Muslim communities, police and other agencies in particular areas of the UK.

Preventing violent extremism – building resilient communities?

The UK has had a strategy for *Countering International Terrorism* in place since 2003 called CONTEST. CONTEST has four principal strands: Prevent, Pursue, Protect and Prepare (HM Government 2006: 1; McGhee 2008a: 51). According to Blick, Choudhury and Weir there are two interconnected aims in this strategy: 'first, gaining vital intelligence that will expose the terrorists; and secondly, engaging with the Muslim communities to obtain that intelligence' (2006: 31). The CONTEST strategy has all the hallmarks of a well-rounded counter-terrorism strategy. Unfortunately, according to Blick et al., the Blair administration gave prominence to 'the hard end of the strategy' such as legislation, measures against 'preachers of hate' and the pursuit and disruption of potential terrorist activities (2006: 31–2; McGhee 2008a: 51). The government (under Gordon Brown) has admitted that 'Prevent' was the least developed of the four CONTEST strands as priority was given to protecting the country from 'the immediate threat to life, rather than to understanding the factors driving radicalisation' (HM Government 2009: 82). This relative neglect of the 'Prevent' aspect of CONTEST was to be addressed within the first few months of Gordon Brown taking office. However, much of the groundwork for the Prevent programme was underway after the new Department for Communities and Local Government (DCLG) was introduced when the Home Office was restructured in 2006. The Preventing Violent Extremism Pathfinder Fund (PVEPF) was launched by the DCLG in 2007. Initially £5 million of funding was made available for distribution among 70 priority local authorities. The aim of the PVEPF programme was to fund projects that were to act as a catalyst for the development of 'bottom-up, community-based programmes to tackle violent extremism' (DCLG 2007b: 4).

The post-9/11 counter-terrorism strategy in the UK has developed in the main at the expense of the appreciation of the wider contexts of 'radicalization' and extremism, more than that, there was a 'lazy parlance' in political discourses that does not adequately differentiate between 'extremism' and 'radicalization' (DEMOS 2006: 41–2). At the

same time, the Blair government's subordination of alternative discourses of the causes of extremism (including the potential link between
British foreign policy and extremism) has hampered the development
of 'partnership approaches' on 'terrorism' with Muslim communities
in the UK (McGhee 2008a). It will be suggested here that the major
obstacle to the Blair government creating an effective partnership with
Muslim communities in the UK was the government's contradictory
approach to Muslim communities as both suspect communities har-
bouring terrorists and as *the* communities they most need to work with
against extremism.

Following the United Nation's Global Counter-Terrorism Strategy
Plan of Action 2006 and the Council of Europe's Convention on the
Prevention of Terrorism 2007 both of which advocated 'community-
relations' approaches to preventing tensions through promoting dialogue and raising public awareness (Davis 2007: 9), the new government
under Gordon Brown took up and ran with the emphasis on 'building community relations' in the DCLG's PVE programme and in the
Countering International Terrorism strategy. As noted, the rebalancing
of CONTEST was to include a greater investment in prevention. For
former Home Secretary Jacqui Smith, prevention was central in the fight
against extremism. Smith stated at the First International Conference
on Radicalization and Political Violence that 'stopping people becoming or supporting terrorists – that is the major long-term challenge we
face' (Smith 2007: 2). This led to the introduction of the PVEPF in 2007.
This funding was made available to enable 'priority' local authorities to
take forward programmes of activities to tackle violent extremism at a
local level (DCLG 2007a: 4). The DCLG's designation of the priority local
authority areas to be targeted for the PVEP funding was based on the size
of the Muslim community in particular areas, for example, areas with
populations of 5 per cent or more Muslims, or those areas with a significant Muslim community concentrated in a few wards (DCLG 2007a: 6)
were to be prioritized. Initially Prevent operated in 70 priority local areas,
though at the time of writing (October 2009) it was operating in 82 local
councils and is set to rise to 94 in 2010 (Dodd 2009: 4).

The PVE pathfinder projects were established in order to encourage
local authorities to better understand and engage in dialogue with
their communities; forge partnerships with police, community and
faith groups; to work more effectively with mosques and 'institutions
of education' (DCLG 2007b: 4). The PVEPF has been created as part of
the DCLG's strategy to deliver its priority remit to enable local communities to challenge the ideas of extremists in order to prevent violent

extremism at the local level and to deliver 'local solutions' to 'local problems' (DCLG 2007a: 4). Rather than shying away from or refusing to engage with what has been described as the felt grievances[9] among some Muslims in Britain (Smith 2007: 15), the PVEPF projects are more in line with the 'battle of ideas' approach advocated by Gordon Brown,[10] which was set out in the department's *Preventing Violent Extremism – Winning Hearts and Minds* report (DCLG 2007c). The projects funded by the PVEPF are varied and wide ranging depending on the needs of particular local areas. According to the DCLG, the funded projects range from promoting the contributions that Muslims make in local communities, to building the capacity of local communities to tackle violent extremism in their area, to protecting specific groups of vulnerable individuals from being targeted by violent extremists (DCLG 2007c: 8).

On paper the PVE programmes seem to be a progressive step forward in Britain's overall counter-terrorism strategy. However, it is at this point that we need to be cautious. When it comes to the Prevent strategy a range of questions must be explored: What does 'engagement', 'capacity' building and 'building resilience against extremism in local communities' (DCLG 2007c: 4) actually mean in practice? How does Prevent compete with the other components of CONTEST on the ground? Suffice to say, the Prevent strategy does not begin and end with DCLG-funded projects but is also part of a wider policing strategy. Looking at reports produced in Hampshire, the county in which I live and work, Hampshire Constabulary and Hampshire Police Authority are very clear in one of their strategic priorities, that is, to protect communities from terrorism and domestic extremism (Hampshire Constabulary 2007: 6). They are also clear about how this strategic priority is to achieved in their Policing Plan, that is, through developing closer 'community engagement' (Hampshire Constabulary and Hampshire Police Authority 2007: 10). What this entails is firstly, the 'identification of vulnerable communities' and secondly, engagement with communities so identified through forging 'partnerships' with them; these partnerships are defined as 'close co-operation, consistency and compatibility when responding to real or perceived terrorist threats' (Hampshire Police Authority Community Affairs Committee 2007: 5). In these reports there is (in line with the interdependent aims of CONTEST) an explicit reference to the relationship between the identification of and engagement with 'vulnerable' or 'priority' communities and the accumulation of intelligence. For example, it was stated in the Local Policing Plan that 'by forging these closer links it will be possible to capture accurate and up-to-date intelligence that can be used to build a picture of the issues affecting our community' (Hampshire Constabulary and Hampshire Police Authority 2007: 10). This raises a number of questions. How will the police use and act upon this intelligence? How will police action taken as a result of this local–community-derived intelligence impact on the priority or targeted communities in question and their potential future relationship with police and other agencies? That is, does the emphasis on intelligence here detract from the other work police forces (and for that matter local authorities and other multi-agency partners) currently do in and with local Muslim communities with regard to engaging with them and empowering them?

Identifying and 'supporting' vulnerable communities

The government is aware of the precarious balancing act that their various departments (e.g. the Home Office and the Communities and Local Government Department), security agencies and the police have to perform in order to address 'Prevent objectives'. In this context these departments, agencies and services are attempting to: support vulnerable individuals and enhance the resilience of communities; implement operations to disrupt propagandists and their networks; while at the same time, attempting to build 'further trust and confidence between police and Muslim communities' (HM Government 2009: 99). However, there are even more precarious balancing acts going on here. Spalek and Imtoual's examination of the multiple and complex roles that the police are expected to perform in the name of CONTEST and Prevent are highly valuable for exploring some of these questions. For example, Spalek and Imtoual suggest that police forces often find themselves caught in-between 'hard' and 'soft' engagement approaches, where the former is devoted to intelligence gathering through internal community surveillance and the use of informants and the latter is devoted to trust-building and community-policing approaches (Spalek and Imtoual 2007: 189). Furthermore, the tension between hard and soft engagement approaches haunts Jacqui Smith's promotion of Prevent in that the former Home Secretary sees the Prevent strategy as comprising of both PVEPF projects and 'community' policing initiatives (which are not mutually exclusive). The tension between 'intelligence gathering', 'Prevention' and 'engagement' is most apparent when Smith talks about finding new 'ways of directly supporting vulnerable people – by intervening with individuals when families, communities and networks are concerned about their behaviour' (Smith 2007: 12). Smith suggested that 'support for vulnerable individuals is best provided by their own communities' and that rather than arresting 'our way out of the problem', 'we need to think about the most effective response – more about rehabilitation, where that will work, and less about the Criminal Justice System' (Smith 2007: 13–14). The government, in their updated *Countering International Terrorism* strategy published in March 2009, attempted to unpack the circumstances and potential causes associated with an individual's vulnerability to extremism, that is:

> Vulnerability is not simply the result of actual or perceived grievances. It may be the result of family or peer pressure, the absence of positive mentors and role models, a crisis of identity, links to criminality including other forms of violence, exposure to traumatic events (here or overseas) or changing circumstances (e.g. a new environment following migration or asylum).
>
> (HM Government 2009: 89)

The spectre of what Tsoukala (2008) called 'the terrorism-immigration-asylum nexus' (see section 1.2) is obvious in this quotation, however, what is less obvious is how the government proposed to 'treat' these 'vulnerable' individuals. It is in the context of the government's attempts to understand different types of vulnerabilities to extremism that they have suggested two types of 'support'. One set of priority programmes will support 'those who are believed to be vulnerable to radicalisation' through programmes providing peer mentoring, diversionary activities and leadership programmes. These programmes will equip participants with 'the knowledge and skills to challenge extremist narratives' (HM Government 2009: 89). However, alongside what they describe as these 'early support' programmes the government has devised 'more intensive interventions' which will focus on people who have already become drawn into violent extremist networks (HM Government 2009: 89). Whereas Jacqui Smith mentioned that rehabilitation programmes normally used for illegal drug users could be modified and developed for these type of 'extremists' (Smith 2007: 12), the government has suggested that the more intensive interventions would build on existing multi-agency support mechanisms at a local level to support vulnerable adults and early intervention work with at-risk young people as part of the Every Child Matters strategy (HM Government 2009: 89).[11] One can only imagine how local Muslim communities would react to these proposals for non-coercive therapeutic interventions to divert those 'at-risk' from extremism in the context of the UK's post-9/11 and post-7/7 counter-terrorism strategies which include shoot to kill policies, dawn police raids, internment policies and control orders. This strategy and political and media discourses on the relationship between Muslims and terrorism have resulted, according to Mythen and Walklate, 'in British Muslims being defined *en bloc* as a risky, suspect population' (2009: 5) which has 'raised the intense scrutiny on Muslims in general and potentially exacerbated the degree of public suspicion directed towards young male Muslims (Abbas, in Mythen and Walklate 2009: 5). In this context how can Muslim communities and more to the point Muslim parents who might be concerned about one of their children's 'activities' be confident that informing the police or an associated organization of their concerns will result in their child being enrolled in a community-based intervention rather than attracting a counter-terrorism police dawn raid on their home?

In the end Prevent is an intelligence gathering strategy. The parallels between the use of co-ordinated dataveillance in the UK's new border controls measures and the Prevent strategies are obvious, both are intelligence-driven systems. The difference is that Prevent depends on 'local community'-derived intelligence. The government does not shy away from the relationship between local intelligence, Prevent and the other strands of CONTEST in their strategy for *Countering International Terrorism* published in 2009. In this document they stipulate that Prevent-related intelligence requirements will require police, security and intelligence agencies to build on their existing programmes, which will involve the sharing of information between these organizations and local partners in order to ensure 'the more comprehensive assessment of areas at risk from terrorism and radicalization and enable authorities to better target Prevent related interventions' (HM Government 2009: 92). Writing in *The Guardian*, Vikram Dodd has voiced a number of concerns about the 'information' or intelligence sharing arrangements under Prevent. According to Dodd (2009: 4), under Prevent, local councils are being encouraged to draw up information-sharing agreements with the police to establish the types of information about PVEPF participants that might be exchanged in local areas. It is as a result of these intelligence-sharing agreements that the Institute of Race Relations (IRR) has reported on 'widespread distrust' with regard to the Prevent programme. Arun Kundnani of the IRR stated that 'many were concerned the programme provided an opportunity for the police to embed intelligence gathering into the delivery of local services, such as youth work' (in Dodd 2009: 4).

Prevent – an example of targeted governance?

The PVEPF projects are linked to particular strategic objectives,[12] for example, 'to measure success' and 'to enable the aggregation and comparison' of 'key local issues' across priority local authority areas (DCLG 2007a: 7–8). Whereas the new border controls are examples of 'targeted exclusion' which come to hone in on particular 'risky' characteristics in particular profiles, the PVEPF projects are targeted, but for the purposes of 'engaging' and including (in terms of 'drawing in' or reaching) particular 'risky' or 'at risk' individuals and their communities in 'the fight against terrorism'. In this light, as well as being set up to build the resilience (DCLG 2007c: 4) of priority areas to combat and challenge extremism through capacity building, awareness training, youth work etc. the PVEPF projects are also to be evidence-driven knowledge systems that are to connect central government to local 'priority' communities (and the 'at risk' or 'vulnerable' individuals in their midst) through what Valverde and Mopas (2004: 245) describe as 'targetted governance' and Rose (2007: 71) describes as 'Preventative interventions'. These evidence-based, intelligence-driven PVE programmes could have particular effects, for example, they could have a transformative effect on designated priority local authorities in that these areas could be transformed into calculable spaces (Miller 1997: 256) that, in theory, can be acted upon by central government from a distance (Rose 1994: 364). Valverde and Mopas (2004: 246) describe this as 'the dream of targeted governance' with its misplaced optimism in believing that 'good information' can and will be collected and will in turn enable 'managers', government departments or police forces 'to target their organization's resources efficiently and with maximum benefit'. The precariousness of such dreams are captured by the DCLG's assumptions that in order to 'measure success' in the form of 'demonstrable changes in attitudes among Muslims and wider communities' it is essential that current local attitudes are mapped 'to provide a baseline for future progress' (DCLG 2007a: 7). This is a tall order for any evaluation team commissioned to monitor the success of a PVEPF project; because attempting to establish an attitudinal baseline for a number of Muslim and non-Muslim communities in an entire local authority area in order to measure the direct impact of a PVEPF project on their 'attitudes' is quite a challenge in itself. Designing surveys that contain what the DCLG describe as 'a common core' to enable aggregation and comparison across local authorities to identify best practice and to identify key local issues introduce, in combination, further challenges. In this light the PVEPF programme is reduced to a calculative regime whose successes or failures are less measured by the quality of the engagement facilitated by the projects and more by the potential for aggregating and comparing data in the context of evidence-based resource distribution *apparati*.

In many ways, the Prevent strategy bypasses the habitual national level engagement with Muslim organizations common under Blair to focus on a wider range of Muslim groups in particular designated as 'at risk' areas through net-widening partnership approaches. One of the remits of the PVEPF projects is to 'develop a more detailed understanding of the range of Muslim and other organizations and key individuals with whom they can work' (DCLG 2007a: 8). In fact the DCLG suggested that PVEPF resources should 'be used to broaden the range of contacts and networks particularly those engaging with young people and women for whom opportunities to express views and participate can be limited' (DCLG 2007a: 8). It is on this basis, according to the DCLG, that Local Forums on Extremism and Islamophobia should be built (DCLG 2007a: 8).[13]

Thus, the PVEPF encourages local projects that will reach deep into Muslim communities in order to engage with the 'hard to reach' or traditionally marginalized groups of women and young people in local areas. However, it is here that we again run up against a tension in the Prevent strategy. Is this attempt to reach ever deeper into Muslim communities just about increasing the representativeness and enhancing the active participation of women and young people? What is the relationship between the latter and the intelligence driven focus on 'at risk' or 'vulnerable' individuals? Engaging young people and women in this light both increases their potential for participating and being represented in local projects and forums; however, it also draws these 'hard to reach' groups into potential intelligence networks through increasing the potential for internal community surveillance into the marginalized, disaffected 'hard to reach' parts of these communities.

Thus, just as Ruth Kelly (former Local Government and Communities Minister) set out to transform the government–'Muslim Community' consultation landscape post 7/7 (McGhee 2008: 78) in response to the view that Muslim leaders had not taken a strong enough stand against extremism, the PVEPF projects can be described as re-instating 'Government through community' in that central government is to be linked to individuals (e.g. 'at risk' or 'vulnerable' individuals) through 'local' public, private, third sector, police and 'Muslim community' partnerships under Prevent. This will no doubt have a transformative effect on the individuals and organizations involved including front line police officers grappling with their conflicting roles; 'Muslim leaders' representing their communities; as well as the ever-widening community groups and all those agencies included in the multi-agency partnerships in local authority areas as they are expected to transform themselves into 'calculating individuals' in 'calculable spaces' subjected to 'calculative regimes' (Miller 1997: 256) set up to measure 'community' resilience against extremism.

Responsibilization, suspicion and intolerance

The PVEPF projects could be conceived as the Labour government (initiated under Blair and implemented under Brown) forcing responsibility for countering extremism onto Muslim communities through a process of devolving responsibility downwards (O'Malley 2004: 73). This responsibility is being articulated less in the accusatory mode of 'Muslims must do more to fight extremism' and more in terms of the responsibility of Muslims and Muslim communities to perform their duty of being 'frontline' 'vigilant watchers' in their Mosques, neighbourhoods and families. This 'vigilant or watchful visuality' (Amoore 2007: 215) is to be taken into their intimate relationships as parents, siblings, cousins, friends and neighbours as they play their part in pre-empting 'future events' through scrutinizing those in their midst for what the former Home Secretaries John Reid (McGhee 2008a: 79) and Jacqui Smith described as looking for 'the telltale signs' of potential extremism, or the vulnerability of 'vulnerable individuals' to extremism.

There is something very distinctive about the PVEPF projects and the ethos of prevention through internal community surveillance in the UK since 2007. A number of other commentators have examined the wider context of suspicion and surveillance that have gripped the post-9/11 world. For example, Judith Butler (2006: 77) describes the facilitation of a 'license for prejudicial perception' and a 'virtual mandate to heighten radicalized ways of looking and judging in the name of national security' in the US post 9/11 which has impacted adversely on the members of Muslim and other misrecognized communities caught up in the tendrils of 'amorphous racism' associated with, as noted above, 'the heightened surveillance of Arab peoples and anyone who looks vaguely Arab' (2006: 39). However, Butler's observations on the US and, for example, those of Vaughan-Williams (2008: 68) with regard to the mobilization of all citizens in the EU to become 'citizen-detectives' who must take up the responsibility of becoming 'agents of surveillance' in the 'battle against terrorism' (70) can be described as strategies that, on the whole, position Muslim communities, as the object rather than the agents of surveillance. The PVEPF projects and the ethos of Prevent in the UK since 2007 are distinctive because they position local Muslim communities and Muslim family members as the primary agents of surveillance on the front line of the battle against terrorism. By so doing, the government is both attempting to counter 'the Othering' of

Muslim communities and their position as a 'suspect community' in the UK through attempting to develop a counter-terrorism partnership approach with 'responsible' Muslims. However, there is a risk that the targeting of and engagement with local Muslim communities in this way could exacerbate tensions and suspicions on both sides.

When it comes to the role that the local members of Muslim communities are supposed to play as agents of surveillance in their own communities Bigo's (2001), metaphor (following Agamben) of the twisted and co-joined figure of the möbius strip offers a means of exploring the potential complexities with regard to relationships and loyalties this could evoke. According to Amoore, Bigo (2007: 219) uses the möbius strip as a metaphor in which the inside and outside are 'interpenetrated' in which one does not know on which face of the strip one is located. This metaphor is in turn useful for the purposes of analysing the ambiguous positioning of individuals in Muslim communities under Prevent. For example, they are positioned as responsible citizens acting in the interest of national security or as parents, friends or neighbours acting in the interest of love and solidarity. Acting under both of these imperatives would result in the negotiation of myriad complexities and consequences for such individuals. Thus, cooperating individuals who act on their suspicions by contacting the police or related agency or those who decide not to act on their suspicions will simultaneously risk being insiders and risk being outsiders on a number of levels with regard to loyalty, responsibility and agency from various perspectives.

There is one further tension that should be briefly examined here, that is, the government's attempts to rally support for their wider counter-terrorism strategy (including Prevent) through their particular articulation of extremism as being akin to a form of hatred, prejudice and discrimination. The government is attempting to co-opt into their counter-terrorism strategy the 'intolerance of intolerance' discourse associated with the hatred and prejudice that has since 2000 become increasingly 'mainstreamed' in service provision and linked to protections in law associated with the incitement, motivation and aggravation of hatred, prejudice and hostility targeted at minorities communities (McGhee 2005). That is, the government is attempting to promote the intolerance of extremism alongside the now familiar intolerance in Britain with regard to other forms of hatred, prejudice and discrimination through insisting that 'the duty on all of us – government, citizens and communities' is to 'challenge those who dismiss our shared values' (HM Government 2009: 97). By so doing the government in their *Countering International Terrorism* strategy of 2009 (under the section 'promoting our shared values') are attempting to ally their Prevent strategy with what they describe as their established 'tradition of building strong, empowered and resilient communities' through 'tackling all forms of hate crime, and promoting equal opportunities' (HM Government 2009: 87). By so doing the government is attempting to rally support for Prevent through stipulating who the target of these strategies are, namely:

> Those who, for whatever reason or cause, reject the rights to which we are committed, scorn the institutions and values of our parliamentary democracy, dismiss the rule of law and promote intolerance and discrimination on the basis of race, faith, ethnicity, gender or sexuality.
>
> (HM Government 2009: 87)

Through this discourse, extremists are relegated to what Beck (1997: 11) would describe as the counter-modern residuum of our dynamic, complex and diverse contemporary societies, who for the sake of 'our' society (and 'our' values, and the institutions these values are articulated through) must be identified, rehabilitated or incarcerated for 'our' protection. Thus the UK's counter-terrorism strategy is itself under the process of rehabilitation from the Blair and Bush's hard-edged 'you are either with us or with the terrorist' approach which was associated with waves of emergency legislation on both sides of the Atlantic (McGhee 2008a) to something much more low key and participative in the form of a coalition of responsible citizens against 'a social evil' that is to be identified by its rejection of 'our' British shared values expressed and epitomized by 'our' enduring institutions. In many ways the quotation above is a rather good place to move onto the next chapters in which the accepting and sharing of British values becomes the ultimate goal of the integration logic of the 'earned citizenship strategy' (Chapter 3). However, as we shall see (in Chapters 2 and 4) the government's commitment to some of these values, especially those pertaining to, for example, equality, tolerance and anti-discrimination is rather more precarious than this statement would have us believe.

1.4 Conclusion

The policies, strategies and justifications for Britain's new border control and preventative counter-terrorism strategies are discursively rich sites, however, as Huysmans (2006) has pointed out these discourses are connected to powerful institutional process with real world effects. In section 1.1 of the chapter I examined examples of the exteriorization and projection of what Massumi (1993: viii) would call the 'ambient fear' that pervades everyday 'domestic' life onto those who seemingly want to penetrate the country's defences, abuse 'our' hospitality and ulti- mately cause 'us' harm. The metaphors of nation and home, and the nation as 'our home', employed here are particularly powerful especially when the resultant politics of fear (Carens 2009: 152) are combined with a culture of indignation (McGhee 2008: 34). The combination of fear and indignation has led to particular effects in the form of introducing a societal indifference to the plight of 'genuine' asylum seekers and refugees who have experienced or have a well-founded fear of being persecuted in the countries they are fleeing from. At the same time, in section 1.3, I examine the 'practical' policy expressions of the interiorization of 'Britain's' fears with regard to 'home grown' al-Qaeda influenced extremist violence. Section 1.3 can be described as an examination of the government's attempts to respond to the fact that the 7/7 suicide bombers were organic, 'home-grown' British citizens, who were members of established Muslim communities. This has involved a shift in strategy from Blair to Brown, from exclusively pursuing extremists (and the inciters of extremists) and preparing and protecting the nation from extremist violence to also emphasizing the need to engage with and form partnerships with Muslim communities in the UK in order to prevent further 'home grown' attacks. However, this shift is not altogether a benign one. Bigo (2008: 2) reminds us that all of the political and professional uses of 'technologies of surveillance which are orientated towards prevention' (and I would add here the low-technology surveillance being encouraged within communities) are the artefacts of the politics of fear, which attempt to maintain 'pub- lic security' through the rather anxious tactics of attempting 'to read the future as a "past future" already known'.

The new border control measures and the Prevent strategies are con- crete examples that help to ground the often theoretical and abstract discussions with regard to 'security' and 'insecurity' in contempo- rary advanced Western societies (some of which will be examined in Chapter 2). Both of these 'strategies' also tell us a great deal about what 'we' fear and how, in practical terms countries such as the UK attempt to pre-empt the potential dangers and threats that could 'harm us'. In this connection, the new border controls, the internal surveillance associated with ID cards and Prevent are associated with a particular abnormalization process, in that they all rely on 'the construction of profiles that frame who is "abnormal"' (Bigo 2008: 2) whether through high-technology systems of dataveillance or through the low-technology imperatives of Muslim communities closely examining their children and neighbours for 'tell-tale' signs of 'radicalization'.

In section 1.2 I noted that the identification process becomes connected to an identity (and a body) which can be further connected to potential effects, for example, not being allowed to board a plane to enter the UK, and in the case of ID cards being excluded from certain benefits and services and ultimately being deported. In section 1.3, the identification process also carries the risk of unpredictable effects and consequences. For example, when a Muslim parent, concerned neighbour or Prevent-funded project worker informs the police or related agency of their suspicions regarding an 'at risk' individual they risk attracting a variety of 'hard' and 'soft' policing interventions to their home, neighbourhood and/or community group with unpredictable consequences for the 'at-risk' individual, his or her family and his or her community.

In the next chapter I will continue to compare and contrast Tony Blair and Gordon Brown's approaches to counter-terrorism, and I will also explore how the discourse of public security has co-opted the language of human security (under Gordon Brown) in an attempt to build a consensus across political parties to join the government to 'defeat' terrorism. I will also examine the relationship between the latter and the continuing attempts (across the Blair and Brown administrations) to fundamentally alter the application of human rights in the UK.

2

Building a Consensus on 'National Security': Terrorism, Human Rights and 'Core Values'

> Last year when I took on this job I said it was my earnest hope that agreeing the answers to these questions could be above party politics. And the Home Secretary, Justice Secretary and I have sought and appealed for a consensus on these issues – not just on terrorism legislation currently before Parliament, but on constitutional reform and on the broad range of issues covered in our first ever National Security Strategy.
>
> Brown 2008a: 9

2.1 Introduction

In this chapter the focus will shift from the examination of 'security' in the form of new border controls and new preventative policing strategies 'with' local Muslim communities to focus on 'security' in political discourse. In this chapter I will explore political discourses with regard to counter-terrorism legislation in the context of specific theoretical and conceptual frameworks, most notably the Copenhagen Peace Research Institute's securitization thesis and the broadening and interpenetration of 'security' in International Relations theory. The chapter, following on from Chapter 1, will also explore the role that 'British core values' and human rights protections are being called to play in the UK's wider counter-terrorism and 'national security' strategies. In many ways this chapter (and the previous chapter) contributes to the recent trend in sociology, in which 'security', and more accurately the mutations, redefinitions, effects and complexities of securities are being critically examined (Carter, Jordan and Watson 2008; McDonald 2008; Bauman 2006).

This sociology of security is in turn related to the emergence of Critical Counter-Terrorism Studies in the interdisciplinary social sciences. It is from these perspectives that we can ask particular questions, for example, what is security? Whose security? And, following on from the previous chapter, what is the relationship between the security of some and the insecurity of others? These questions provide the backdrop for the analysis contained in this chapter and some of the chapters that will follow.

There has been a great deal written on Britain's post-9/11 counter-terrorism legislation and its impact on British society. In this chapter I want to explore developments indirectly linked to the controversies over indefinite detention without charge, control orders and the extension of pre-charge detention up to 42 days. One aspect of this chapter will be the exploration of relationship between particular developments associated with Tony Blair's (who had a parliamentary majority) and Gordon Brown's (who did not have a parliamentary majority) very different attempts to create a consensus (both in terms of cross-party, and a wider 'national' consensus) on 'security', especially with regard to counter-terrorism. However, the primary purpose of this chapter is to explore what could be described as a securitized conception of 'British shared values' and human rights in the context of social threats to 'national security'.

This chapter is primarily an exposition on the relationship between the shifting definitions of securities and threats in the government's consensus-building activities around counter-terrorism policy. In so doing I will explore the impact of the government's consensus-building activities on (1) human rights policy (and the state's duty to protect those in its jurisdiction in this context) and (2) the shifting articulation of what are presented as 'British shared values'. It will be argued here that it is through redefining, or rebalancing, human rights and explicitly expressing the core values 'of the nation' that the government is attempting to reaffirm (or more accurately redefine) its raison d'etre (based on its claim to citizens' obedience on the promise to protect its subjects against threats to their existence) in the context of 'globalized' threats and dangers. It will be suggested here that the government is attempting to reassert itself in a world of 'new' global realities and security challenges (Cabinet Office 2008; Booth 2005) which are associated with 'broadening' (following Buzan et al.) out into (and simultaneously the dedifferentiation, following Bigo) what have been described as the various domains or sectors of 'security' including the economic, the political, the military, the environmental and the societal sectors (Buzan et al. 1998: 7). In this chapter, I will focus on the government's attempts to reconceptualize 'security' in the National Security Strategy (*The National Security Strategy of the United Kingdom: Security in an Interdependent World*) of 2008 in both 'state' and 'human' security terms, in order to prioritize what it defines as its positive obligations, in particular (1) the defence of the core values of the nation which are articulated through Britain's institutions (for example, parliamentary democracy, the rule of law) and (2) the protection of the right to life and ensuring the safety of the citizenry in its jurisdiction in the context of global insecurities.

In the main, this chapter unpacks, what Gordon Brown in the quotation above describes as the co-ordinated 'security' strategy, he, as Prime Minister, the Home Secretary (in this case former Home Secretary Jacqui Smith) and the Justice Secretary (and Lord Chancellor) Jack Straw have been rolling out since taking office in 2007. That is, to seek and appeal for a consensus on national security, and as we shall see, also a consensus on the correct application of human rights.

The chapter comprises three sections, each dedicated to examining the role of each of these members of the government with regard to the roles they play in rolling out Brown's new national security strategy. As well as critically exploring the definitions, mutations and effects of security, each section examines particular conceptual, rhetorical and 'policy' tensions, for example the relationship between the Copenhagen Peace Research Unit's thesis on securitization and desecuritization (and Blair and Brown's rhetorical styles), the shifting relationship between the concepts of national security and human security and the relationship between the protection of the civil liberties of the individual and the state's duty to protect the rights of all those in its jurisdiction through increasingly 'pre-emptive' interventions in the debates on Britain's evolving human rights policy.

Section 2.2 will examine the relationship between the securitizing and desecuritizing elements of Gordon Brown's recent speeches in which he is attempting to create a consensus on security between the executive, parliament and the judiciary. Brown's efforts will be contrasted with Tony Blair's infamous 'rules changing' speech in the aftermath of 7/7 in which Blair employs securitizing language for particular aims, namely to reduce the likelihood of opposition from parliament and the courts with regard to the post-7/7 counter-terrorism provisions that he planned to introduce. The processes of securitization and desecuritization will be examined here, following Huysmans (2007) as particular techniques of government, that is, techniques for marginalizing opposition and creating consensus. In contrast to securitizing theory of Buzan et al. the intention here is to locate the analysis of securitization, following

Bigo (2002, 2001) as 'a field effect' involving a range of different actors (politicians, 'security' professionals and media commentators) rather than viewing 'security' and the processes of securitization 'as being of a different realm' (2002: 67) made possible through isolated speech acts.

Section 2.3 examines former Home Secretary Jacqui Smith's consensus-building activities in the form of the parliamentary debates on the extension of pre-charge detention to 42 days. Smith, in contrast to Brown, combines securitizing with desecuritizing speech acts to encourage parliament (in a similar vein to Blair) to support the new provisions. This section will include an analysis of the broadened conceptualization of 'security' that includes an appreciation of 'human security' (rather than just 'state security') in the National Security Strategy (2008). This section will also examine Smith's attempts to reassure other parties and the general public that the government is attempting to bring a more balanced perspective to terrorism and counter-terrorism which is to be infused with an emergent discourse of 'human welfare'. It will be suggested here that Smith co-opts the discourse of human security (that is, the universal concerns with regard to 'freedom from fear' and 'freedom from want') found in the Prime Minister's new national security strategy and transforms it in order to create a discourse that more closely resonates with the concerns of the citizen-consumers of advanced liberal democracies such as contemporary Britain. The result of Smith's approach (following Bush and Blair) is that it leaves parliament being held to ransom. The choice Smith puts forward to parliament is that they either support the executive to protect 'our' core values and 'the lives of everyone' against terrorists or that they choose to protect the civil liberties of the terrorist suspects potentially at the expense of everyone's rights, including everyone's 'right to life'.

Section 2.4 examines the parallel process being led by Justice Secretary (and Lord Chancellor) Jack Straw (but was initiated by Straw's predecessor, under Blair, Lord Falconer, see McGhee 2008a: 139) in which appeals to 'our' potential shared victimhood in the context of the unprecedented nature of the threat from 'the new terrorism' have resulted in recommendations for devising a human rights policy that coincides with the government's pre-emptive security strategies (Ericson 2008) which are being redesigned in the name of 'public security'. In this context 'public security' becomes a matter of protecting 'the right to life' of the many, as set out by Jacqui Smith, as opposed to protecting the civil liberties of the few. It will be suggested here that the broadened out definition of 'security' in the National Security Strategy and the calls to rebalance human rights is evidence of a new hierarchy of rights

(Parekh 2006) in the UK in which personal safety and public security are fast becoming the ultimate 'shared values'.

2.2 Counter-terrorism in the UK: From Securitization to Desecuritization?

In this section of the chapter I will examine the relationship between the legacy of the securitization of terrorism under Tony Blair and Gordon Brown's attempts at desecuritizing 'terrorism' and counter-terrorism. The aim of this section of the chapter is to explore the differences between the Blair and Brown governments' approaches to terrorism through the use of securitization and desecuritization theory. The main objective of doing this is to provide a theoretical framework for the exploration of the relationship between securitized and desecuritized consensus-building strategies under Blair and Brown.

But what is securitization? Securitization has been defined thus by Buzan, Wæver and de Wilde:

> If by means of an argument about the priority and urgency of an existential threat the securitizing actor has managed to break free of procedures or rules he or she would otherwise be bound by, we are witnessing a case of securitization.
>
> (1998: 25)

According to Buzan, Wæver and de Wilde, securitization is not fulfilled only by the breaking of rules, nor is securitization achieved solely by pronouncements on real or imagined existential threats (1998: 25). Successful securitization is achieved when existential threats legitimize the breaking of rules (Buzan, Wæver and de Wilde 1998: 25). According to Taureck, successful securitization consists of three stages, the (1) identification of existential threats; (2) emergency action; and (3) effect on inter-unit (or societal) relations by breaking free of rules (2006: 2). As a result of these stages 'the issue' is moved out of the sphere of 'normal politics' into the realm of 'emergency politics' where the issue can be dealt with swiftly and without some of the normal (democratic) rules and regulations of policymaking taking place. This section of the chapter comprises two subsections, the first will briefly examine (with the intention of contextualizing the analysis below) the relationship between the securitization thesis with regard to the lack of parliamentary scrutiny and opposition to one of the most controversial pieces of legislation in the UK's recent legislative history: the Anti-Terrorism, Crime and

Security Bill in 2001 in order to contextualize the examination of the relationship between the securitization thesis and Tony Blair's specific speech acts in the aftermath of 7/7. In the second subsection I will examine what I will refer to as Gordon Brown's (in contrast to Blair) attempts to promote a desecuritized consensus on counter-terrorism in the UK.

Tony Blair – a securitizing agent?

If one reads Helen Fenwick's account of the passage of the infamous Anti-Terrorism, Crime and Security Bill through the House of Commons in the aftermath of 9/11, then Buzan et al.'s securitization thesis seems to be pertinent. According to Fenwick, this Bill can be described as 'smuggling a range of new powers into law under the guise of the urgent need to combat terrorism' (2002: 729). The Anti-Terrorism, Crime and Security Bill, according to Fenwick, was introduced to the House of Commons as an 'extraordinary measure' to be adopted in the face of 'an apparent emergency' (2002: 79). In the context of the immediate aftermath of 9/11 this qualification of extraordinariness was accepted by the House of Commons; furthermore it also accepted the rather surprisingly limited amount of time (relatively speaking) that the Bill was granted in the parliamentary debate timetable – a mere 16 hours to scrutinize a Bill of 124 pages (Fenwick 2002: 79). Yet another surprise was that the House of Commons did not impose a single amendment on the government (Fenwick 2002: 729). Even if one takes into consideration that the government enjoyed a parliamentary majority at that time, the sheer range of what Fenwick described as 'illiberal measures' (2002: 729) that had been adopted in this Bill, including internment without charge of foreign national terrorist suspects (McGhee 2008a), one can only assume that the 'consensus' achieved in the House of Commons during the Anti-Terrorism, Crime and Security Bill, was more than just a case of 'speech act' securitization but rather securitization as what Bigo calls 'a field effect' (2002: 69). This Bill was introduced in the aftermath of a spectacular event, which was captured and constantly replayed by the world's media, namely 9/11, which had been presented in the persuasive and terrifying rhetoric of the clash of civilizations (Huntington 1993) and resulted in the seismic shifts in the interpenetration of the two great 'security' *dispositifs*: geopolitics, addressed in terms of sovereign territory, and biopolitics, associated with 'life' addressed in terms of population (Dillon 2007: 5). As such, the Bill was introduced in the context of heightened emotions and heightened security concerns replete with the simplified enemy (foreign national Muslim) constructions and tailor-made solutions, namely, the deportation or internment of foreign national terrorist suspects (McGhee 2008a: 15–20).

I consider Buzan et al.'s securitization thesis to be a useful starting point from which to further explore the complex negotiations in what Bigo describes as the field of political, professional and media discourses, that is, as a struggle, between what he calls the 'managers of unease' (2002: 67). It should be noted that securitization for Buzan et al. is more than mere politicization in that securitization involves the presentation of an existential threat, requiring emergency measures and justifying actions outside the normal bounds of political procedure (1998: 23–4). It is through examining securitization (and, for that matter desecuritization) as a political process associated with either marginalizing opposition and/or consensus building that we are able to explore the complexity of such processes, and for the purposes of this chapter, their relationship with particular effects. The brief exploration of the relationship between the securitization thesis and the passage of the Anti-Terrorism, Crime and Security Bill provides the context from whence to explore Tony Blair's deliberate attempt to generate parliamentary consensus (through marginalizing opposition) on emergency measures in response to a particular event, namely, the 7/7 suicide bombings in London in 2005.

Tony Blair's August Media Briefing in 2005 offers a good example of attempted 'speech act' securitization in the context of his justification for his government's post-9/11[1] and new counter-terrorism strategy. This media briefing on 5 August 2005, less than one month after the 7/7 bombings, was made famous by Blair's statement: 'let no-one be in any doubt, the rules of the game are changing' (Blair 2005: 1). During the briefing Blair satisfied many of Buzan et al.'s criteria (in the form of internal and external conditions) of a successful securitizing speech act, including 'internal conditions' associated with the construction of a plot replete with 'existential threat, a point of no return, and a possible way out' (1998: 33). The first of the external conditions to be satisfied by Blair was one of Buzan et al.'s criteria that the securitizing actor should be a figure of authority; however, it is the importance of Buzan et al.'s second external or 'facilitating condition' that I wish to focus on, that is, the ability of the securitizing actor to connect their securitizing activities to certain objects 'that are generally held to be threatening' (1998: 33). Rather than 'directly' threatening objects or individuals (for example, actual violent extremists), or even threatening events (such as 7/7), the security threat that Blair took the opportunity to 'conjure' was those individuals 'indirectly' responsible for 'terrorism' through their activities of inciting and proselytizing extremism in Britain. In this speech Blair also managed to display his frustration at not being able to respond to what he describes as the publics' demands that he should do something about the proselytizers of extremism. That is,

> [t]ime and again over the past few weeks I've been asked to deal firmly with those prepared to engage in such extremism, and most particularly with those who incite it or proselytize it.
>
> (Blair 2005)

The substantial political (and legal) effects that Blair set out to justify in response the 'intersubjective establishment' (Buzan et al. 1998: 25) of the existential threat of incited terrorism was the continuation of his government's 'controversial' action with regard to the deportation of terrorist suspects, and those who incite extremism, despite the restriction placed on the government by Article 3 of the ECHR.[2] At the same time, the 7/7 bombings provided Blair with the opportunity not only to introduce rule-changing provisions with regard to taking action against so-called preachers of hate but also gave him the opportunity to attack, and to marginalize, those who had in the past attempted to restrict what he calls 'controversial' actions, namely the courts and parliament, especially the House of Lords. The plot, characterization and dramatization that was at the heart of Blair's August 2005 media briefing was an example of a reflexive securitization process which attempted to call into question, in the light of the recent atrocities, the power of the courts and parliament to undermine the executive's previous actions as being based on 'scare-mongering':

> The action I am talking about has in the past been controversial, each tightening of the law has met fierce opposition, regularly we have been defeated in Parliament or in the Courts ... but for obvious reasons, the mood now is different, people do not talk of scare-mongering.
>
> (Blair 2005: 1)

Even this classic example of reflexive 'speech act' securitization must be contextualized in 'the field' of its emergence; 'the threat' that Blair was attempting to deal with was more than just the indirect 'inciters' of hatred who must be stopped from influencing more 'home grown' suicide bombers in the UK. Blair was also presenting those who had opposed his government's previous attempts to protect the nation from harm as a threat. Rather than viewing the process of securitization here as 'a specific strategy of a dominant actor' (Bigo and Tsoukla 2008: 8); Blair's speech should be instead understood as what Bigo calls a 'conversion' operation (2002: 69). It is undoubted that Blair attempted to introduce a new batch of emergency legislation that would be 'rule-breaking'; this is obvious through his 'rules of the game are changing' rhetoric. However, the securitizing 'work' Blair was engaged in here was rather more complex, in that he was attempting to speak the ultimate 'truth' (and have the last word on national security) through employing the events of 7/7 as a conversion operative in a contested political field. Blair's objective here was to validate 'his' particular 'truth' with regard to what the government needed to do to defeat terrorism and thus to devalue alternative truths in order to 'produce a hierarchy of threats' (Bigo 2002: 69). The conclusion that one can draw from this interpretation is that Tony Blair's securitizing actions in this media briefing were not really devoted to generating a consensus, in the form of a dominant discourse that would marginalize opposing and alternative discourses. Rather than seeking a consensus by way of agreement and compromise, Blair's securitizing activities were dedicated to gaining permission to act unfettered by what Berman would call 'irksome restrictions' (2003: 192; McGhee 2008a: 38–9). By so doing Blair was attempting to grant himself and his government the permission to fight terrorism as they saw fit. In the next section I will contrast Gordon Brown's attempts at consensus building with those of Tony Blair.

Gordon Brown – a desecuritizing agent?

In contrast to Tony Blair, Gordon Brown's approach to terrorism and counter-terrorism does not place the executive in conflict with parliament and the courts. Brown seems to be less concerned with exploiting the intersubjective resonance that comes with successful securitization associated with threats or atrocities. In fact Brown, in his speech acts, can be accused of attempting to close the distance created between the executive, parliament and the judiciary that had opened up under Blair. Furthermore, it should be noted that Brown's speeches as Prime Minister were in the context of the government losing their parliamentary majority in 2007.

Rather than examining the place of securitization in Brown's recent speeches as Prime Minister, I am going to focus on the processes of desecuritization in these speeches. Brown includes a number of what can be described as desecuritizing statements in his speeches. For example, in his Security and Liberty speech in June 2008, he drew an explicit line between his approach and those of his predecessor by stating: 'to say we should ignore the longstanding claims of liberty when faced with the urgent needs of security is tempting to some, but never to me – it would be to embark down an illiberal path that is as unacceptable to the British people as it is to me' (2008: 4); another example can be found in his speech on Liberty in October 2007 in which he again attempts to distance himself from Blair's approach to counter-terrorism by insisting on transparency and proper scrutiny by parliament of new counter-terrorism legislation:

> [T]he key to making these hard choices in a way that is compatible with our traditions of liberty is to, at all times, apply the liberty test, respecting fundamental rights and freedoms, and whenever, action is needed by government, it never subjects the citizen to arbitrary treatment, is transparent and proportionate in its measures and at all times also requires proper scrutiny by, and accountability to parliament and the people.
>
> (Brown 2007: 8)

I have suggested earlier that this type of approach is an example of desecuritization. But what is desecuritization? The relatively under-theorized processes associated with desecuritization (relative to the now familiar analysis of securitization) have been described in various ways. For Huysmans, following Wæver (1995) desecuritization is a process of unmaking securitization (2006: 126). For Aradau, also following Wæver (1995), desecuritization is a matter of adopting democratic 'unexceptional' procedures in policy and law making in response to the potentially 'undemocratic', urgent and often exceptional policies whose introduction is made possible by securitization (2004: 400). I think Aradau's interpretation is closer to Wæver's brief mention of the processes of desecuritization as being a matter of desecuritizing 'issues that have become securitized' (1995: 58). Rather than 'unmaking' securitization I view this process as rather more selective. For example, Gordon Brown's approach to terrorism and counter-terrorism, as we can see from the quotations above, is a matter of adopting some unexceptional procedures in response to some of the exceptional, urgent or emergency procedures adopted by his predecessor. This is less a case of 'unmaking securitization' in that Brown's apparent desecuritizing intentions and consensus-building ambitions are made possible through and in reaction to the Blair's administration's 'securitization' of the issue of 'terrorism'. Gordon Brown is not the first senior member of the Labour government to reflect on the acceptable balance between liberty and security in the post-9/11 world. The former Home Secretary David Blunkett, in his foreword to the discussion paper *Counter-Terrorism Powers: Reconciling Security and Liberty in an Open Society* in 2004, said:

> My first responsibility as Home Secretary is to do everything I can to ensure our common security but is this security worth having if the price is a series of unacceptable restrictions on our hard-won freedoms?
>
> (Blunkett, in Home Office 2004a: Foreword).

However, Gordon Brown, unlike Blunkett, does not leave questions such as these open to the inevitable securitizing logic that fills the vacuum created in the aftermath of atrocities, which in the case of the Blair administration post 9/11 led to 'executive justice' (Hillyard 2006: 5) and conflict with the judiciary (Lord Phillips 2006: 4). Rather, Brown provides a definitive answer, that is, governments must put forward counter-terrorism provisions not because they are 'tough' or 'populist' but because they are 'necessary' (Brown 2008a: 3). At the same time, these 'necessary measures' must be treated unexceptionally (in procedural terms) with a view of achieving a settlement with regard to liberty and security. The following quotation from Brown is a prime example of this desecuritizing approach:

> I argued then, and I believe now, that by preserving the primacy of the courts, backed up by proper oversight and, in the end, parliamentary scrutiny, we can achieve a settlement that ensures both our tradition of liberty and our need for security.
>
> (Brown 2008a: 3)

It is here that we begin to see the consensus-building strategy adopted by Brown which could be described as a successful case of desecuritization, which like Blair's securitization strategy is also designed to operate as a field effect (Bigo 2002: 67) across the executive, parliament, the judiciary and ultimately the general public through media dissemination. Brown's desecuritizing speech acts are also made with the intention of Brown becoming a 'conversion operator' (Bigo 2002: 69). However, Brown's speeches are not for the purpose of 'achieving sufficient effects' (that is, bring about a conversion of the field) resulting in an audience being 'more tolerate of the violations of rules' (Buzan et al. 1998: 25) as in Tony Blair's post-7/7 media briefing. Rather,

Brown's intention is to create sufficient effects to make an audience (for example, other political parties, the judiciary and 'the general public') support him in the fight against terrorism through the adherence to rules and procedures. Brown's speeches on terrorism, when viewed in this light, can be described as attempting to provide an antidote to the illiberalism of Blair's version of the 'war on terrorism'. This contrast between Blair and Brown's strategic 'conversion' roles in these securitizing and desecuritizing strategies is significant in their own right. However, the objective of exploring these different strategies is for the purpose of examining the extent of the influence of Brown's desecuritizing strategy on the members of his cabinet (for example, the Home Secretary and the Justice Secretary).

In the next section I will continue to explore the 'consensus'-building activities of the Brown administration through examining the place of human security in former Home Secretary Jacqui Smith's appeals for support in the extension of pre-charge detention to 42 days.

2.3 National security, 'core values' and the protection of 'life' and well-being

This section of the chapter will analyse aspects of the National Security Strategy and examine Jacqui Smith's speeches to the House of Commons during the debates on the Counter-Terrorism Bill on 11 June 2008. It will explore the symbiotic relationship in these parliamentary debates and in the guiding principles of the National Security Strategy between a discourse of 'shared' or 'core' values and a discourse that attempts to bring the terrorist threat 'home' in terms of the necessity of protecting the 'life' and 'well-being' of British citizens. It will be suggested here that Jacqui Smith's consensus-building activities are a case of 'the inter-subjective establishment of threat' (Roe 2005: 790) through employing both securitizing and desecuritzing speech acts that attempt to employ what Bauman (2006) calls 'derivative fear' to tap into what Giddens (1993) calls ontological security.[3]

The National Security Strategy introduced by Gordon Brown in 2008 includes a considered discussion on a number of contemporary threats to national security, for example, climate change, international finance, organized crime and population movement.[4] In the introduction to the National Security Strategy it was stated that the scope and approach of the strategy reflects the broadening of the view of national security which in the past focused on 'the protection of the state and its vital interests from attacks by other states' to also 'include threats to individual citizens and to our way of life, as well as the integrity and interests of the state' (Cabinet Office 2008: 3–4). What was presented as 'our single overarching national security objective' in the National Security Strategy reflects this broadening out of national security to include the more personal or 'human' aspects of security, that is,

> [o]ur single overarching national security objective of protecting the United Kingdom and its interests, enabling its people to go about their daily lives freely and with confidence, in a more secure, stable, just and prosperous world.
>
> (Cabinet Office 2008: 5)

In many ways this statement gives a flavour of the widened, broadened and de-differentiated concept of 'national security' included in this strategy. It will be argued here that this strategy presents a globalized contextualization of British national security 'in an interdependent world' and attempts to emphasize the more human and personal aspects of 'security'. The National Security Strategy can be described as the receptacle for the government's interpretation of many of the academic debates on the definition of 'security' (or more accurately securities) that have emerged in recent decades. This strategy therefore can be described as attempting to reconcile a number of what have been described as 'cleavages' in academic definitions of security (Huysmans 2006b: 3). For the most part these debates have clustered around the split between the 'narrow' versus the 'broad' definition of security and this has come to be known as the 'widening debate' (Krause and Williams 1997, in Huysmans 2006: 3) in academic International Relations debates. During these academic debates challenges were raised with regard to the remit of 'security studies' as being dedicated to just military activities and defence or whether security should be widened to focus on other interrelated sectors. Buzan (1983, 1991), and eventually Buzan et al., as noted earlier, were pivotal in widening out 'security' to examine what they called the interactions between a range of interdependent sectors (1996: 7).[5] At the same time, Bigo refers to another shift in the academic study of 'security' with regard to the influence of social constructionism, post-structuralism and deconstructionism in International Relations. For Bigo, the latter resulted in the empiricist scholars in the discipline of International Relations being challenged with regard to the 'essentialism' and the forms of dualisms (for example, international/national, external/internal, state/societal, security/insecurity, us/them) that structured their scholarship (Bigo 2001: 96). For Bigo, the result of this process is that 'the question of security is not reducible to national security and even less to the traditional questions of defence' (2001: 96). With the merging of 'internal' and 'external' securities in an increasingly interconnected world, the interactive 'sectors' described and categorized by Buzan et al. are not sustainable; for Bigo, 'it becomes impossible to oppose, as two different faces, national and state security on the one hand, and societal and identity security on the other hand' (Bigo 2001: 95). In many ways, the National Security Strategy in conjunction with Jacqui Smith's appeals for consensus in the House of Commons, as will be noted later, reflects the blurred boundaries found in the academic definitions (and cleavages) of 'security'.

However, as well as widening the analysis of security questions across a range of sectors another shift became apparent which is even more pertinent to the analysis of the parameters of the National Security Strategy in the UK. According to Ole Wæver, it was during the 1980s that a general move was witnessed that was intent on broadening 'the security agenda' (1995: 47). The result being that there was a shift from the strict focus on the security of 'the state' (national security) towards a broader or alternative focus on the security of 'people, either as individuals or as a global or international collectivity' (Wæver 1995: 47). According to Zygmunt Bauman, this shift in academic debates mirrors the parallel shift in 'the state's' relationship with its subjects. According to Bauman, 'the state' having founded its raison d'etre and its claim to citizens' obedience on the promise to protect its subjects against threats to their existence have found themselves in the position of not being able to deliver on its promise (2006: 4). As a result of this situation 'the state', according to Bauman, in the context of, for example, the fast globalizing and increasingly extraterritorial threats that assail its populace, has been obliged to shift the emphasis on 'fear protection' from dangers to social security which emphasizes the dangers associated with 'personal safety' (2006: 4). It will be suggested here that although the National Security Strategy should be praised for its heroic attempts at attempting to reconcile the different debates and cleavages between broad, wide, narrow, state and human securities, this strategy has a particular role to play in the Gordon Brown government's attempts to build a consensus on national security, especially with regard to the emphasis on the human and personal aspects of security and the role of 'core' or 'shared values' in counter-terrorism policy. In summary the broadening out of security is evidence of the recognition that definitions of insecurity and threat can no longer only be conceived at the level of the state and in the relationship between states (Thomas 2000: 9). However, it will be argued here that the 'single overarching national security objective' found in the National Security Strategy does not signal the eclipse of 'state-centred' security for what has been described as 'people-centred' or 'human security' (Wæver 1995: 47; Axworthy 2001: 19) in the form of a wholesale shift from statist discourses of national security (Aradau 2004: 393) to more intimate and emotive discourse of human security (Falk 2004: 10). Rather, what this process leads to is a particularly strong discourse associated with the need to protect 'core' national values through strategies that prioritize public security.

'Human security' has been described as lacking a precise definition, and for being an elusive concept (Betts and Eagleton-Pierce 2005: 5; Paris 2001: 88). However, this has not stopped the concept from gaining ground in UN, EU and now in UK policies. In fact, according to Paris, this definitional imprecision has increased rather than decreased the salience of 'human security' as a rallying call and campaign slogan (2001: 88). Furthermore, the salient appeal of human security has in turn been articulated with what Malmvig describes as the positive side of securitization processes associated with social and political mobilization in the face of imminent dangers (2005: 358) within states. It is to these processes that I intend to turn my focus in the UK. It will be argued here that the de-differentiation of the designated 'security' sectors becomes articulated in the form of the government's discourse of national core values as the entities 'we' most need to protect and as 'our' ultimate source of security in the face of unprecedented threats. The National Security Strategy includes it own attempt to build a unified response to and consensus on 'the single national security objective', that is:

> This National Security Strategy shows that the Government is committed to working with the whole of society, to build confidence in our core values, our shared approach, and our strong security capabilities. It sets out a new clearer understanding of what security means and how we need to work together … to manage risks, harness the opportunities of globalisation, and achieve the single overarching national security objective.
>
> (Cabinet Office 2008: 60)

This is a consensus-building statement through and through. However, in what follows I want to explore the interplay between the defence of (and building confidence in) core values in the National Security Strategy and the defence of personal well-being (and ultimately 'life') in human security terms, in the text of the Counter-Terrorism Bill of 2008 and in Jacqui Smith's defence of the Bill in the House of Commons. It will be argued here that it is in the combination of these two elements where a 'deeper' more resonate and affective national security consensus-building strategy can be observed and which will ultimately lead to proposals for introducing wide-ranging changes in the UK's human rights policy (see section 2.4). In the section dedicated to 'guiding principles' in the National Security Strategy it was stated that:

> [o]ur approach to national security is clearly grounded in a set of core values. They include human rights, the rule of law, legitimate and accountable government, justice, freedom, tolerance, and opportunity for all. Those values define who we are and what we do. They form the basis of our security, as well as our well-being and our prosperity.
> (Cabinet Office 2008: 6)

Before challenging the government's assertions that their national security strategy is 'grounded' in core values, including human rights and the rule of law (see section 2.4), in this section I will explore (1) the relationship between the definition of a 'grave and exceptional terrorist threat' in the text of the Counter-Terrorism Bill and (2) the interplay between the discourse of British 'core values' and the protection of 'life' and 'well-being' in Jacqui Smith's speech in the House of Commons during the Counter-Terrorism Bill of 2008.

The definition of a 'grave and exceptional terrorist threat' can be found in Section 1 of the Counter-Terrorism Bill. In this Bill 'grave exceptional terrorist threat' means an event or situation involving terrorism which causes or threatens (a) serious loss of human life, (b) serious damage to human welfare in the UK or (c) serious damage to the security of the UK (Smith Hansard [Commons] 11 June, 2008). The combination of state and human security here are obvious, however, subsection 1 (b) upgrades the focus on 'freedom from fear' and 'freedom from want' associated with human security discourse to include events and situations that threaten 'human welfare', that is, human welfare as defined for the purpose of securing lives and perhaps even the lifestyles enjoyed in advanced Western democracy. Expected definitions of basic human welfare are included here, for example, causing or threatening to cause human illness or injury in physical security terms (Donohue 2008: 30) and the disruption to the supply of food, water, energy, fuel and health services. However, the following are also included: disruption to communication systems, transportation facilities and the supply of money, all of which have also become central to our capacities to defend ourselves and also to live in advanced Western democracies (but are not matters of life and death). In many ways the broadening of the objectives of security and the expansive definitions of exactly what is at stake with regard to 'grave exceptional terrorist threats' can be described as being an attempt to humanize and personalize potential threats. By so doing the security threat is brought 'home' through presenting the potential impacts of terrorism as being relevant to how 'we' in Britain live today. There are parallels to be made here with former Home Secretary David Blunkett's emotive employment of 'home' and the 'abuse of hospitality' in his attempts to conjoin the 'social problem' of asylum with the threat of terrorism in the previous chapter. This is a similar strategy to what Bonnie Honig calls the 'the politics of home' (1996: 257) which is evident in the personalization of 'grave and exceptional terrorist threats' in that this is an attempt to ground the repercussions of particular existential threats in formal legal terms (in the Bill) in order to make the threat 'real' and to personalize insecurities (Douzinas 2007: 184). There is a great deal of political purchase to be made from the process of consensus building through personalizing and humanizing threats in this way. Rather than just the existential threat (of, for example, unprecedented terrorist activities), it is the aftermath of potential attacks that are being 'played up' and dramatized in very personal 'human' terms here. This is an example of the performativity associated with the simultaneous processes of defining 'security' and through this process of also constructing identities (Campbell 1998; Wæver 1995). According to Campbell, representations of security and discourses of threat tell us who we are, what we value and what (and more accurately whom) we should be afraid of (Campbell 1998). This is not as Buzan et al. would have us believe, a matter of constructing a 'we' identity in the 'societal sector' where individuals identify themselves as members of a community in processes that should be viewed as being distinct from, but are often entangled with, the explicitly political organizations 'concerned with government' (Buzan et al. 1996: 119). In Buzan et al.'s and Wæver's formulations, according to McSweeney, 'identity describes the society, and society is constituted by identity' (1996: 87). In contrast to this formulation of societal security in and through identity, the government in the National Security Strategy and in the Counter-Terrorism Bill is in the process of reformulating security as 'national security' through their promotion and reinforcement of 'core values' and the general publics' commitment to accepting and sharing these values as a primary defence to myriad threats. This is a matter of the government attempting to construct identities through encouraging everyone in the UK to identifying with 'our' core values which are expressed and articulated through Britain's historically enduring institutions (see also Chapter 5). However, the primary core, shared and common value that is emerging here is not the abstract and general core values listed in the National Security Strategy but rather the value of personal safety in and through the strategies that promise 'public safety'.

Jacqui Smith's consensus-building work during the debates on the Counter-Terrorism Bill partly follows Gordon Brown's example in that the former Home Secretary's statements are peppered with desecuritizing speech acts, for example, for Smith, 'Our response to terrorism must continue to be based on those values and liberties, ardently pursued through our democratic framework, primarily through our Criminal Justice System' (Smith, Hansard [Commons] 11 June 2008: Col 328). However, Smith 'spices up' these reassuring desecuritizing statements with what amounts to a securitizing technique including rhetorical structures specified by Buzan et al. in which 'survival' and the necessity of action are presented in apocalyptic terms along the lines of: 'if the problem is not handled now it will be too late, and we will not exist to remedy our failure' (Buzan et al. 1998: 26). However, it will be suggested here that the rule-changing action Smith is intent on introducing in her appeals for parliament's support for the government's extension of pre-charge detention of terrorist suspects from 21 days to 42 days is above and beyond the specifics of these provisions. Smith, in this speech, seems to be intent on paving the way for something far more significant than these controversial powers. I believe it was her intention to fundamentally shift the balance between individual civil liberties and 'public security' in contemporary Britain in her quest for introducing pre-emptive measures against 'terrorist suspects'. This is where Jacqui Smith and Jack Straw (see section 2.4) can be seen to be working in tandem. Smith's intention, following Gordon Brown and the tenets of the National Security Strategy, is, that when opposing terrorism, the government must not lose sight of 'our' values, that is,

[f]or me, getting the balance right between individual freedom and collective security must always be at the heart of what we do. Our response must reinforce our shared values, not weaken them, because it is on those values that our security ultimately depends.

(Smith, Commons [Hansard] 11 June: Col 328)

Thus it is 'our' core values that are under threat and 'our' core values are what will ultimately save us. Furthermore, the processes normally given over to 'the construction and articulation of a collective sense of identity' (McSweeney 1996: 86) in the face of considerable threats, in Smith's speech, can be described as being relegated to a 'by-product' of the ultimate goal, namely the protection of what 'the we' stands for and stands to lose, which is presented here as 'our' shared values. The government's strategy, which is evident in Smith's appeals for consensus and support for the Counter-Terrorism Bill seems to be a strategy dedicated to 'domination' through recourse to the role the government has taken up as defenders of Britain's core values. According to Graham M. Smith it is through the intersubjective establishment of the threat to its particular conception of 'core values' that one group establishes its dominant position in relation to other groups (in Roe 2005: 790). According to Smith:

> The ability to define a security threat to the core values of an order, and to implement or impose security measures to defend or perpetuate those core values, is simultaneously to enable certain ... groups to take hold of the core values of an order, that is, to define the order itself, and to attack ... potential challenges to that order, or potential power rivals.
>
> (Smith, in Roe 2005: 790)

It would appear that Jacqui Smith's performance in the House of Commons on 11 June 2008 followed Graham M. Smith's hypothesis rather closely. The former Home Secretary's strategy of domination can be observed in the next passage where her appeals to parliament to work with the government are presented in terms of 'the House' doing 'the right thing for this country's security'. However, there is one further twist that should be noted in the next passage, and that is the former Home Secretary's replacement of the 'defence of core values' with the even more resonate calls with the protection of 'everybody's right to life', that is:

> It is the job of the Government, Police and Prosecutors to protect the public from terrorist attack, and thereby to defend everybody's right to life, but today, it is the job of Parliament to give them the tools to do that. We need the support of the House for the proposals in the Bill. We need the support of the House to do the right thing for this country's security.
>
> (Smith, Commons [Hansard] 11 June 2008: Col 328)

It is Smith's employment of 'everybody's right to life' in her appeal for unity, support and consensus on 'getting the balance right' between individual freedom and national security needs, which in this instance would be evidenced by parliament supporting the government's Counter-Terrorism Bill, which is of particular interest here. In many ways this is like the speech acts employed by Tony Blair, in that they are a complex example of securitization through the process of attempting to convert myriad positions on counter-terrorism in the parliamentary field into a unified consensus in the form of 'the House' granting the government permission to act as it sees fit. That being said, Smith's strategy differs from Blair's in that she wants parliament on board (in contrast to Blair wanting parliament and the courts to back off to allow him to fight terrorism in his way). Whereas Blair craved the power and responsibility to take on 'terrorists' and 'extremists' unilaterally, in the context of the government no longer enjoying a parliamentary majority, Smith's approach can be described as a responsibilization strategy that (like the Blair and Bush administrations) offers a limited choice of options for 'the House'. That is, the House of Commons can either act responsibly (that is, supporting the government) and in the process uphold and defend British 'core values' and thus safeguard the lives of everybody, or they can act irresponsibly with the opposite effect.

Furthermore, it should be noted that 'the right to life' is not just a colloquialism, a shorthand way of presenting, for example, the rights associated with protections against physical insecurities (threats to life and limb). The right to life as enshrined in Article 2 of the ECHR[6] is fast becoming the ultimate trump card (as we shall see in the next section) in speeches made by the former lord chancellor Charles Falconer (under Tony Blair) and the current lord chancellor Jack Straw.

2.4 Deciding whose rights come first

In this final section of this chapter I will explore the impact of the broadening definitions of 'security' on the discourse of 'shared values' and on suggestions for the application of human rights. I agree with Douzinas when he writes that contemporary Western governments are in the business of assiduously cultivating 'a climate of fear' through maintaining 'personal insecurity' as an 'ever-present existential condition' (2007: 184). Huysmans describes 'security' in this context as a 'technique of governing danger' (2006: 7); similarly Bigo describes, as noted in the previous chapter, these processes as 'the management of unease' (2002: 64). For Douzinas the ever-present existential condition of personal insecurity in, for example, Jacqui Smith's speech, offers the government the dream of an 'open-ended authorisation for all kinds of preventative and protective action' (2007: 184) which can be used to skew, as Blair did, institutionalized tensions between judicial, executive and legislative powers in favour of the executive (Huysmans 2006: 12). Increasingly the latter has been carried out in the name of protecting 'the law abiding majority' from danger in the name of public security. This discriminatory discourse which evokes the rights of 'the law abiding majority' over the rights of 'criminal' and 'extremist' minorities is an extension of the Bush and Blair administrations' 'war on terror' mantra: 'you are either with us or you are with the terrorists'. As we shall see, the moralistic strategy of placing the protection of the lives of the 'law abiding majority' at the heart of the 'war on crime' and especially 'the war on terror' is an example of what Malmvig describes as the negative side of the processes of securitization (Malmvig 2005: 358; Wæver 1995: 57). That is, the aspect of securitization that 'brings closure and hypersensitivity to an issue' is in turn associated with particular political effects, namely the tightening of control and the closing down of debates 'by securitizing actors' (Malmvig 2005: 358). Aradau takes these observations further by suggesting that the discursive work of securitization processes involves more than just the contestation over meanings and actions. For Aradau, securitization is a process of ordering that closes off forms of social antagonisms and struggles for justice and delegitimizes their claims in these terms (Aradau 2006: 82). Securitization is therefore part of an artificial, temporary (emergency) consensus-building technique which, as noted in section 2.3 of this chapter, can both promote 'core values' such as human rights and the rule of law which were listed as some of the guiding principles of the government's National Security Strategy, and simultaneously, as will be noted, promote changes with regard to some of these 'core values', for example, the application of human rights in Britain in the name of what appears to be Britain's ultimate core value: public safety. I agree with Zedner's summation that the employment of the 'public interest' or 'public security' by governments is the 'trump card against which any individual claim to liberty cannot compete' (2005: 513). According to Huysmans, when viewed in this way both securitization (and the desecuritizing speech acts of politicians in the context of previously successful securitization), becomes, as suggested in Chapter 1, 'a technique of Government' (2006: 6) a means of mobilizing certain meanings that modulates these meanings in certain ways (2006: 7). This is no more evident than when politicians want to influence the balance between the civil liberties of individuals and 'collective' or 'public' security.

Much has been written on the liberty/security balance or sliding scale, where 'the people' are willing (or persuaded) to give up some freedom/ liberty in a 'state of emergency' in order to secure their 'freedom' in the long term (Dworkin 2003; Waldron 2003; Zedner 2005; Thomas 2003) within the liberty/security binary opposition (Neal 2007: 3). Most of these authors have suggested that 'the balance metaphor' is misleading and diverts attention away from, or encourages indifference to, the reality of, for example, the impact of the 'war on terrorism' on the reduction of the rights of often vulnerable minority groups, foreign nationals, asylum seekers and certain members of Muslim communities (Thomas 2003; Dworkin 2003; Kundnani 2007; Fekete 2005; McGhee 2008a). Others, who have been involved in analyzing public or social attitude surveys (in Britain), for example, Conor Gearty (a co-author of a recent British Social Attitudes Survey), comments on the wider 'field effect' (see section 2.2) evident among the general public where 'the very mention of something being a counter-terrorism measure makes people willing to contemplate the giving up of their freedoms' (in BBC News 2007). However, as Dworkin (2003) so clearly stated, when 'the public' think they are giving up their freedom they are actually giving up the freedoms of others; it is undeniable that certain sections of the population, namely foreign nationals (foreign national Muslims in particular) in the US and UK are at the head of the queue when it comes to the risk of having their human rights violated.

It is in the context of this indifference to the plight of those whose rights and freedoms 'we' are willing to relinquish[7] that I want to examine 'the balance', or more accurately, the rebalancing metaphor with regard to human rights further with regard to other, related political effects. I agree with Donohue, when she says that 'rights and security' are far more complex than the customary trade-off implies (2008: 29). Whereas Donohue's emphasis is on the relationality between discrete rights, and that 'restrictions that affect one right, for instance, resonate in others' (2008: 29), I want to focus on the effect on all human rights and civil liberties enshrined in the ECHR articles that were incorporated into the Human Rights Act of 1998 when one right in particular, 'the right to life', becomes the prism through which all other rights are to be viewed and ultimately applied.

According to the Department for Constitutional Affairs, in their review of the implementation of the Human Rights Act, the problem with human rights in contemporary Britain is that key decision takers are 'getting the balance wrong by placing undue emphasis upon the entitlement of individuals' (2006: 39). The result being that judges in British courts, as well as judges sitting in the European Court of Human Rights,[8] were accused of paying insufficient regard to 'the overarching importance of a State's duty to maintain public security under Article 2 of the European Convention on Human Rights' (2006: 39). The recommendation made by the Department for Constitutional Affairs was that the government should consider using the Human Rights Act to effect a rebalancing (within the UK's margin of appreciation) in the way Article 2 (the right to life) is applied in relation to other articles (2006: 39; McGhee 2008a: 137–8). The calls to strike a new balance between individual rights and public security is just one of a series of reflexive rebalancing processes observable in contemporary Britain associated with responses to an existing disequilibrium (for example, the public's mistrust of human rights and the alleged inappropriate application of human rights protection)[9] and an external threat (for example, the threat from al-Qaeda) (Zedner 2005: 508). This emphasis on public security in the calls to rebalance human rights have emerged since 9/11 and has gathered pace since the 7/7 attacks in London in 2005. It was also evident in Lord Falconer's (the former Lord Chancellor under the Blair administration, see McGhee 2008a: 139) defence of the Human Rights Act. Lord Falconer, in his Royal United Services Institute speech in the series *Legislating for Terrorism*, advocated a re-prioritization of human rights and specific aspects of the European Convention, namely Article 2 (following the Department for Constitutional Affairs recommendations) in order to better equip the state in the fight against terrorism, that is,

> the first duty of Government is to protect its citizens. And faced with new and changing threats the Government must develop its response. New steps must be taken in order to meet these changing circumstances and to continue to provide protection to the public.
>
> (Lord Falconer 2007: 3)

The current Lord Chancellor, Jack Straw (who was the minister responsible for introducing the Human Rights Bill through parliament in 1997–8) reiterated many of his predecessor's (Lord Falconer) points in his Mackenzie-Stuart Lecture at Cambridge University in October 2007, including an emphasis on a government's ultimate duty, that is, 'Governments must act to protect life, and laws must change to meet the imperatives of national security' (2007: 4).

In this lecture Straw focuses on 'the new terrorism' and 'the new terrorist' with the intention of advocating a new human rights policy in Britain to respond to 'new circumstances'. According to Straw, the ECHR was established 'to protect the citizens of Europe from ever again experiencing the horrors of totalitarianism' after the Second World War (2007a: 2). Contemporary Europe and Britain, according to Straw, need new ways of protecting themselves from the horrors of 'al-Qaeda inspired terrorism', that is, 'the threat from al-Qaeda inspired terrorism is wholly asymmetrical; our diplomatic, military, security, law enforcement and legal/judicial systems were never designed to counter it. It has made it harder to protect our citizens' (Straw 2007a: 4).

Straw's depiction of the threat from al-Qaeda is an exemplar of 'the new terrorism thesis' (Burnett and Whyte 2005: 6) which contrasts 'nation-state terrorism' (of which ETA in Spain and the IRA in Northern Ireland are examples) with the activities of al-Qaeda which are understood as being transnationally oriented and organized (Beck 2006: 113). In many ways Straw's depiction of 'the new terrorists' and 'the new terrorism' and the limitations placed on states to defend themselves from these new phenomenon is a well-trodden path taken by senior members of the Labour government under Blair. Various Home Secretaries (Straw, Blunkett, Clarke and Reid) have all pronounced on the need to strengthen legislation, strengthen democracy and balance rights in 'the new war on terror' since 1999 (McGhee 2008a: 38–9).[10] At the same time, it is in the context of new threats such as these that the new broadened definitions of 'security' (see section 2.3) are being devised to respond to.

In his Mackenzie-Stuart lecture Straw's main message on human rights (in the context of contemporary geopolitics) is that the government will do its 'utmost to secure the safety of the British people' (2007a: 5). According to Straw, 'far from undermining how we strike the balance in the new situation, a human rights framework used intelligently – can help us resolve these tensions' (Straw 2007a: 4). The 'intelligent use' of what Straw describes as 'twenty-first century rights' to address our changing circumstances is a question of application rather than a question of the principles that underpin human rights (Straw 2007a: 5). This prioritization of public security (driven by the executive) over the rights of the individual (protected by the judiciary) does carry risks. The former and current Lord Chancellors are engaging with what Ignatieff describes as the question as to what role human rights should play in deciding public policy during terrorist emergencies (2005: viii).

The rebalancing of human rights protections away from the rights of the individual to prioritize public, human or personal security is an example of the logic of 'the lesser evil'. This comes down to striking a balance between 'our' security and 'their' liberty, of ensuring the rights of the many through sacrificing the rights of the few (Dworkin 2003).

By rebalancing human rights in this way, the anomaly of emergency measures could fast become a turning point (Mamdani 2005: 2003) in which human rights, which prior to this point have been associated with the protection of the weak, the vulnerable and the marginalized, that is, the 'people who need human rights protection the most' (Gearty 2006: 5), will become associated with the protection of the rights of the law abiding majority. For Gearty, the supposed lack of conflict between counter-terrorism laws and civil liberties, defined as 'defending everybody's right to life' (see section 2.3), is an ominous development which flows from the redefinition of human rights, the material effect of which is to excuse repression as necessary to prevent the destruction of human rights values (Gearty 2006: 108; McGhee 2008a: 140). As a result of this 'dangerous embrace' between counter-terrorism laws and human rights, 'messing about aggressively with people, suspending the ordinary processes of law, narrowing the civic space so as to exclude alternative points of view all turn out to be okay from a human rights perspective' (Gearty 2006: 108; McGhee 2008a: 141). This is no more apparent than in the pre-emptive turn in UK counter-terrorism. The pre-emptivity with regard to new border controls and the early intervention policing strategy under Prevent (see Chapter 1) are examples of the wider pre-emptive turn in UK policymaking. As will be noted in the next chapter, a pre-emptive logic also haunts the managed migration strategy which will be described as a proactive immigration policy designed to exclude those immigrants who are deemed to pose the risk of being the problematic (in social, cultural and economic terms) communities of the future.

Pre-emptivity has been an abiding feature of post-9/11 counter-terrorism in the UK since the introduction of the Anti-Terrorism, Crime and Security Act 2001 (Donohue 2008; Fenwick and Baker 2007). According to the Privy Counsellor Review Committee's review of the Anti-Terrorism, Crime and Security Act 2001 the powers associated with indefinite detention without charge of foreign national 'terror suspects' introduced in the Act were particularly problematic as they are 'more likely to interfere with the rights of the individual than conventional police powers because they seek to pre-empt terrorism, that is to allow intervention before a specific crime has taken place, as well as punish crimes after the event' (Privy Counsellor Review Committee 2003: 25).

Pre-emptivity was once again at the forefront of debates on finding the balance between individual civil liberties and public security in the extension of pre-charge detention to 42 days in the Counter-Terrorism Bill of 2008. The provisions of this Bill were premised on 'the need for early intervention' to allow the police in the name of 'defending everybody's life' 'to step in early to prevent a plot from coming to fruition' (Smith Hansard [Commons] 11 June 2008: Col 318).[11] What can be observed here is a relationship between the pre-emptivity of counter-terrorism and the performativity associated with what Bigo describes as the management of unease (2002: 63). At the same time, counter-terrorist pre-emptivity, and the rebalancing of the relationship between individual civil liberties and 'public' security in the name of 'defending everybody's life', can be viewed as being a rhetorical structure of securitization and the hybrid securitizing and desecuritizing structures introduced by Jacqui Smith (see section 2.3) in that these 'precautionary risk practices' (Amoore and de Goede 2008: 10) are beyond the certainties of logic and calculation and instead involve imaginative or 'visionary' techniques (O'Malley 2004: 5) which summon forth emergent or possible existential threats. These, in turn, lead to 'a politics of pre-emption' which legitimizes pre-emptive interventions (Amoore and de Goede 2008: 12–13).

In this light, the provisions of the Counter-Terrorism Bill are an example of what Ericson describes as 'pre-emptive security' which requires the reconfiguration of existing laws through the enactment of new laws or through devising new uses for existing laws in order to erode or eliminate traditional principles, standards and procedures of law 'that get in the way of pre-empting imagined sources of harm' (Ericson 2008: 57). Therefore, it is once again (see Chapter 1) through preventing harm (and in the process defending everybody's right to life) that the police are being allowed to act pre-emptively. It is here that the fragile balance between 'individual' civil liberties and 'public' security, which under Blair was occasionally distorted, is to become under Brown, Smith and Straw permanently rebalanced and enshrined in the language of a state's 'ultimate duty' (Home Office 2006a: 1). If this ultimate duty, as described by the government as an 'emerging duty in international human rights law' (Home Office 2006a: 1)[12] was beginning to gather pace under Blair and Falconer, we can see that under Brown, Smith and Straw the rebalancing of civil liberties and public security, in the name of the state acting upon its 'onerous positive obligations to take effective steps to protect the lives and physical integrity of everyone within their jurisdiction against the threat of terrorist attack' (Home Office 2006a: 1), could become a fait accompli.

The state's ultimate duty to protect the lives and physical integrity 'of everyone' in the name of the hybrid combinations of national and human security, that is, 'public security', is fast becoming 'our' ultimate value in Britain. As such this 'ultimate duty' and concomitantly 'ultimate value' in combination is becoming what Bourdieu would describe as 'a strong discourse' (1998: 95). According to Peck and Tickell, certain discourses are designated as 'strong discourses' in part by virtue of their self-actualizing nature and in part by virtue of their self-evident alignment with the primary contours of contemporary political-economic power (2002: 382). In my view, the interpretation of the right to life that I have examined in this chapter amounts to the securitizaton not of the right to life but rather the securitization of 'the right to the protection of life' (Xenos 2007: 4). This 'ultimate duty' is also, as Zedner (2005) has pointed out, the ultimate 'trump card' as discourses such as these are strong and therefore difficult to oppose because they, unlike other discourses, have 'all the powers of a world of power relations' behind them (Bourdieu 1998: 95). This is perhaps the ultimate danger in what Gearty (2006) refers to as the dangerous embrace between human rights and counter-terrorism. Public security and the state's ultimate duty to provide it is evidence of what Alkire describes (benignly) as the deep interconnections between 'human security' and 'human rights' (2003: 38). However, there is more to it than that; the interpretation of the state's ultimate duty under ECHR Article 2 is an example of what Bigo describes as 'reassuring and protective pastoral power' (2002: 72) which introduces a number of material effects associated with 'proactive, anticipative, and morphing techniques and aims' (2002: 72) designed to master chaotic futures 'with minimalist management focusing only on risky groups (so identified) or groups at risk' (Bigo 2002: 72). In Chapter 1 I noted the impact of this politics of unease management on the life chances of groups deemed 'risky', for example, asylum seekers attempting to enter 'fortress Europe' and on 'the state' rolling forward into Muslim communities (and arguably the intimate relationships among Muslim families and neighbours) in the name of preventing extremism in 'at risk' individuals. In this chapter, the pre-emptive politics of public security should be understood as being an example of reassuring pastoral power, in the context of twenty-first century biopolitics. This twenty-first century biopolitics in contrast to early twentieth-century biopolitics should not be merely understood as a strategy associated with the goal of maximizing 'population quality' (Rose 2007: 57). Rather these are strategies dedicated to maximizing what 'we' value the most: 'personal safety'[13] through 'public security' in the context of 'new' global realities (Booth 2005) in the context of shifting definitions and understanding of 'security' (McDonald 2008: 49).

2.5 Conclusion

This chapter has brought a number of developments together with the intention of examining Gordon Brown, (former) Home Secretary Jacqui Smith and Justice Secretary (and Lord Chancellor) Jack Straw's attempts at building a consensus around 'security' in contemporary Britain. I have decided to explore the ever broadening concept of 'security' tangentially in this chapter through the analysis of political discourses of security and insecurity with a view to examining some of the major themes of the book, namely, the performativity of 'core' or 'shared' values discourse in interdependent areas of public policy: counter-terrorism, immigration and integration and citizenship; and the shifting human rights culture in contemporary Britain. In order to do this I compared and contrasted the desecuritizing gestures of the Brown administration with the more explicitly securitizing rhetoric under Tony Blair. I also examined Brown and his former Home Secretary Jacqui Smith's apparent desire to close the distance (created by Blair) between the executive, parliament and the judiciary through attempting to garner support from the judiciary and parliament (and ultimately 'the general public') through their attempts to reassure the latter that their approach to counter-terrorism will strike an acceptable balance between civil liberties and 'public safety'. That being said, I proceeded to contextualize their apparently reassuring consensus-building rhetoric within the political effects and opportunities that have arisen in the process of broadening out and 'humanizing' the discourse of security in their National Security Strategy and in section 1 of the Counter-Terrorism Bill which employed 'core values' and 'the right to life' as trump cards in an attempt to convert 'the field' to their particular (and dominant) position. In so doing, these politicians have manipulated a highly sensitized 'field' which has resulted in the promotion of 'personal safety' as 'our' ultimate value in the context of strategies to ensure 'public safety' as the ultimate duty of the government.

In the next chapter the focus will be once again on border controls and anxieties about particular 'foreigners' and immigrant communities when I examine the combination of the managed migration points system with proposals for extending the naturalization process of becoming a British citizen in contemporary Britain.

3
Restoring Public Confidence – Managed Migration, Racialization and Earned Citizenship

3.1 Introduction

As yet, Europe does not have a co-ordinated 'managed migration' strategy. According to Graham Watson MEP,[1] Europe has 27 different immigration systems 'one for each of the EU's twenty-seven Member states'; this is despite the fact that 'what happens in one country inevitably affects the others' (Watson 2008a: Foreword). Watson notes that there is a sharp contrast between the levels of cooperation in the new EEA border regimes 'to fight illegal migration' (see Chapter 1), but relatively little by way of coordinated policy (apart from some EC Directives) to manage immigration across Europe (2008a: Foreword).[2] Furthermore, a number of EU states have introduced sweeping changes to their immigration policies and naturalization processes in recent years. According to Joppke, the impetus for these processes gained momentum in the wake of the post-9/11 worries over 'Muslim terror' and what he calls concerns over 'failing immigration integration in Europe' (2007: 41). As a result of these twin concerns a number of European countries imposed 'new "civic integration" courses and tests on newcomers' (Joppke 2007: 41). For example, in 2006 the Netherlands introduced civic integration examinations as part of their requirements for residency; in 2007 France introduced a compulsory 'welcome and integration contract' for all permanent foreign residents; in 2007 Spain issued its first strategic plan for Citizenship and Integration; also in 2007 Germany launched its National Integration Strategy (Borders and Immigration Agency 2008: 17). According to Joppke, the 'Dutch' model[3] has been the most influential civic integration strategy in Europe, variants of the Dutch model are now in force in Austria, Denmark, France, Portugal and France, among other countries (Joppke 2007: 44). In all instances, according to Joppke, the introduction of civic integration strategies in these European countries has been in response to 'worries about the unity and integration of ethnically diverse societies', and many states have responded to this 'with campaigns to symbolically upgrade citizenship, which may also include a re-tightening of access' (2007: 39). In this chapter I will explore the implementation of the twin public-reassurance strategies of 'up-grading' the naturalization process and the new measures associated with the processes of 'tightening' 'access' in Gordon Brown's Britain.

This chapter will once again explore the continuities between the Blair and Brown administrations,[4] in this instance the focus will shift from counter-terrorism strategies to immigration and naturalization strategies. In fact in this chapter I will explore how Gordon Brown and the first Home Secretary to serve under him, Jacqui Smith, have extended, for example, Prime Minister Blair and his various Home Secretaries' (especially David Blunkett and Charles Clarke) immigration and citizenship policies. This chapter focuses more on the security and citizenship themes of the book. I will return to the theme of human rights in Chapters 4, 5 and 6. Whereas Chapter 2 focused on the relationship between the populist discourse of 'public security', the discourse of shared values and human rights policy, this chapter explores the attempts by the Blair and Brown governments for attempting to restore 'public confidence' in the immigration system through introducing evermore selective, exclusive and restrictive immigration policies and also introducing (and proposing to introduce) citizenship examinations and other requirements such as English language tests on those applying for British citizenship.

Policy reform in the areas of immigration and integration are just one of a number of rebalancing strategies unfolding in contemporary Britain, as noted in the previous chapter. For Zedner, government discourses associated with 'rebalancing' usually take two forms: (1) rebalancing can presuppose a prior imbalance in the form of an existing disequilibrium; or, (2) can be introduced in response to external factors 'that can be said to tip the balance out of kilter' (Zedner 2005: 511). The Home Office's *Controlling our Borders: Making Migration Work for Britain* White Paper of 2005 (which will be examined later) and their 'Securing the UK Border: Our Vision and Strategy for the Future' paper published in March 2007 (examined in Chapter 1) are exemplars of reflexive and proactive rebalancing strategies that are cognizant of the policy failures of the past. However, the proposals introduced in these documents are also proactive in that the interrelated immigration and border control strategies they include are in part legitimized through their remit of heading off 'threats' or 'social bads' (side effects) that might have an adverse impact on the nation's future. The threats and social bads that these strategies are attempting to prevent are, in the case of *Controlling our Borders*, reducing future internal disequilibria presented by the government in 'community cohesion and integration' discourse as the continuing non-integration, social exclusion and associated economic marginalization of established minority ethnic and religious minority immigrant communities through a highly selective managed migration strategy. On the other hand the 'Securing the UK Border' strategy, as noted in Chapter 1, is an example of the securitization of migration (Huysmans 2006; Rumford 2008; Bigo 2002, 2006a, 2006b) which is dedicated to attempting to reduce future external threats in the form of terrorist attacks through setting up a system of offshore borders that will prevent 'failed' asylum claimants, known terrorist suspects (or those with any connection to terrorists or extremist organizations) from entering or re-entering Britain. This chapter will examine the former strategy, that is, the Labour government's managed migration strategy, which was introduced by Tony Blair and Home Secretary Charles Clarke in 2005. I will analyse the proposals made by Gordon Brown with regard to how the managed migration strategy was to work in tandem with his proposals for introducing the next phase in the UK's civic integration process, namely the earned British citizenship strategy. The managed migration strategy in combination with the new proposals for earned British citizenship, especially those aspects pertaining to permanent immigration to the UK, is reflexive in that it attempts to ameliorate what the government presents as the internal disequilibria (for example, the non-integration, 'segregation', lack of community cohesion and persisting 'race inequalities' mentioned earlier); however, post 7/7 this has also included concerns over 'public security' (see Chapters 2 and 5): future internal threats in the form of the potential disloyalty and unpatriotic acts of British born/home grown and naturalized citizens. The institutional reflexivity (Lash 1994; Giddens 1994), or more accurately government reflexivity (Dean 1999), associated with attempting to reduce the side effects and unintended consequences of previous immigration and 'integration' policies are also articulated through biopolitical concerns (associated with for example, regulating 'chain migration'), but even wider than this, the justification for these strategies are often made in the name of continuing 'societal' safety and prosperity.

In this chapter I will suggest that the proposals for combining the re-tightening of access under the managed migration points system and the upgrading of naturalization in the next phase of the UK's ongoing civic integration strategy requires analytical concepts that can match the complexity of these developments. It will be suggested here that these combined strategies necessitate a shift in the conceptualization of institutionalized racism in British post-war immigration legislation to reflect the multidimensionality and multilayered nature of the discourses which justify selectivity through racialized, cultural, and integrative criteria of desirability and undesirability. In this chapter these processes will be described as examples of institutional racialization (Rattansi 2005).

Managed migration, as articulated here, will be contextualized within the rationalities of what has become known as neoliberal globalization, in that this strategy is dedicated to selecting the migrants or immigrants that will 'work for Britain' on an economic level while mitigating the potential risks of immigration. Furthermore, the new approach to managed migration in combination with proposals for introducing earned citizenship naturalization processes proposed by Gordon Brown attempt to balance the economic utility of the points-based managed migration strategy by attempting to ensure that 'migration benefits us as much socially and culturally as it does economically' (Brown 2008: 3). This chapter will examine the articulation, following Parekh (2008), of a multilevel 'economic' and 'civic/cultural' integrationist agenda in Gordon Brown's recommendations for combining the managed migration strategy with his proposals for the new earned British citizenship/naturalization processes. By so doing I will explore both the managed migration point system and the proposals for the introduction of the three 'citizenship stages' (temporary residents, probationary citizens and full citizens) in the 'earned citizenship' strategy. It will be noted here that the earned citizenship proposals will extend the citizenship testing regimes introduced by David Blunkett considerably.

The interplay between the highly selective (and therefore exclusive) managed migration strategy and the new earned British citizenship proposals provides an opportunity for examining the relationship between what can be described as the interrelated 'security' threats and fears that have come to crystallize around new and established 'communities of immigration' in Britain. These communities, in particular have been the subject of problematization with regard to their alleged weak sense of citizenship, economic viability and potential extremism (McGhee 2003, 2005a, 2008a). In this light the primary aim of this chapter is to map the shift from Blunkett's model of civic assimilation with its Cantle-esque emphasis on dialogic participation to Brown's model of civic nationalism with its post-7/7 fuelled emphasis on loyalty, duty, responsibilities and 'shared values'. The secondary aim of this chapter is to explore the multilayered and multidimensional processes of institutional racialization (as opposed to institutional racism) associated with the justification of the restrictions on non-EU, low-skilled, potential chain migrants to the UK. At the same time I intend to tentatively tease out the relationship between these processes of institutional racialization and what Dean (2007) describes as the interplay of indiscrete and heterogeneous regimes of power in advanced liberal democracies, thus building on observations in previous chapters.

The chapter will be divided into three sections. Section 3.2 will examine the relationship between the episodes of social disorder in Oldham, Burnley and Bradford and the findings of the Cantle-chaired Community Cohesion Review (which reported on these episodes of social disorder) and the emergence of David Blunkett's British citizenship strategy.

Section 3.3 examines the emergence of the concept of managed migration from 2005 onwards and explores the proposals made by Gordon Brown and the then Home Secretary, Jacqui Smith, for dramatically extending the citizenship strategy introduced by David Blunkett. In this section I will advocate the shift from examining these developments as an example of institutional racism. It will be suggested here that institutional racialization is an appropriate analytical tool for appreciating the multilayered 'integration' discourse in operation when managed migration is combined with the next stage of civic integration in the form of the earned citizenship strategy.

Section 3.4 will contextualize the proposed 'earned' and 'contractual' citizenship testing regime within the 'you are either with us or against us' shared British values discourses that have emerged post 7/7. In this section Brown's 'patriotism of common purpose' and Jacqui Smith's compulsory shared values discourse (in what she called the 'deal of citizenship') will be explored. This section of the chapter will end with a brief discussion on power and the existence of what Agamben describes as heterogeneous and indiscrete regimes of power (sovereign, disciplinary and biopower) in debates on these interdependent immigration and citizenship strategies.

3.2 Shoring-up British citizenship and increasing integration through participation

In many ways, the Labour government's desire to tighten or restrict access and to 'up-grade' the processes of naturalization was born in the aftermath of the episodes of social disorder that occurred in the summer of 2001 in Oldham, Burnley and Bradford. There has been a great deal written about these events and their aftermath (including my own work, McGhee 2003, 2005a, 2008a).[5] It would not be an exaggeration to say that these disturbances have spawned 'an industry' with the agenda of enhancing citizenship, increasing integration and building community cohesion. Concerns over the alleged weakness of British citizenship (especially in established immigrant communities) was a central component of the former Home Secretary David Blunkett's response to the disturbances in Oldham, Burnley and Bradford in 2001. The problem, according to Mr. Blunkett was that

> [t]he UK has had a relatively weak sense of what political citizenship should entail. Our values of individual freedom, the protection of liberty and respect for difference, have not been accompanied by a strong, shared understanding of the civic realm. This has to change.
>
> (Blunkett, 2001: 2)

The solution to this imbalance between respect for freedom and liberty and the development of shared understanding in the 'civic realm', according to the former Home Secretary, was through developing

> a stronger understanding of what our collective citizenship means, and how we can build that shared commitment into our social and political institutions.
>
> (Blunkett, 2001: 2)

What Blunkett was trying to achieve here was to introduce a process where British citizenship would be 're-nationalized' (Joppke 2007: 39) in the context of 'a historically thin sense of citizenship' (Joppke 2008: 536). Blunkett's comments can be described as laying the groundwork for the Labour government's various projects in recent years of replacing the emphasis on the respect of diversity, as an end point of political tolerance and political unity in a multicultural, multi-ethnic and multi-faith context, with a new project that insists on forging a new level of meta-allegiance and loyalty (McGhee 2005a). Joppke describes the latter as a centrist policy of civic integration with respect to immigrant communities (2004: 243). For Parekh integrationist strategies such as these attempt to reconcile the demands of unity and diversity in multicultural societies (2000: 199) through attempting to forge commonality in the public realm in the form of a shared political culture 'which includes its public or political values, ideals, practices, institutions, mode of political discourse, and self-understanding' (Parekh 2000: 200). According to

Blunkett, this is a matter of encouraging flexible or complex meta-loyalties above and beyond competing micro-loyalties, for example:

> There is no contradiction between retaining a distinct cultural identity and identifying with Britain. But our democracy must uphold fundamental rights and obligations to which all citizens and public authorities adhere. Citizenship means finding a common place for diverse cultures and beliefs, consistent with the core values we uphold.
>
> (Blunkett, 2001: 2)

These comments made by the former Home Secretary resonate with the analysis and construction of the social problems of segregation and antagonism between the allegedly spatially proximate yet culturally distinct communities of Oldham, Burnley and Bradford made by the Community Cohesion Review Team, chaired by Ted Cantle. The Community Cohesion Review was commissioned (by the Home Office) to examine the factors that led to the eruption of violent clashes between Pakistani-Muslim, White Communities, members of far-right organizations and police in the spring and summer of 2001 in these areas. They were also commissioned to propose how these problems could be ameliorated. Citizenship, or more accurately the establishment of a 'greater sense of citizenship' based on principles common to all groups was central to the recommendations made by the Community Cohesion Review in relation to not only Oldham, Burnley and Bradford but the whole of the country:

> We believe that there is an urgent need to promote community cohesion, based upon a greater knowledge of, contact between, and respect for, the various cultures that now make Great Britain such a rich and diverse nation. It is also essential to establish a greater sense of citizenship, based on (a few) common principles which are shared and observed by all sections of the community. This concept of citizenship would also place a higher value on cultural differences.
>
> (Community Cohesion Review 2001: 10)

According to the Community Cohesion Review report, White and Pakistani communities in Oldham, Burnley and Bradford were united in their ignorance and hostility towards each other and they were described as living a series of 'parallel lives'. Thus the alleged non-integration of 'host' and settled immigrant communities, experienced as 'segregation', separation and lack of 'contact' between these communities were viewed by the Community Cohesion Review as the root of the problems leading to the disturbances. There has been a great deal of criticism of the assumptions inherent in this report, as I have previously noted (see McGhee 2008a). For example, according to Kalra, 'segregation' discourse in the Cantle-chaired Community Cohesion Review report is tantamount to a drastic simplification of the problems being experienced in towns like Oldham and Burnley and in the city of Bradford. Kalra suggests that the 'comically simple' thesis proffered by Cantle amounts to something of the order of 'these people do not live together and therefore this is the reason they do not get on and therefore riot' (Kalra 2002: 25). Other commentators such as Kundnani (2001a; 2001b) and Amin (2002) have also noted that in the local reports, for example, the Bradford District Race Review (2001) and in the national reports such as the Community Cohesion Review report that 'segregation discourse' has focused too much on 'Asians' as segregated from Whites, rather than the process of Whites segregating from racialized groups (Kalra 2002: 24). 'White flight' and the fear of racial harassment (Kundnani 2001a: 107) are two dynamics in the 'segregation discourse' that are de-emphasized in these policy reviews.

It is not only social scientists who have criticized community cohesion discourse, organizations representing ethnic and religious minority groups have also criticized the community cohesion agenda. For example, the Commission on British Muslims and Islamophobia (CBMI) was critical of the overemphasis of 'the contact hypothesis' in the Community Cohesion Review report. According to the CBMI the contact hypothesis is grounded in the 'naïve faith that if only there were more contact between different communities all would be well' (2004: 62). The CBMI suggests that the community cohesion agenda got off to a poor start, for it appeared unambiguously to be based on negative views and stereotypes of British Muslim communities and to be proposing mere assimilation rather than genuine inclusion (2004: 63).

Despite these criticisms, the 'failed integration hypothesis' so central to the various Community Cohesion reports and strategies produced in the aftermath of the disturbances in 2001[6] has been very influential on the citizenship strategies for 'new' migrants in Asylum and Immigration policy in the UK. According to Jock Young, the disturbances in Oldham and Burnley and the 'riots' in Bradford in 2001 are the most pivotal events leading to the Home Office regarding 'integration' as the key issue in their immigration and asylum strategy (2003: 449). This was evident in the *Secure Borders – Safe Haven* White Paper (2002):

> The reports into last summer's disturbances in Bradford, Oldham and Burnley painted a vivid picture of fractured and divided communities, lacking a sense of common values or shared civic identity to unite around. The reports signalled the need for us to foster and renew the social fabric of our communities, and rebuild a sense of common citizenship, which embraces the different and diverse experiences of today's Britain.
>
> (Home Office 2002: 10)

The result of this observation was that the 'integration' of 'new' migrant communities in asylum and immigration policy, as well as the de-segregation of 'established' migrant communities in community cohesion discourses was to be achieved through a common policy solution: the establishment of an inclusive sense of common citizenship underwritten by 'shared values'. In turn, in asylum and immigration policy, the emphasis in the process of attaining British citizenship began to have a distinct 'community cohesion' flavour especially through the emphasis of the 'new citizenship pedagogy' on building the capacity in 'new citizens' for effective engagement and 'active citizenship'. This was to be achieved by transforming the naturalization process from a bureaucratic process into 'an act of commitment to Britain and an important step in the process of achieving integration into our society' (Home Office 2002: 32). The acquisition of English language and knowledge of 'British life' were presented as the key to successful integration of 'new' migrants, as without them, according to the Home Office, migrant communities were ill equipped to take an active role in society (Home Office 2002: 32).[7]

David Blunkett, when Home Secretary, outlined his integrative concept of 'active citizenship' (as opposed to 'assimilation' and 'multiculturalism') in a paper published on the Foreign Policy Centre website:

> An active concept of citizenship can articulate shared ground between diverse communities. It offers a shared identity based on membership of a political community, rather than forced assimilation into a monoculture, or an unbridled multiculturalism which privileges difference over community cohesion.
>
> (Blunkett 2002: 6)

The former Home Secretary is correct when he says he was not advocating a model of 'forced assimilation'. Rather what was on offer here is an invitation to a variety of 'civic assimilation' masquerading as what Parekh would describe as the reciprocity associated with two-way ('host' and 'migrant') integration strategy (2008: 89).

The project of 'integration with diversity', which was first introduced in the *Secure Borders – Safe Haven* White Paper, is a model of civic assimilation based upon the communitarian ideal of forging allegiance to core principles shared by all, through the effective engagement of responsible 'active citizens' located in 'active communities'. Concomitantly, integration with diversity was a major component of the government's project of 'civil renewal' at the heart of the Home Office's subsequent strategies, for example, in the 'Strength in Diversity' consultation document it was stated that

> [c]ivil renewal is at the heart of the Government's vision of life in our 21st century communities. It aims to reconnect citizens with the public realm by empowering them to influence the development of solutions to problems affecting them. It is vital that barriers to participation – from lack of confidence and capacity to express one's views to prejudice which lead to exclusion – are tackled so that the aspiration for wider engagement can be translated into reality.
>
> (Home Office 2004b: 19)

It is important to reflect on what was driving this project of civil renewal with its strategies dedicated to making the engagement between diverse groups (and between these groups and government) more effective. Blunkett's statements with regard active citizenship and active communities reflect his adherence to Third Way principles associated with participatory models of democracy, which when combined with his model of citizenship and integration, takes the form of a republican model of 'popular participation' through dialogue. Dialogue in this model is the path to greater understanding and greater participation and hence the means to the end of the republican ideal of an actively engaged citizenry. The Home Office's 'Strength in Diversity' consultation strategy is a prime example of the government's take-up of Cantle's 'community cohesion' discourse this is evident in their desire to 'manage' the alleged sources of 'non-integration' and hence non-participation through the vehicles of shared citizenship, increasing participation and dialogue. That is:

> To build a successful integrated society we need to promote an inclusive concept of citizenship, which goes further than the strictly legal

definition of nationality and articulates the rights and responsibilities we share. Building this wider notion of active citizenship through participation, volunteering and civic action, underpinned by a sense of shared values, is one of the main ways in which we can strengthen the relationships and connections between communities.

(Home Office 2004b: 6)

Behind the explicit communitarian flavour of this quotation with regard to establishing the correct balance between rights and responsibilities and the necessity of sharing core values (this will be further developed in Chapter 4), David Blunkett took a rather pragmatic approach in his route to upgrading citizenship through the naturalization process. The focus of David Blunkett's citizenship strategy was less on the deliberative quality of identities (and for that matter values) forged (and modified) in interaction with others (Gutman 1994: 7) than on a rather more 'practical' intervention in which basic skills (English-language proficiency and a superficial 'knowledge of life in the UK') becomes the means whereby civic responsibilities and shared values could be taken up. Thus the ability to speak English forms the bedrock of the dialogic, participatory and active citizenship elements advocated in Blunkett's citizenship/integration discourse. The provision of English language training for new and established migrants was described in the *Strength in Diversity* consultation strategy as a means of providing 'practical support' that would 'overcome the barriers to integration' that could face those newly arrived in the UK (Home Office 2004b: 18). English language and citizenship tests (based on the knowledge 'of life in the UK') were introduced in the Nationality, Immigration and Asylum Act 2002. The first ever citizenship ceremonies were held on the 26 February 2004.

The relationship between English language skills and the idea of a culture of active and responsible citizenship in the Blunkett's citizenship/integration discourse also resurfaced as being central to the findings of the Commission on Integration and Community Cohesion's (CICC) interim statement and final report published in 2007 (McGhee 2008a, 2008c). In the latter English-language proficiency was linked with enhancing participation in civic culture in new and especially in established immigrant groups. In both Blunkett's and the CICC's proposals and recommendations the acquisition of language skills and 'knowledge' of the UK became the means whereby naturalizing immigrants could participate in the communitarian dream of creating unity in diversity through rebalancing responsibilities and rights and establishing core values. In the next section the emphasis on English-language proficiency and increasing participation and dialogue between communities found in the Cantle-Blunkett's civic assimilationist discourse (and to a certain extent in the CICC's recommendations) is relegated to the category of 'taken for granted skills' new citizens are expected to possess. Gordon Brown wants more from immigrants than just the ability to speak English and to have knowledge of 'life in the UK'. Brown wants would-be citizens to 'become British' at a deeper level.

3.3 Managed migration and earned citizenship

Elements of community cohesion discourses which emphasize the forging of 'unity in diversity' through the establishment of core principles common to all and the new citizenship provisions introduced in the Nationality, Immigration and Asylum Act 2002 can also be found in the Labour government's managed migration and new immigrant contract strategies that have emerged since 2005. The points-based managed migration system introduced in the *Controlling our Borders* White Paper of 2005 by Tony Blair and Charles Clarke and the new earned citizenship proposals introduced by Gordon Brown and Jacqui Smith in the *Path to Citizenship* Green Paper in February 2008 are both designed to restore 'public confidence' in Britain's immigration systems. According to Blair, in the foreword to the *Controlling Our Borders* White Paper, 'The challenge for the Government is to maintain public confidence in the system by agreeing immigration where it is in the country's interests and preventing it where it is not' (Home Office 2005). This process was started in the *Secure Borders – Safe Haven* White Paper in 2002 where it was stated that 'we need to bring order to the disparate flows of people by developing legal routes of entry for those who will benefit our economy' (Home Office 2002: 26). However, in The *Controlling our Borders* White Paper of 2005 the government's thinking with regard to introducing a different type of immigration system based on their selection of the particular types of immigrants 'Britain wants' came to fruition in the form of an Australian style 'immigration points system' (Home Office 2005: 16).[8] In his foreword to the *Controlling our Borders* White Paper Tony Blair connected the failings in the immigration and asylum system (in the past) to the wider threats facing Britain at that time. Blair suggested that the government must act to bolster public confidence in their asylum and immigration policy, as failure to do so could threaten Britain's 'traditional tolerance' to asylum seekers and generosity to new immigrant groups. According to Blair, this threat to traditional British tolerance comes from the publics' growing feelings of indignation associated with 'those who come to live here illegally by breaking our rules and abusing our hospitality' (Blair in Home Office 2005: 5). Behind all of the rhetoric of 'abuse', 'immigrant criminality' and reflexivity with regard to the necessity of better managing 'the system' is a politics of fear in that this is an approach that feeds off the fear in society 'that uncontrolled immigration will inevitably lead to 'racial tensions' (Geddes in Walters 2004: 239). Furthermore, as indicated earlier, this is also a culture of indignation associated with anger, that Britain's 'hospitality' to incomers is being abused to the detriment of 'indigenous' citizens which can be described as an example of what Honig calls 'a politics of home' (see Chapter 2).

Blair can be positioned in the foreword to the *Controlling Our Borders* White Paper in the tradition of 'ambivalent' British post-war immigration policy making (Steel 1969). That is, policy making dedicated to maximizing economic gains of immigration while simultaneously trying to diminish the possibility of the immigrant workforce acquiring a social and political presence in Britain (Kundnani 2007: 143). What can be observed in the form of the 'cautious opening towards immigration in the UK' (Walters 2004: 244) in both the *Secure Borders – Safe Haven* 2002 and *Controlling Our Borders* 2005 White Papers a positive case was made for allowing certain forms of migration and disallowing others. This is evidence of what Walters calls 'a particular form of neo-liberal reasoning – within a discourse of globalization' (2004: 244). The managed migration strategy, when read in this light, is dedicated to promoting the maximization of the economic gains of immigration (through matching particular immigrants with particular British economic needs) on the one hand, and on the other hand promoting the minimization of the possibility of new immigrants negatively impacting on the economic prosperity (and security) of Britain. The mantra 'mitigating risks, maximising benefits' even in calls for 'progressive migration policies' (Watson 2008: 73) can be read as a neoliberal globalization statement. Managed migration strategies stem from the recognition that the global market-induced displacement of people cannot be left to market forces but 'must be managed for the First World's benefit' (Fekete 2009: 21). It is in this spirit, according to the White Paper, that the government intended to

> replace out-dated and confusing rules with a clear and modern points system so we only allow into Britain the people and the skills our economy needs. Those who want to settle permanently in the UK will have to show they bring long-term benefits to our country.
>
> (Home Office 2005: 6)

Although other related issues were also covered in the White Paper such as border controls (see Chapter 1) and revisions to the asylum system, the main focus of this White Paper was on permanent immigration. According to the White Paper permanent migration raises a different set of issues to temporary migration in that permanent immigrants make a larger contribution to British society than temporary migrants, however, they are also more likely to start families and therefore also make greater use of public services (Home Office 2005: 21). The latter justifies the careful control of permanent immigration (Home Office 2005: 21). The following criteria were stipulated for permanent immigrants to the UK in the White Paper: 'permanent migrants must be as economically active as possible; put as little burden on the state as possible; and be as socially integrated as possible' (2005: 21). Low-skilled permanent migration was at the forefront of the government's suggested changes to permanent settlement. In the executive summary of the *Controlling our Borders* White Paper it was stated that 'our starting point is that employers should look first to recruit from the UK and the expanded EU before recruiting migrants from outside the EU' (Home Office 2005: 9). Thus non-EEA low-skilled permanent migration schemes were singled out as being particularly problematic. These were to be 'phased out in the light of new labour available from the European Union' (Home Office 2005: 9) especially the new European Accession countries, including, for example, Poland under the Worker's Registration Scheme introduced by the UK after the Accession of eight European Countries in May 2004. From this we can deduce that the primary 'risk management solution' in the new political rationality of 'what we now call neoliberal globalization' (Larner 2008: 49) as articulated in this White Paper was to focus on the phasing out of non-EEA low-skilled permanent immigration into the UK. This phasing out of low-skilled non-EEA immigration was combined in the White Paper with a strategy that would encourage the flows of highly skilled and skilled migrants from a global reserve 'army' of labour when the UK's economy needed them.[9]

It is important that the restrictions on non-EEA low-skilled migration in the *Controlling Our Borders* White Paper be put into context. It will be suggested here that these restrictions are directly related to the ongoing debates in the UK with regard to the necessity of building community cohesion and increasing integration between communities (which stemmed from, as noted earlier, the disturbances in Northern England in 2001). Furthermore, the latter is also related to concerns with regard to 'race inequality' which are in turn linked to concerns about 'the Muslim underclass' (McGhee 2008a: 154–5) and *the* Muslim question expressed as an alleged tension between loyalty to Britain and loyalty to the Muslim *ummah* (see McGhee 2008a: 31–2). The seeds of the justifications for these particular restrictions can be found in the *Secure Borders – Safe Haven* White Paper, which as well as referencing the disturbances in 2001 as *the* events that justified the proposed reform in immigration and naturalization policy also includes a brief but rather significant statement when viewed through the lens of the proposals for restricting non-EEA immigration in the 2005 White Paper: 'We must plan for the future. Failure to ensure the successful integration of those settling in the UK today will store up problems for future generations' (Home Office 2002: 28). The Home Office can be described as employing a discourse akin to what Portes and Zhou call 'segmented assimilation' (1993: 74) which is associated with the divergent 'integration' patterns of second generation immigrant groups in some of their statements on successful and unsuccessful integration. For example, the Home Office have noted: 'sharp differences in the relative prosperity of recently settled ethnic minority communities are already becoming apparent. Our objective is to secure social cohesion and equality of opportunity between communities' (Home Office 2002: 28). When we fast-forward to the *Controlling Our Borders* White Paper of 2005, the emphasis on domestic policies associated with 'managed integration' and 'race' equality in the 2002 White Paper has shifted to a more restrictive, 'tightening of access' immigration policy. When contextualized, the subtext (and risk mitigation strategy) of the *Controlling Our Borders* White Paper can be read as: Britain must stop 'importing' 'social problems' in the form of immigrant communities who have not integrated properly into British society, who are dependent upon state welfare, and who do not seem to serve the country's interests.[10] From this we can deduce that the solution to the alleged social problem of immigration in the UK is to reduce permanent immigration from non-EEA countries. Therefore the social problem of immigration (and hence integration, community cohesion, 'race' inequality, and so on) in the *Controlling Our Borders* White Paper seems to be closely associated with non-EEA permanent immigration. This is an example of a 'social problems' inflected racialization process (Murji and Solomos 2005: 3) in which racialized meanings are attached to particular issues (for example immigration) and to particular social groups namely low skilled, non-EU migrant immigrants and their families. Within this racialized, classed, 'cultured' and potentially gendered framework the common sense – practical solution that emerges to solve Britain's immigration (and ultimately the alleged community cohesion and integration problems) – is to encourage more EEA (assumed European, White,

Christian) migration and discourage non-EEA (assumed non-white, ethnic and even religious minority) migration.[11] Furthermore, under the section 'Ending Chain Migration' in the White Paper it was stated that 'we will end the practice where those who have settled on a family reunion basis can themselves immediately sponsor further family members' (Home Office 2005: 22). Rather than 'ending' chain migration this policy is designed to postpone chain migration as it will only be possible for an immigrant to be reunited with his or her family in Britain after they have settled for five years or have successfully achieved a sustainable level of economic prosperity and have gained British citizenship (2005: 22).[12] The regulatory instrument in the form of the new points system amounts to, in the first instance, discrimination on the grounds of 'economic utility' (Billig et al. 2006: 30) whereby only 'assimilable' (in economic terms) immigrants and their families will be allowed into the UK. The subtext of the new points system is that Britain will be able to deselect the immigrants and their families who might in the future impact adversely on the prosperity of the nation.

On the surface this seems like an example of institutionalized racism as described by Robert Miles. Miles described institutional racism (which was introduced by Carmichael and Hamilton 1968) as the circumstances where explicitly racist discourses are silenced but nevertheless become embodied (institutionalized) in the continuation of exclusionary practices (Miles 1989: 85). Institutionalized racism, for Miles, should not be used to refer to the exclusionary practice, rather institutionalized racism is an analytical device for examining 'the fact that a once present discourse is now absent and that it justifies or sets in motion exclusionary practices' (1989: 85). In this way the new discourse is expressive of a previously explicitly racist discourse (1989: 85). The exclusionary practices suggested in the *Controlling Our Borders* White Paper with regard to avoiding non-EU low-skilled migration are evidence of the survival of the institutionalization of racial difference in the UK's post-war immigration legislation in order to restrict 'coloured' immigrants from the Commonwealth in the name of easing social tensions (Solomos 2003: 14; Ong 2006: 121). The selectivity of the managed migration strategy and the proposals to postpone chain migration can be tentatively described as institutionally racist biopolitical interventions that will result in the active exclusion of non-EU low-skilled would-be immigrants. According to Dean, biopolitics is a politics concerned with the administration of life and populations; it is concerned with the social, cultural, environmental, economic and geographic conditions under which humans live (1999: 99). Therefore, biopolitics is concerned with the family, with housing, living and working conditions, patterns of migration, levels of economic growth and the standards of living (Dean 1999: 99). According to Ong, citizenship requirements and immigration policies are also 'the consequences of Foucauldian biopolitics' (2006: 120) in that these areas of public policy in which the state attempts to regulate the conduct of subjects as a population (by age, ethnicity, occupation, and so on) and as individuals (in the form of sexual and reproductive behaviour) are often legitimized through the state attempting to maximize the security and prosperity of the nation as a whole (Ong 2006: 120). It will be suggested here that rather than institutional racism the processes above could be better described as institutional racialization (Rattansi 2005: 289) within an overarching biopolitical strategy.

Institutional racialization better captures the complexity of what Modood describes as the elaborate articulations of racisms, including compound 'cultural racisms' (Modood 2005: 15) in these proposals. According to Rattansi, institutional racialization, in contrast to institutional racism, opens up the investigation 'to articulations and complexity, rather than being nudged to closure by a focus on a singular disadvantaging operational feature' (2005: 290). Thus institutional racialization permits the analysis of the common sense justifications for restricting certain types of immigrants through the chains of equivalence associated with social problems inflected racialization discourses which portray non-EU low-skilled immigrants as undesirable on not only 'race' grounds but also on the grounds of their potential civic, cultural, economic and even reproductive/familial 'undesirability'. These observations with regard to institutional racialization can be contextualized within what Butler described as post-9/11 'amorphous racism' and Sivanandan called the enduring 'xenoracism' associated with the winners and losers in what Fekete describes as 'the global management of migration' (2009: 21). In many ways the government's solution to 'the problem of permanent immigration' can be further contextualized within the Home Office's 'future risk assessment' and 'risk management strategy' associated with concerns with regard to some immigrant groups (and their descendents). I have suggested earlier that the Home Office is employing a discourse akin to that developed by Portes and Zhou in the form of their concept of 'segmented assimilation' (1993: 74). Portes and Zhou introduced their concept of segmented assimilation to describe what they observed as a typology of vulnerability (and the availability of resources) that determined the 'outcomes' in terms of the successful and unsuccessful adaptation of second-generation groups of immigrants in the US (1993: 74). According to Portes and Zhou, the process of growing up in America for the members of second-generation immigrants from numerous immigrant communities 'oscillates between smooth acceptance and traumatic confrontation' (1993: 75). For Portes and Zhou, whether the adaptation of the group is either 'smooth' or 'problematic' depends on (1) the characteristics that the immigrants and their children bring with them; and (2) the social context that receives them (1993: 75). The examination of racialization in the managed migration strategy provides the opportunity for exploring the government's 'common sense' restrictions on those immigrants whose characteristics have been 'deemed' to be difficult to assimilate and whose lack of 'integration' (on a number of levels) is compounded by the recognition that the UK is increasingly becoming a 'hostile' context for some immigrant communities, namely Muslims. Thus in the context of post-9/11 amorphous racism and the xenoracism of the new border control measures (see Chapter 1) the racialization of the managed migration strategy can be described as being justified by a compound integration discourse which presents immigrant 'incorporation' through a particular articulation of society on a number of levels: political, economic, social, moral and cultural (Parekh 2008: 85). I will suggest that Parekh's observations with regard to selective immigrant integration, where immigrants might decide to 'integrate' at some of these levels but not at others (Parekh 2008: 85), is currently under revision. I will suggest that the government's managed migration strategy in combination with the earned citizenship proposals are evidence of the government (rather than immigrants) demanding 'immigrant integration' at all levels of society.

In many ways the managed migration strategy which was introduced in the Immigration, Asylum and Nationality Act 2006 (and came into force in March 2008) and the English language and knowledge of the UK citizenship tests introduced in the Nationality, Immigration and Asylum Act 2002 have enabled the evolution of the British integration and citizenship strategy into its most recent phase as proposed by Gordon Brown and former Home Secretary Jacqui Smith in February 2008. Brown and Smith's new citizenship strategy was also promoted as a vehicle for 'increasing public confidence' in immigration policy. This legitimization strategy is evident in *The Path to Citizenship: Next Steps in Reforming the Immigration System* Green Paper which was introduced by Jacqui Smith on 20 February 2008. Following Liam Byrne's (the minister of state for Borders and Immigration) suggestion that the new border controls were developed as a direct consequence of responding to public demand (see Chapter 1), it was suggested in *The Path to Citizenship* Green Paper that 'listening to and responding to the concerns of the British people is at the heart of the changes we propose' (Border and Immigration Agency 2008: 11).[13] The new proposals for British citizenship were outlined by the Prime Minister in his speech at the Camden Centre in London titled 'Managed Migration and Earned Citizenship' which was delivered to coincide with the publication of the Green Paper. In this speech Gordon Brown stipulated that becoming a British citizen should not just be a matter of the applicant's choice but should depend on their ability to actively enter into a contract with Britain whereby they accept the responsibilities of being a British citizen and thereby 'earn' the right to be a British citizen (Brown 2008: 1). It was suggested in *The Path to Citizenship* Green Paper and in the Prime Minister's speech to mark its launch that the new citizenship proposals were being designed in tandem with the managed migration points system. For example, in the Green Paper it was stated that 'we propose that just as we are changing the way we judge who should come to Britain, so too must we change the way we ask newcomers to earn the right to stay' (Border and Immigration Agency 2008: 12). Furthermore, according to Gordon Brown, the existing citizenship requirements and tests were insufficient. He acknowledged that 'we' already ask people who want to settle in Britain, or want to become citizens here, to show that they understand some of the key things about what is it to be British by passing a test called 'knowledge of Life in the UK' and 'we' also demand a minimum standard of English. However, Brown stipulated: 'I believe we must now do more – and demand more' (Brown 2008: 5–6). The problem for Brown is that the existing citizenship tests 'do not make enough of a distinction between those who want to reside here temporarily and those who want to become full British citizens' (2008: 5).[14] What Brown proposed was that newcomers should pass through three stages to become 'full British citizens'. First they enter as temporary residents, then if they wish to stay in the UK and have resided in the UK for five years they can become a new category, that is, 'the probationary citizen' (Brown 2008b: 5). It is at the point of applying to become a probationary citizen that applicants will be asked to provide evidence of their continuing economic contribution and they will have to pass knowledge of UK and English language tests that currently apply for settlement in the UK. Those who pass these tests will become probationary citizens, however, those who fail these tests and do not satisfy these requirements, according to Brown 'will lose their right to stay in the UK' (Brown 2008b: 6).[15] Those who successfully pass the first round of tests and become probationary citizens can, after a minimum period of one year, be subjected to a further round of tests to become full citizens or permanent residents (Brown 2008b: 6). A little more detail is given in the Green Paper concerning the requirement for progression through the three stages:

> Under our proposals, the journey to citizenship will enable migrants to demonstrate a more visible and more substantial contribution to Britain as they pass through successive stages. At each stage, the journey will incorporate appropriate requirements that determine whether a migrant can progress.
>
> (Border and Immigration Agency 2008: 6)

It was proposed in the Green Paper that probationary citizens could demonstrate their commitment to the UK by playing an active part in their community (Border and Immigration Agency 2008: 7). Demonstrating active citizenship (which was central to David Blunkett's policy reforms) was presented in the Green Paper as the means whereby probationary citizens could fast-track to full citizenship (Home Office 2008: 25). Apart from the proposals that probationary citizens might fast-track to full citizenship by demonstrating active citizenship through playing an active part in their communities there is little detail in the Green Paper or in the Prime Minister's speech on 20 February 2008 about what the final round of testing for full citizenship will consist of. What we know, from the Green Paper and from the Prime Minister's speech is that the process of becoming a full British citizen will work in tandem with the selectivity and economic utility model associated with the managed migration strategy and will employ the existing knowledge of the UK and English-language proficiency requirement as a first tier of test (from temporary resident to probationary citizen). In the rest of the chapter I will bring together the major themes present in Brown's recent speeches and in the Green Paper which provide some clues as to the discursive context which might inform the creation of the 'full British test' in which the focus on ensuring the continuing prosperity of the nation in the managed migration strategy is joined with concerns over national security, especially steps to reduce the possibility of future internal disequilibria (Zedner 2005) emerging in settled immigrant communities.

3.4 Citizenship: Rights, responsibilities, shared values and Britishness

According to Liz Fekete, many of the debates that have emerged across Europe with regard to 'race relations', immigration and citizenship in recent years have coalesced around 'events' specific to each country (2004: 18). In this regard, 2001 was a very 'eventful' year for the UK. As already noted, the social disorder in Oldham, Burnley and Bradford in the summer of 2001 and the reports and reviews on these episodes of social disorder (especially the Community Cohesion Review chaired by Ted Cantle) have been repeatedly used by the Labour government to legitimize their increasingly selective managed migration policy. At the same time these disturbances have been used to justify the necessity of transforming naturalization into a process that emphasizes the acquisition of responsibilities rather than just the rights through the processes of accepting and sharing 'British values'. Former Home Secretary Jacqui Smith explicitly stated what she described the 'deal for citizenship' in the foreword to the *Path to Citizenship* Green Paper:

> There is a deal for citizenship. This is a country of liberty and tolerance, opportunity and diversity – and these values are reinforced by the expectation that all who live here should learn our language, play by the rules, obey the law and contribute to the community.
>
> (Border and Immigration Agency 2008: 5)

For Smith, the Green Paper was intended to outline the government's plans for migration reforms with the intention of reinforcing 'our shared values' (2008: 5). In the Green Paper, the relationship between restoring public confidence in the immigration system and in naturalization requirements and inculcating British shared values into would-be applicants for British citizenship was explicitly linked:

> There is a simple ambition behind our proposed reform of the immigration system: to place the values of the British people at the heart of the journey newcomers take towards citizenship. To do this, we are clear that we must listen to and take account of the views of the public in developing our reforms.
>
> (Border and Immigration Agency 2008: 14)

In Chapters 4, 5 and 6 I will continue to explore what was described in the Green Paper as the activities across government for 'developing policies to strengthen our shared standards and values' (Border and Immigration Agency 2008: 11) with regard to and the development of a British Statement of Values which will inform (and underwrite) a potential British Bill of Rights and Responsibilities (Chapters 4 and 6). The point that I want to make with regard to Jacqui Smith's foreword and the Green Paper in general is that the process of accepting and sharing (see Tony Blair in Chapter 5) particular 'British' values becomes central to 'the deal' for citizenship. From this we can deduce that the ambition of the 'earned citizenship' proposals is to make the testing of newcomers' 'commitment' to particular shared values more explicit and therefore enable the assessment of an applicant's sense of responsibility and potential civic contribution to Britain.[16]

Whereas David Blunkett's integration with diversity strategy was described as a civic assimilationist strategy in which the promotion of uniformity in the public realm was to be achieved through relegating 'diversity' to the private realm of 'the family and civil society' (Parekh 2000b: 200), Brown and Smith in their attempt to combine the earned citizenship proposals with the Managed Migration points system take Blunkett's civic assimilationist model into uncharted territory. Whereas Smith emphasized the commitment to shared values in this instance, Brown's contribution to this centripetal politics of creating unity in diversity was to introduce a civic nationalist theme in the new earned citizenship contract proposals which were to be infused with his desire to promote patriotic Britishness. Brown's speech on 20 February 2008 echoes a number of his post-7/7 speeches. According to Brown:

> Geographically, Britain is a group of islands; historically, it is a set of ideas that have evolved over centuries: brought together uniquely across traditional boundaries and today united not by race or ethnicity but by distinctive values that have, over time, shaped the institutions of a multinational state.
>
> (Brown 2008b: 2)

Brown is attempting to promote a particular image of Britain hereby distinguishing between two types of 'nationalisms', that is, 'ethnic nationalism' and 'civic nationalism'. According to Billig et al. civic nationalism, in contrast to traditional 'ethnic nationalism', depicts the nation as based on shared values, not shared ethnicity (2006: 4). Similarly, Michael Ignatieff made the distinction between civic and ethnic nationalism thus: ethnic nationalism 'defines the nation in terms of ethnic origins and birth' (Ignatieff 1996; 219). On the other hand, civic nationalism 'defines the nation not in terms of ethnicity but in terms of willingness to adhere to its civic values' (Ignatieff 1996: 219). But it should be noted that in the first instance Britishness is and is not an identity in Brown's formulation. Britishness is not expressed in terms of who 'we', the British, are, but rather, in terms of what 'in particular' 'we', the British, stand for. This is a noticeable shift between the *Secure Borders – Safe Haven* White Paper of 2002 and *The Path to Citizenship* Green Paper of 2008. In the former, as noted by Joppke, the emphasis is on 'citizenship as identity' and that the questions of 'unity and integration' (in the face of immigration and diversity) are to be answered by putting 'citizenship as identity ... to the top of the political agenda' (Joppke 2007: 534).[17] In the 2008 Green Paper, as noted earlier, the emphasis shifts subtly from an identity-centred discourse of citizenship to a shared values-centred citizenship strategy dedicated to formulating 'what we stand for'. I will take up this shifting and interdependent relationship between identity and values in the emergent discourses of Britishness in Chapter 5.

It must be noted, however, that Brown's formulation concerning Britishness, diversity and integration are reflected through the rather dark prism of 7/7. According to Brown, it is the events of 7 July 2005 that 'lead us to ask how successful we have been in balancing the need for diversity with the obvious requirements of integration in our society' (Brown 2006: 2). According to Brown, it is in looking to the future, that is, to Britain's ability to meet and master the challenges of the global economy (and also the international, demographic, constitutional and social and security challenges ahead) 'that requires us to rediscover and build from our history and apply in our time the shared values that bind us together and give us common purpose' (2006: 3). The themes of Britishness, shared values, common purpose and competing understandings of patriotism have been (see Chapter 1 and 2) and will be explored in numerous places throughout the book (but especially in Chapters 4, 5 and 6). What should be noted here is Brown's references to the 'social problems' associated with integration and diversity, that is, the consequences of immigration are also linked to the 'economic' and 'security' challenges that Britain might face in the future. Following on from previous chapters, this is another example of the pre-emptive politics of security, however, rather than employing these discourses in a strategy designed to rebalance human rights in the name of 'public security' (see Chapter 2), Brown is attempting to restore the public's confidence in the immigration system and process of obtaining British Citizenship (and ultimately restore confidence in the Labour government itself). This process of restoring public confidence through 'tough', restrictive and selective immigration policies and extended naturalization processes also comes to involve a number of regimes of power. For example, in the proposed combination of the managed migration and earned citizenship strategies there is evidence of what Dean, following

Agamben, describes as indistinct and heterogeneous regimes of power (Dean 2007: 94; Morton and Bygrave 2008:2). In many ways, taking on the role of responding to and restoring public confidence in the immigration system and the process of acquiring British citizenship, the government in its excluding (certain applicants) and removing (failed applicants) activities is attempting to demonstrate its willingness to engage in sovereign decisions with regard to the prosperity of 'the body politic'. At the same time, in their determination that newcomers should earn their right to become citizens through proposals for more extensive testing regimes there is evidence of governmental power in the form of a politics of obligation associated with the inculcation of compulsory 'shared British values'[18] which are in turn articulated with biopolitical strategies and sovereign decisions dedicated not to the maximization of population quality as in early twentieth-century biopolitics but to the maximization of what Ong (2006) describes as population security and prosperity. What can be observed here is therefore the continuation of neo-biopolitical policies in the name of both public security through the rebalancing of human rights in the context of counter-terrorism (see Chapter 2) and through the attempt to increase public confidence in the immigration system and naturalization process through more selective and extensive systems with regard to managing the flows of immigrants into the country and with regard to their potential journey to citizenship.

3.5 Conclusion

This chapter maps the continuity and shifts in immigration policy in the UK since 2001. Two sets of events (in the context of wider references to unprecedented mobility and globalization) in particular are referenced by 'policy makers' in their attempts to legitimize the launch of new immigration and naturalization policy reforms. That is: (1) the alleged non-integration of settled ethnic and religious immigrant communities, for example, in towns and cities like Bradford, which was emphasized in the reports in the aftermath of the social disturbances in 2001; and (2) the threat from seemingly integrated 'home grown' extremists from within settled minority ethnic and religious minority (in particular Muslim) communities which have come to be epitomized by the 7/7 bombers (this theme will be further developed in Chapter 5). The discourses surrounding these events have in turn been feed into the reflexivity evident in the legitimization of immigration reforms which (under David Blunkett as Home Secretary) took the form of attempting to correct previous immigration and integration policies, which allegedly failed to integrate immigrant communities sufficiently. At the same time, the discourses surrounding these events continue to shape the recent attempts at promoting a new type of British patriotism and British citizenship which is to be uncoupled from ethnic identity and be replaced within a clear framework of rights, responsibilities and duties introduced by Gordon Brown. As well as mapping out the shifts between Blunkett's dialogic, active 'civic' assimilation strategy and Brown's recommendations for how his earned British citizenship proposals could work with the existing managed migration strategy this chapter has also attempted to map out the necessity of engaging in conceptual shifts, for example, from institutional racism to institutional racialization to adequately examine the trajectory of these policy developments. At the same time, in this chapter I have also attempted to explore the relationship between the processes associated with institutional racialization in these policies and the heterogeneous regimes of power operating in advanced liberal democracies such as the UK.

Following Rattansi (2005, 2007), this chapter has attempted to examine immigration and naturalization policy regimes and discourses as multilayered and multidimensional phenomena which are complexly articulated and will, no doubt, have myriad effects on diverse social groups in the future. The result being that rather than viewing the economic and civic/cultural integration strategies associated with the managed migration strategy and earned British citizenship proposals just as examples of institutional racism and what Kundnani describes as 'integrationist racism' (2007: 144), we can begin to explore these strategies and proposals as exhibiting racism, culturalism and inferiorization articulated in wider discourses (Meer and Noorani 2008; Anthias and Yuval-Davis 1992). For example, class (linked to concerns with, for example the social exclusion and economic marginalization associated with, for example, '*the* Muslim underclass'); gender (linked to concerns, for example, over arranged marriages with foreign spouses, dependent 'wives' with low human capital);[19] and, family (linked to, for example, concerns over 'chain migration', the intergenerational transmission of disadvantage and the potential 'radicalized' malcontent of the second- and third-generation members of settled communities). These multidimensional examples of institutionalized racialization in the discourses surrounding the disturbances in Oldham, Burnley and Bradford and in the discourses surrounding 7/7 present the alleged threat to Britain's continuing prosperity and security as coming from particular social groups, namely, low-skilled, would-be permanent immigrants from outside of the

EEA. These discourses also clearly suggest the means of minimizing the threat to Britain's prosperity and security from this category of immigrant, that is, a strategy that restricts the possibility of future low-skilled, non-EU immigrants from settling in Britain. Thus managed migration becomes just another example of pre-emptive border control (see Chapter 1).

In the next chapter the focus of the book shifts to examine the government's intentions of bolstering public security and addressing the civic deficit (in terms of a strengthening British citizenship and making responsibilities explicit) through the creation of a potential Bill of Rights (and responsibilities) and the associated Statement of Values that is to form the preamble of the Bill of Rights. However, it is in Chapter 5 that I will examine the relationship between Britishness, shared values and belonging in greater detail.

4
Security, Citizenship and Responsibilities – Debates on a Bill of Rights in the UK

4.1 Introduction

The process leading up to the creation of a Bill of Rights is a momentous occasion for any nation. In this chapter (and the next two chapters) I will explore different aspects of this process through an examination of what the government and the Conservative opposition party in the UK intend to use the potential British Bill of Rights for. In many ways, this chapter can be described as an exploration of the tension between what I will call here 'civic rights' (or the rights of citizenship) and human rights. Thus this chapter develops, albeit in a very different policy arena, some of the themes already developed in previous chapters, for example, hierarchical thinking with regard to human rights (deciding whose rights come first) and the necessity of 'strengthening' the sense of citizenship and articulating the balance between rights and responsibilities in Britain. In addition to these themes, it will be suggested in this chapter that these debates and proposals for a Bill of Rights in the UK are the site for the emergence of a clash between two types of politics: a 'politics of citizenship' and a 'politics of human rights' in which the 'dual commitments of liberal democracies, that is, to international human rights and collective self determination' (Benhabib 2001: 363) are in tension. This tension between the universal and the particular, with regard to civic rights and human rights, is part of what Žižek refers to as 'the rebirth of the old distinction between human rights and the rights of citizens' (2002: 95). For Žižek this involves programmes which repackage the political rights of citizens as a mere 'secondary gesture' (2002: 95). This attempted repackaging of the rights of citizens will be explored in this chapter with regard to debates on the conditional relationship between rights and responsibilities. However, in this chapter

I will also explore the distinction between 'citizens' rights' and human rights in the context of the radical exclusion (under the 'war on terrorism') where the treatment of foreign born 'terrorist suspects' can be best described in Arendtian terms (following on from Chapter 2) as a matter of deciding who has 'the right to have rights' in the name of public security (McGhee 2008a: 25).

As has been noted, the debates on the potential Bill of Rights bring together a number of themes already encountered in previous chapters of the book, for further consideration. For example, the necessity of increasing 'public security' (Chapter 2); strengthening citizenship through making responsibilities, duties and 'British values' explicit (see Chapter 3); the attempt to win over the general public through shifting 'the balance' of rights in their favour (Chapter 2); as well as, the ongoing project of attempting to establish who 'we' are in Britain through various citizenship and 'national identity' forging strategies (see Chapter 3 and especially Chapter 5). As a result the debates on a potential British Bill of Rights or British Bill of Rights and Responsibilities are a particularly important repository of Gordon Brown's government and David Cameron's shadow cabinet's hopes and fears for the nation's future. The result being that, for example, the potential Bill has been hijacked by various agendas from the moral authoritarianism which render rights contingent on responsibilities to the xenophobic attempt to place British citizens' rights ahead of non-British citizens. Thus in this chapter I will also explore the 'rights' and 'value' trouble these proposals lead to. The main problem with many of these proposals is that they could contravene the universality principal of human rights through adding elements of exclusivity and conditionality into the British Bill of Rights and Responsibilities.

However, there is evidence of an alternative version of the Bill of Rights in the form of the JCHR ideas for what they call a UK Bill of Rights and Freedoms that offers a glimmer of hope, beyond the regressive and inward vision of our main political parties. In many ways the JCHR's draft Bill is a forward- and outward-looking corrective to the machinations of the government and the opposition with regard to different plans for the Human Rights Act and for the potential Bill of Rights.

In this chapter I will explore the emergence of debates on the British Bill of Rights in the context of government and opposition's ambivalence to the Human Rights Act evident in, for example, David Cameron's calls for the Human Rights Act to be scrapped (see section 4.2) and Jack Straw's suggestions for employing the Bill of Rights in the process of rebalancing rights to better protect the British people from harm, especially from 'new varieties' of terrorism (see also Chapter 2). It is in this context that the following questions should be asked: what is the new Bill of Rights for? What is it supposed to do for Britain?[1]

This chapter, like the previous chapters, explores a particular image of Britain from the perspective of politicians (this will be examined further in Chapter 5). In this image a concoction of forward-looking, backward-looking, inward-looking and outward-looking views can be observed with regard to contemporary Britain and the place of human rights and 'shared values' in it. The debates surrounding the potential Bill of Rights, as noted earlier, offers a significant archive which projects for us an array of 'political mindsets'. For example, the tabloid collusive ambivalence of the Labour government with regard to the Human Rights Act and their authoritarianism with regard to the British Bill of Rights and Responsibilities; to David Cameron's explicit hostility to the Human Rights Act; and eventually to the JCHR's attempts to salvage the potential Bill of Rights from party political short-sightedness, illegality and jingoism.

The chapter will consist of three main sections. Section 4.2 will explore the relationship between the Human Rights Act and the potential Bill of Rights in the post-9/11 context. Section 4.3 will examine the government's rationale for introducing a Bill of Rights at this time. In this section I will examine how the Ministry of Justice is attempting to use what they call a British Bill of Rights and Responsibilities as a vehicle for (1) bolstering 'public security', (2) for making responsibilities explicit and (3) for strengthening citizenship. I will also explore the JCHR's alternative UK Bill of Rights and Freedoms which challenges the relationship between 'public security' and the Ministry of Justice's proposed Bill of Rights; the JCHR also insists on the uncoupling of 'Britishness', citizenship criteria and contingent responsibilities from the Bill of Rights. Section 4.4 consists of an exploration of the initial signs that the potential Bill of Rights in the UK could be introduced alongside Lord Goldsmith's (the former Attorney General) recommendations in his Citizenship Review for the development of a statement of rights and responsibilities for citizens and the creeping influence of the unfolding 'integrationist' strategies in the Netherlands (see Chapter 3) in the form of Jack Straw's interest in developing a British version of the controversial Dutch Charter of Responsible Citizenship. Section 4.4 will include an analysis of the Green Paper, *Rights and Responsibilities: Developing a Constitutional Framework* published by the Ministry of Justice in 2009. Of particular note here will be the shift in emphasis from the Bill of Rights and Responsibilities to a non-legalistic declaration (or charter) of Rights and Responsibilities. It will be suggested here that the shift from a formal Bill of Rights to a non-legal charter or declaration (of responsible citizenship) is an attempt, by the Ministry of Justice, to resolve some of the opposition that they have faced with regard to the tensions they have introduced between the rights of citizens and human rights in their proposals for a British Bill of Rights and Responsibilities.

4.2 The Human Rights Act – a (precarious) stepping stone to the Bill of Rights?

The Human Rights Act of 1998 has been described variously by Jack Straw as 'not having an easy childhood', and as being 'an Aunt Sally; unfairly blamed for a host of other issues' especially through misreporting on the part of the media and sometimes through the misapplication of the act by public authorities (2009: 3). Ultimately the Human Rights Act was 'a victim of circumstance' (Straw 2009: 3) given that it was implemented barely a year prior to the 9/11 attacks in the US. As a result of 9/11 and the ensuing 'war on terror' the same government that had introduced the Human Rights Acts pre 9/11 came to see the act, in the post-9/11 context, 'as an obstacle in the so-called "war on terror"' (Klug 2007a: 4). When we realize how closely connected the Human Rights Act and the potential British Bill of Rights are in, for example, the Labour party's recent history, the government's orientation to human rights and the Human Rights Act will have a particular bearing on the questions: what is the new Bill of Rights for? What is it supposed to do for Britain? I shall deal with these questions in the next section. In this section I want to spend a little time exploring the relationship between the Human Rights Act and a potential British Bill of Rights. Francesca Klug, in numerous speeches and articles released between 2007 and 2009, has traced the relationship between the Act and the potential Bill. Klug heads off the Eurosceptic backlash against the Human Rights Act (mostly led by the Conservatives under David Cameron) as being a foreign (European) imposition when she reminds us, as did the *Governance of Britain* Green Paper, that British lawyers drafted the ECHR (Klug 2009: 8, Ministry of Justice 2007: 60).

According to Klug, the late Labour leader, John Smith, committed the Labour party to a British Bill of Rights as early as 1993. Smith suggested a two-stage approach to the development of a Bill of Rights. The first step in John Smith's plans for the introduction of a substantial package of human rights in the UK was to create an Act of Parliament which would incorporate the ECHR into British law. With the introduction of the Human Rights Act the process that began under Atlee with the ratification of the ECHR in 1951, followed by the Wilson government in 1966 granting individuals the right to directly petition the European Court of Human Rights in Strasbourg (Klug 2007a: 3), would be complete. The second stage, the stage we in Britain are currently in (or potentially entering) is to introduce a British Bill of Rights. The introduction of a British Bill of Rights was first suggested at the Labour Conference at the NEC in 1993 by the then Home Affairs spokesperson, Tony Blair, who in support of an all-party commission, called for the drafting 'of our own Bill of Rights', following the incorporation of the ECHR into UK law (in Klug 2007a: 3). The 1997 Labour Manifesto reflected the first part of this process and the Human Rights Act was introduced the following year (Klug 2007a: 3).

A year after the implementation of the Human Rights Act the 9/11 attacks occurred in North American cities. The Human Rights Act has had a poor childhood indeed in that the act has suffered from post-9/11 ambivalence and lack of sustained support on the part of the government. The act has also been the focus of an extremely hostile media (especially sections of the tabloid press) who have taken every opportunity to publicize cases associated with an alleged misapplication of human rights in the courts, that have allegedly given undue consideration to the rights of 'the undeserving' (Russell 2007: 3). Klug has suggested a degree of collusion, post 9/11 and especially post 7/7, between senior members of the cabinet and this hostile media reporting, by suggesting that at times the former Prime Minister Tony Blair sounded 'like a cheer leader for the tabloids negative spin' on the Human Rights Act (Klug 2007c: 14). As well as what Klug describes as 'the tabloid onslaught against the Human Rights Act' which government ministers compounded by showing little or no appetite to rebut these impressions (Klug 2007a: 5), there is also evidence that the Human Rights Act was bedevilled by poor public consultation and a general lack of preparation prior to implementation.[2] For example, according to the Audit Commission's report, *Human Rights: Improving Public Service Delivery* published in 2003, 58 per cent of public bodies surveyed had no clear corporate approach to human rights (2003: 21).

It is the ambivalent relationship between the government, the opposition and the Human Rights Act that I want to briefly focus on here. In Chapter 2 I have already explored the calls from the Prime Minister, Justice Secretary and Home Secretary for rights to be rebalanced in Britain in favour of public security over the rights of individuals (especially terrorist suspects). These processes must be kept in mind when the new Bill of Rights is being advocated. It is the attempt to prioritize the rights of British citizens over non-British citizens in the debates on the Bill of Rights that is of interest to me. In this regard I want to first turn to the opposition leader, David Cameron's views on a Modern British Bill of Rights, before returning to the government's agendas (in the next section). Ken Clarke has famously described David Cameron's ideas for the Bill of Rights as being based on xenophobic, legal nonsense[3] if he intends the Bill of Rights to be used as 'a get out clause' from the ECHR (in Klug 2007b: 2). It was during his *Balancing Freedoms and Security – a Modern British Bill of Rights Speech*, at the Centre for Policy Studies in June 2006, that David Cameron announced his party's intention to scrap the Human Rights Act and to replace it with what he calls 'a Modern Bill of Rights to define the core values which give us our identity as a free nation'. Cameron's intention in this speech was to attempt to outdo the government's increasingly tough stance on terrorism and to court public opinion in the context of the confusion with regard to the alleged misapplication of the rights included in the Human Rights Act (as reported in some aspects of the media). For Cameron, it was the Chahal ruling issued by The European Court of Human Rights in 1996[4] that epitomized the failure of ECHR case law (compounded in the UK by the Human Rights Act) with regard to governments making judgements in the public interest if these impacted adversely on the rights of individuals, such as terrorist suspects.[5] That is:

> A Home Secretary must have more flexibility in making a judgment in the public interest, balancing the rights of terror suspects against the rights of British citizens. At present the jurisprudence from cases such as Chahal prevent this happening. And the Human Rights Act compounds the problem. I believe it is wrong to undermine public safety – by allowing highly dangerous criminals and terrorist to trump the rights of the people in Britain to live in security and peace.
>
> (Cameron 2006: 11)

This was not Cameron's only attack on the Human Rights Act, in August 2007, in an article in the *Telegraph*, Cameron responded to the judgement to not allow Learco Chindamo (the killer of the Head Teacher Philip Lawrence) to be deported to Italy with the following:

> It has to go. Abolish the Human Rights Act and replace it with a British Bill of Rights, which sets out rights and responsibilities. The fact that the murderer of Philip Lawrence cannot be deported flies in

the face of commonsense ... it is a glaring example of what is going wrong in our country. What about the rights of Mrs Lawrence?

(Cameron, in Hope and Gammell 2007: 1)

According to Liberty, in reality this case had little to do with the Human Rights Act and was more about the right to free movement of people under EU law (Russell 2007: 3). It should be noted that Cameron's solution to what he perceives to be the miscarriages of justice as a result of the inappropriate application of the human rights in British courts is different to the suggestions for rebalancing rights made by Jack Straw and Jacqui Smith (see Chapter 2); whereas Straw and Smith advocate the prioritization of 'public security' through emphasizing ECHR Article 2, the right to life, above other rights, Cameron wants to 'scrap' the Human Rights Act altogether and replace it with a Modern British Bill of Rights and Responsibilities (Cameron 2006: 14). For Cameron,

> a modern British Bill of Rights needs to define the core values which give us our identity as a free nation. It should spell out the fundamental duties and responsibilities of people living in this country both citizens and foreign nationals. And it should guide the judiciary and the government in applying human rights law where the lack of responsibility of some individuals threatens the rights of others. It should enshrine and protect fundamental liberties such as jury trial, equality under the law and civil rights. And it should protect fundamental rights set out the European convention on human rights in clear and more precise terms.
>
> (Cameron 2006: 16)

Cameron's initial ideas for his Modern British Bill of Rights have many of the hallmarks of the government's own Bill of Rights and Responsibilities, especially the relationship between security, shared values, citizenship and responsibilities (which will be examined in the next section). The major difference is that the Labour party and later the government's intention, from John Smith in 1993 to the publication of the *Governance of Britain* Green Paper in 2007, is to build on (and not abolish) the Human Rights Act, that the Human Rights Act should be seen as a stepping stone, in the form of what Michael Wills (Justice Minister) refers to as 'the next stage' (2008a) in the UK's human rights story.

Although there is cross party support for British Bill of Rights it should be noted that this potential document has become the repository for both the hopes and fears of the nation. The Bill of Rights is seen by the government and also by the opposition as a major component of future British national security and citizenship strategies and as providing the opportunity for making 'British values' and the responsibilities and duties that come with rights more explicit.

4.3 Security, responsibilities and citizenship – the government and the Bill of Rights

The government, unlike the opposition has no plans for scrapping the Human Rights Act, but there have been a great deal of statements (see Chapter 2) with regard to amending the Human Rights Act in respect of the interpretation of the ECHR (Klug 2007c: 14). Despite this, the Bill of Rights and Responsibilities is seen by the government as an opportunity for addressing Britain's alleged (1) responsibilities deficit, (2) civic deficit and (3) public security deficit. It will be argued here that the government's attempt to use the potential Bill of Rights to address each of these three 'deficits' is problematic because they create tensions between a domestic or territorially bound 'politics of citizenship' and a universal 'politics of human rights'. In this section I will examine further the place of 'public security' (referred to here as 'pubic safety') in particular; the relationship between rights and responsibilities and the relationship between what has been called the British Bill of Rights and Responsibilities and the processes of forging of a sense of Britishness (and British national identity) and strengthening British citizenship.

The determination to enhance 'public security' in the Bill of Rights

It was in the *Governance of Britain* Green Paper that the relationship between the potential Bill Of Rights and Duties and 'public security' was introduced:

> The government itself recognized in its review last year of the implementation of the Human Rights Act,[6] the importance which must attach to public safety and ensuring that government agencies accord appropriate priority to protection of the public when balancing rights. A Bill of Rights and Duties might provide a means of giving greater clarity and legislative force to this commitment.
>
> (Ministry of Justice 2007: 61)

To add to this Jack Straw stipulated in his Mackenzie-Stuart Lecture that, 'Britain faces a new set of challenges, both internationally and at home, which requires us to look again at our mechanisms of rights' (2007a: 2). From this statement and the statement in the Green Paper we can see that the Bill of Rights and Responsibilities is a component in Straw's wider project of rebalancing of rights in favour of public security (see Chapter 2). According to Liberty, statements such as these undermine the Human Rights Act by suggesting, as David Cameron has, that the Act pays insufficient regard to public safety and national security (Russell 2007: 9). Liberty does not accept these criticisms of the Human Rights Act; it suggests that

> public protection is at the core of the human rights framework. Not only do rights instruments like the 1998 Act play a vital role in protecting individuals against abuses by the state; they also require the state to take positive steps to protect the rights of those within their jurisdiction, including from the actions of other private individuals. The Human Rights Act requires criminal laws to be put in place to protect people from committing serious offences like murder, terrorism and rape.
>
> (Russell 2007: 10)

Liberty also reminds us that most of the rights included in the Human Rights Act are not absolute and that 'one of the legitimate reasons for placing proportionate legal restrictions on the rights protected is public safety' (Russell 2007:10). The JCHR has also opposed the government's ambitions for rebalancing the Human Rights Act in favour of 'public safety'; in their 2006 report, *The Human Rights Act: The DCA and Home Office Reviews*, the JCHR demonstrated 'that there was no evidence that such an amendment to the human rights framework was necessary' (2006: 35–9). In their *Bill of Rights for the UK?* report, the JCHR stated that 'a surprising number of witnesses in our inquiry were opposed to a Bill Of Rights on this ground alone: they were concerned that the real motivation behind the proposal was to dilute the protections for human rights already contained in the Human Rights Act' (2008: 19). The JCHR, in an attempt to reassure these witnesses and to send a clear message to the government, placed the following in bold in their report:

> In our view it is imperative that the Human Rights Act not be diluted in any way in the process of adopting a Bill of Rights. Not only must there be no attempt to redefine the rights themselves, for example, by attempting to make public safety or security the foundational value which trumps all others, but there must be no question of

weakening the existing machinery of the Human Rights Act for the protection of convention rights.

(JCHR 2008: 20)

The JCHR's recommendations in the 2008 and 2006 reports was that the government must start acting consistently with regard to the Human Rights Act, if they are to successfully build on 'its achievements'. For example, government ministers cannot on the one hand talk about building upon the achievements of the Human Rights Act, while also pandering to a hostile media's characterization of the Human Rights Act 'as some sort of terrorists' charter' (in JCHR 2008: 20). Jack Straw admitted during his evidence to the JCHR that addressing this characterization of the Human Rights Act and the public's misperceptions 'is part of the framework for the current debate' on the Bill of Rights and Responsibilities (Straw, in JCHR 2008: 20). The JCHR's consistent position with regard to the government's attempts to correct public misperceptions about the current regime of human rights protections under the Human Rights Act is that they 'should seek proactively to counter public misperceptions about human rights rather than encourage them by treating them as if they were true' (JCHR 2008: 14). The government cannot have it both (or all) ways; they cannot promote human rights at the same time as attempting to correct/rebalance the application of human rights (see Chapter 2). By so doing they undermine the Human Rights Act. As Shami Chakrabarti (Director of Liberty) notes, 'we must be wary of those who dangle bright and shiny Bills of "Rights" while demanding a "rebalancing" in favour of responsibilities' (2009: 2).

The explicit articulation of responsibilities in the Bill of Rights

The presentation of the potential Bill of Rights as the 'next stage' in the evolution of Britain's human rights culture, as suggested by Michael Wills, is all about responsibilities, or more accurately the better articulation of the balance between the rights to which we are entitled and obligations we owe each other (2008a: 2). Jack Straw was even more explicit in his oral evidence to the House of Lords Constitution Committee about the next stage in Britain's human rights policy especially with regard to the need to better educate the public that rights go with obligations and responsibilities. According to Straw:

That side of the equation was taken for granted by the drafters of the European Convention, which were British lawyers – almost exclusively British lawyers – and I think in today's world we need to take better account of that, so that is what we are seeking to do and so not to undermine the Human Rights Act and still less the European Convention, but to see ways in which it can be supplemented and complemented and a mutual obligation is brought out.

(Straw 2007b: 38)

The better articulation of rights and responsibilities is not new; the alleged responsibilities deficit in Britain has been a feature of New Labour's moral communitarianism as far back as 1995. For example, Tony Blair's lecture, *The Rights We Enjoy Reflect the Duties We Owe*, of 1995 depicted what Driver and Martell refer to as the new Labour perception that in the post-war years Britain was too eager to extend the scope of individual rights without any corresponding concern with the responsibilities attached to these rights (Driver and Martell 1998: 130). To overcome the alleged responsibilities deficit, Labour's communitarianism was, according to Driver and Martell, strongly laced with ideas of reciprocity and strong values (1998: 118). For Driver and Martell (1998: 119), the 'new social morality' associated with New Labour's communitarianism was founded on their belief in the existence of shared values. In an article written in 1997, Driver and Martell describe New Labour as being torn between what they describe as conformist and pluralist versions of communitarianism (1997: 27). I think this is an accurate description of 'early' New Labour. However, if we fast-forward from the early days of the New Labour to Tony Blair's last year in office as Prime Minister, in the post-7/7 context we see that rather than being 'torn' between conformist and pluralist versions of communitarianism, the government has shifted into an explicitly conformist and morally prescriptive discourse with regard to 'shared values' (see also Chapters 3 and 5). Citizenship, responsibilities and duties are all intermingled in Blair's 'you are either with us or with the terrorists' conditional approach to integration.

When it comes to the government's promotion of the Bill of Rights and Responsibilities, the communitarian concerns with regard to the responsibilities deficit and the attempt to make the acceptance and sharing of particular values a condition of citizenship are a central feature. Schinkel's analysis of the shifting weight between what he describes as the formal aspects and moral aspects of citizenship in Dutch integration discourse is a useful comparison for examining a similar shift in emphasis in contemporary Britain. Formal citizenship, according to Schinkel, is associated with our 'juridically codified rights and duties' derived from being 'citizen-members of states' and moral citizenship is 'a counterfactual ideal of citizen-participation' associated with an extra-legal and normative concept of 'the good citizen' (2008: 17). Although Schinkel is careful to point out that every formal conception of citizenship is going to entail aspects of moral citizenship, the distinction he is making is analytical and serves the purpose of exploring the relative weight given to formal or moral aspects of citizenship (2008: 18). If we move our attention away from 'integration' strategies and discourses for a moment (we will return to Schinkel's analysis of Dutch citizenship and integration strategies and the proposals for a Dutch Charter of Responsible Citizenship later) to the central focus of this chapter, the Bill of Rights and Responsibilities, we shall see that when it comes to the government's and the opposition's promotion of Bill of Rights and Responsibilities in the UK, the relative weight or emphasis between the formal and the moral has shifted to the latter.

There are problems with the ambition, coming from both David Cameron's opposition party and from Jack Straw and the Ministry of Justice, to better articulate the responsibilities that come with rights, and attempting to use the Bill Rights and Responsibilities to reverse the alleged responsibilities deficit in contemporary Britain. For example, David Cameron suggests we need 'a modern Bill of Rights that ... balances rights with responsibilities' and which 'spells out the fundamental duties and responsibilities of people living in this country' (Cameron 2006: 2); while in the *Governance of Britain* Green Paper the government stated that a 'Bill of Rights and Duties could provide explicit recognition that human rights come with responsibilities' and must be exercised in a way that 'respects the human rights of others' (Ministry of Justice 2007: 61). Liberty challenged this portrayal of a culture of rights without responsibilities in contemporary Britain. As with their criticism of the government's pandering to the misperception that individuals' rights are being prioritized over 'public safety', Liberty reminds us that with few exceptions the rights in the Human Rights Act are not absolute, which means that individual's rights can be restricted for a number of legitimate reasons; the result being that it is permissible to make laws which restrict a person's rights in order to ensure compliance with individual's responsibilities to society (Russell 2007: 8). At the same time Liberty reminds us that there is a mass of criminal and civil laws that have existed for centuries which ensure that people act in accordance with their responsibilities to the state and other individuals (Russell 2007: 8). These laws already operate to punish those who breach the criminal law and provide redress where a person violates civil law responsibilities to others, that is, by acting negligently (Russell 2007: 8).

The problem, according to Liberty, is that David Cameron and Jack Straw's ambitions of trying to make these implicit and embedded responsibilities, obligations and duties explicit and 'easily understood' (Ministry of Justice 2007: 54) by the public and new citizens alike, could be perceived as making individual rights 'in some way contingent upon compliance with one's responsibilities' (Russell 2007: 9). It is at this point that the inclusion of civic politics of responsibilities, duties and obligations and the universality of human rights protections are seen to be incompatible, when expressed in this manner, for these purposes, in a Bill of Rights. The JCHR has similar concerns to Liberty, in particular it was the potential for undermining the principle of universality through the overemphasis of the conditionality of rights (on the contingency that duties or responsibilities are performed) that resulted in the JCHR stating: 'rights cannot be contingent on performing duties or responsibilities' (2008: 6). According to the JCHR, a number of the witnesses called to their inquiry expressed concerns that the 'inclusion of responsibilities and the Bill of Rights might mean that only the "deserving" would have full rights entitlement' (2008: 69).

Jack Straw told the JCHR, that the long-standing desire to ensure that people realize that with rights come responsibilities was 'the first reason why the government is interested in moving beyond the Human Rights Act to a Bill of Rights' (JCHR 2008: 68). Straw informed the JCHR that he wanted to be able to confront people, who, in his view, have asserted their rights 'selfishly', that is, without any regard for the rights of others, with a text which says, 'yes, you have rights, but you also have responsibilities'. Straw stipulated to the JCHR that he was 'really keen on getting that out specifically' (Straw, in JCHR 2008: 68). The JCHR recognized the importance of responsibilities to the debates on the new Bill of Rights, but suggested that the government's thinking about the relationship between rights and responsibilities was 'extremely muddled' (2008: 71). The JCHR suggests that once again the government's intention to address an alleged deficit with regard to responsibilities (as with the alleged 'public security' deficit) gives sustenance to the myths surrounding the Human Rights Act, as suggested by David Cameron and others that rights have been overemphasized at the expense of responsibilities. According to the Committee:

> By insisting on the importance of 'responsibilities' in any new Bill of Rights, Ministers tread a fine line between educating the public on the one hand and giving sustenance to the myths about the Human Rights Act which have been so damaging to the legislation.
>
> (JCHR 2008: 71)

According to the JCHR, the government's 'muddled' thinking, yet determination to link rights to responsibilities, has left the Committee with a distinct sense of unease (2008: 71) and a realization that once again 'the language of responsibilities is a rhetoric which plays well with those in the media and the public at large who are hostile to the Human Rights Act and indeed to any form of legal protection from human rights' (JCHR 2008: 71). The JCHR's position is unequivocal on the matter of the relationship between responsibilities and rights: 'human rights are rights as people enjoy by virtue of being human: they cannot be made contingent on the prior fulfilment of responsibilities' (JCHR 2008: 71).

A Bill of Rights for British citizens?

At this stage it would be helpful to acknowledge the parallel and interdependent process that is to accompany the potential Bill of Rights. That is, the formulation of the British Statement of Values. There has been a great deal said about British shared values and the British Statement of Values in recent years, from Tony Blair's ultimatum that British values will be 'shared and accepted' (see Chapter 5) to the centrality of British values in Jacqui Smith's 'deal of citizenship' in the foreword to the *Paths to Citizenship* Green Paper (see Chapter 3) and as what 'we' need to protect and the things that protect 'us' in the *National Security Strategy* (see Chapter 2). In many ways, the government's 'on and off' support of 'human rights' (or more accurately the Human Rights Act) has resulted in the relationship between the British Statement of Values and the Bill of Rights becoming increasingly unclear. Members of the government such as former Home Secretary Jacqui Smith can be described as attempting to uncouple the British Statement of Values from the process associated with introducing the Bill of Rights in order to get their authoritarian 'accept and share' 'or else' message across. For this reason it is important to stipulate that the government's intention behind suggesting that a British Statement of Values should be created was that this process, in particular the national debate that was promised on shared values, would inform and underwrite the Bill of Rights. According to the JCHR, the intention was that the government's consultation on 'the values the British people consider to be fundamental' would be used to form the preamble to the Bill of Rights (JCHR 2008: 34). In many ways the Statement of Values, the Bill of Rights and the preamble to the Bill of Rights are all interdependent processes in the textual representation of 'the imagined community' of the nation through what Benedict Anderson (1991) calls the 'cultural artefacts' that fashion who 'we' are, and more to the point, what 'we' are supposed to stand for (this will be further developed in Chapter 5). It is my intention here to explore the role of, and implications for, the addition of the prefix 'British', which has been attached by the government to these 'textual imaginings' (or re-imaginings): The Statement of British Values and the British Bill of Rights and Responsibilities.

The 'Britishness' and the use of 'British' by the government here is a source of contention. The JCHR suggested the removal of the prefix 'British' to both the Statement of Values and the Bill of Rights. The JCHR anticipates difficulties associated with establishing a Bill of Rights on the basis of a statement of 'British' values. The main reason being that this label 'may or may not be accepted' by those people 'who consider themselves to be, for example, "English", "Scottish", "Irish" or "Welsh", but not "British"' (JCHR 2008: 29). The JCHR's recommendations for dropping the 'British' prefix can be viewed as coming from an appreciation of the tensions associated with what Miller calls 'nested nationalities', that is, co-existing 'territorially-based communities' which exist in the framework of a single nation (2000: 129). According to Miller, despite these territorially based communities co-existing reasonably well, there could be historically enduring tensions and structures of feeling which could bring the identification with and loyalty to 'the overarching national identity' into conflict with the identification with and loyalty to 'the sub-communities within the larger nation' (Miller 2000: 129).

Jack Straw's justification for employing the adjective 'British' to the potential Statement of Values and the Bill of Rights, in his witness statement to the JCHR can be described as yet another strategy to head off (yet also colludes with) hostile media reporting and public attitudes with regard to human rights:

> The 'British' adjective in my view is important because there is the implication in the air that these human rights which equal in some people's minds, not mine or yours, with a terrorists' and criminals' charter, or a European imposition and by that Europe is meant 'the Other', that somehow we are not part of Europe. I think it is important that we break that down.
>
> (Straw, in JCHR 2008: 29)

The JCHR took an alternative view; as noted earlier, they saw the adjective 'British' as being counterproductive in that it could be detrimental to social cohesion and could be a source of divisive (2008: 29). They also viewed the adjective 'British' as suggesting a link with British citizenship, which for many of the rights within the Bill of Rights, would be inappropriate.[7] The connection between British citizenship, the British Statement of Values and the potential British Bill of Rights and Responsibilities was made by Justice Minister Michael Wills. In a statement that demonstrates the connection between what Anderson calls the textual and the national imaginings through artefacts (in both a progressive and defensive sense) Wills suggested that the Statement of Values provides the stepping stone between the Human Rights Act and the British Bill of Rights and Responsibilities. For Wills the British Statement of Values would explicitly articulate previously implicit responsibilities and would also explicitly express 'our national identity':

> Our national identity matters ... it was only the years after the Second World War that we went through a period of introspection, lacking in self-confidence when such discussions were often regarded with embarrassment. We are now far more successful and self-confident as a country and the government believes the time is right to find a way to express who we believe ourselves to be in a way that is inclusive and commands broad support.
>
> (Wills 2008a: 3)

For Wills this is a pre-emptive strategy, in terms of the government getting in there first, facilitating a national debate before this process could be overtaken by 'others':

> If we don't do this, others will. National identity matters to people. If there isn't a national process to discuss it, in ways that are inclusive of everyone on these islands, then there is a risk that this territory will be colonized by sectarian and sometimes even poisonous views.
>
> (Wills 2008a: 3)

Once again, as in some of the other chapters in this book, policy is being made in response to a perceived future threat, which justifies the government taking actions, launching a debate and in this instance proposing a national discussion. In contrast to the concerns with regard to the fear of a sectarian and poisonous, far right/extremist co-option of the discussion on national identity, values and human rights found in Michael Wills' speech, Jack Straw's primary concern (as noted above) is to reverse what he describes as the selfish use of rights in British society, that is, where rights are increasingly viewed as commodities (Straw 2008a: 5). Thus the potential discussion of the Statement of Values and the Bill of Rights is bound up in these two examples with pre-emptive-defensive or reflexive-corrective motivation associated with 'getting in there first' mentality or undoing the mistakes 'we have allowed' in the past.

Giving the process of formulating a Statement of Values and a Bill Of Rights and Responsibilities a 'British spin' has other consequences. Alongside concerns with regard to the government's attempts to use the Bill of Rights to bolster public security and make responsibilities more explicit, there is the concern that the emphasis on 'Britishness' and the addition of the prefix 'British' to the Statement of Values and the Bill of Rights sends the wrong messages, and once again flies in the face of universality (Russell 2007: 5). Liberty views the emphasis on Britishness, as suggesting that the 'British' Bill of Rights would only protect the rights of British people. They view the prefix 'British' as yet another, ill-advised response to criticisms, for example, launched by David Cameron that the Human Rights Act protects the rights of foreign citizens to the perceived detriment of British citizens (Russell 2007: 5). Once again the tension between citizenship and human rights and in particular the distinction between those who should and should not enjoy human rights protections emerges here. For Hannah Arendt, decisions such as these should be conceptualized as a matter of deciding who has 'the right to have rights' (Arendt 1979: 226).[8] In an Arendtian sense, Liberty, in their response to the proposals for a British Bill of Rights and Responsibilities, stated that 'people have basic rights by virtue of being human' (Russell 2007: 5). Liberty attempted to block any move that would prioritize the rights of the citizenry over the rights of others (for example, Third Country, non-EU foreign nationals) who are resident in the UK in the name of preventing further human rights abuses. Liberty, in the following statement, reminds us just what is at stake and why human rights should never be a privilege one group enjoys and others do not: 'as the Belmarsh internment policy and treatment of asylum seekers have demonstrated, it is indeed non-citizens that are most often in need of human rights protections' (Russell 2007: 5). Liberty is adamant that the privileging of the citizenry and subjects over others is a line that Britain should not cross again and certainly should not write into a potential Bill of Rights. The primary concern associated with connecting the Bill of Rights too much to citizenship rights is that potentially this could lead to what Judith Butler describes as the deprivation of legal protections for some people to which other people, namely subjects, are entitled to under national and international law (2006: 77). For Butler, echoing Liberty's (and Arendt's) concerns, 'these are surely populations that are not regarded as subjects, humans who are not conceptualised within the frame of a political culture in which human lives are underwritten by legal entitlements' (2006: 77). This potentially creates a situation where some humans become (in their entitlements to legal protection) 'humans who are not humans' (Butler 2006: 77) in the distinction between human rights and the rights of citizens (Žižek 2002: 95).

Liberty's intervention in this regard is that a Bill of Rights and a Statement of Values cannot be used to shore up a sense of 'Britishness' if the result of this is that such a process is perceived as a means to prioritize the rights of British citizens. The JCHR is also opposed to the British prefix with regard to the Statement of Values and Bill of Rights. The JCHR recognizes that the formulation of a Bill of Rights is a significant event of 'national definition' (2008: 28). According to the JCHR, a national Bill of Rights is an expression of national identity and in the process of drawing up a Bill of Rights invites reflection about what 'binds us together as a nation' (2008: 28). However, the JCHR was not persuaded that the term 'British' Bill of Rights is a helpful description of the government's proposal. The JCHR's primary concern, echoing Liberty's, was that giving the Bill of Rights the prefix 'British' could encourage an inward-looking view that human rights are linked to nationality or citizenship rather than being universal in their application (JCHR 2008: 30). The JCHR suggests instead that the term 'UK' Bill of Rights would be more accurate and appropriate and would also serve to demonstrate that the rights it contained are 'owned' by all of the people (Scottish, English, Welsh and Northern Irish, and more recent communities of immigration) of the UK (JCHR 2008: 30). At the same time they suggest the removal of 'Responsibilities' and the addition of 'Freedoms' to the title of the Bill to represent the location of the UK Bill of Rights and Freedoms within established human rights conventions, which following Klug, would signify that the Bill of Rights, would provide both a unifying force, but not at the expense of recognizing 'the contribution of many countries, and most religions and cultures, to the human rights values recognized throughout the world today' (Klug 2007a: 13).

In many ways Liberty's report and especially the JCHR report *A Bill of Rights for the UK?* have taken on the role of filtering out the prioritization of the rights of some over the rights of others, and the discourses of responsibilities, Britishness and citizenship from the government's proposed British Bill of Rights and Responsibilities. The JCHR has performed the task of removing the contingency, exclusivity, restrictiveness and non-universality of the proposed Bill of Rights to propose their own UK Bill of Rights and Freedoms which is universal, inclusive and outward-looking (through referencing existing human rights conventions and standards). Moreover, the JCHR's recommendations could also lead, and there is some evidence that this idea is beginning to gather some momentum, to the uncoupling of the government's strategies for increasing a sense of obligations, duties and responsibilities through the process of strengthening British citizenship from the processes associated with introducing the Bill of Rights. This will be further explored in the next section.

4.4 A Bill of Rights or a declaration of responsible citizenship?

As noted earlier, there are a number of similarities between the citizenship and integration strategies found in the Netherlands and those found in the UK. Schinkel's work has been extremely useful for mapping out these parallels. According to Schinkel, the shifting emphasis on the moral aspects rather than the formal aspects of citizenship in the Netherlands have had a specific function and target. Like in the UK, in the Netherlands the strategies of citizenship and integration have become increasingly merged in a moralizing strategy targeting 'newly arrived citizens' (Schinkel 2008: 22). Just like the proposals for the introduction of 'earned' British citizenship (see Chapter 3), in the Netherlands newly arrived immigrants are required to first gain what Schinkel calls 'moral citizenship' in order to apply for 'formal citizenship', the latter being 'the crowning achievement of their becoming-citizen' (2008: 22). However, perhaps the most significant aspects (for the focus of this chapter) of Schinkel's account of the shifting nature of citizenship processes in the Netherlands (and their parallels with the UK) is what he has to say about the Dutch authorities' concerns about established immigrant communities. Muslim communities are central to these concerns. Muslim communities are presented as people 'who have formal citizenship status but who lack "integration"', which is constructed by some politicians and the media in the Netherlands in 'cultural racist terms' as being 'as a consequence of their lack of "cultural adjustment"' (Schinkel 2008: 22). For Schinkel, in the case of established immigrant community groups, many of which already have formal citizenship status, 'the real prize' for the government is achieving 'the loyalties involved in moral citizenship' (2008: 22). As noted by Liz Fekete (2004), policy proposals and developments such as these are usually linked to particular events in particular countries. In the Netherlands the event that has impacted most significantly on the unfolding Dutch integration and citizenship strategies in recent years was the killing of the Dutch film director and columnist Theo van Gough by a Moroccan-Dutch man, Mohammed Bouyeri, in Amsterdam on 2 November 2004. According to evidence found at the scene of the murder, there was a strong suggestion that Bouyeri had been motivated to perpetrate this murder by 'extremist Islamist ideas' (Van den Brink 2007: 350). According to van der Brink, this horrific murder 'did not so much spark a debate about the very real dangers of Islamist terrorism. Rather, it gave rise to a debate about the question as to whether Muslim immigrants can be good citizens at all' (van der Brink 2007: 351). As a result of this incident and these concerns with regard to 'the Muslim presence' in the Netherlands, the Dutch have initiated the process of developing a Charter of Responsible Citizenship (Schinkel 2008: 24). In many ways, Jack Straw and the Ministry of Justice seem to be more influenced by the proposals with regard to the Dutch Charter of Responsible Citizenship than the recommendations made in a high-profile, wide-ranging, British-based review of citizenship conducted in Britain in 2007–8, namely, Lord Goldsmith's Citizenship Review (2007–8). One can only surmise that by 'going Dutch' the Ministry of Justice wants to be seen as associating Britain's integration and citizenship strategies with one of the toughest and most 'anti-Muslim' immigration (and now citizenship strategies) in the EU (Fekete 2009: 80).

In many ways, Lord Goldsmith's review of citizenship is a complement to the Prime Minister and Home Secretary's focus on transforming new immigrants into British citizens through their three-tier earned citizenship strategy (see Chapter 3). However, Lord Goldsmith's review and recommendations also focus on the wider challenges of strengthening a sense of citizenship and commonality for all in the UK. However, in my opinion, Lord Goldsmith's recommendations do not lead to the strengthening of 'our common bond of citizenship' through a Bill of Rights. Rather, in my view, many of Goldsmith's recommendations lead us down the paths to something like a British (or UK) Charter of Responsible Citizenship which could exist alongside, for example, the JCHR's suggestions for a UK Bill of Rights and Freedoms. I think the development of a Bill of Rights along with something like a Charter of Responsible Citizenship is an option given the government's intentions with regard to strengthening British citizenship, better articulation of the relationship between responsibilities and citizenship and their desire to bring an element of national redefinition to the process.

There are some signs that Jack Straw is beginning to think along these lines, and that he has begun to realize that there is stiff opposition, as already noted, from the JCHR and organizations like Liberty with regard to his plans for (a) better articulating rights with responsibilities and (b) undertaking a project of national identity, national citizenship and national value system definition in and through the processes of formulating a Statement of Values in the run up to introducing a Bill of Rights. However, Jack Straw seems more interested in the process of creating a Dutch-style Charter of Responsible Citizenship in the UK than following up some of the recommendations made in Goldsmith's review. The initiation of the Dutch Charter of Responsible Citizenship has been described, by commentators in the Netherlands, as a process that will strengthen citizens, further protect citizens, and importantly for our discussion, 'raise awareness concerning their rights and duties' (Van Raalten 2007: 2). Jack Straw noted that the Dutch Charter of Responsible Citizenship 'is not intended to be a formal document with direct legal or even normative effect. It aims to stimulate social change by increasing individuals' understandings of their responsibilities to one another and to society as a whole' (2009: 7). All that being said, in my opinion there are strong parallels between the Dutch Charter of Responsible Citizenship, Jack Straw's understanding of the latter and Lord Goldsmith's recommendations for developing 'a narrative, non-legalistic statement of the rights and responsibilities of citizenship' in Britain (Lord Goldsmith 2008: Executive Summary). Like the Dutch Charter of Responsible Citizenship, Lord Goldsmith advocated a narrative statement of British citizenship that intends to both simplify and clarify 'the package of rights and responsibilities which demonstrate the tie between a person and a country' (2008: 6). For Lord Goldsmith, access to citizenship for new immigrants should be rigorous and could, like the earned citizenship proposals, include a 'credit-based' modular system for the acquisition of citizenship which will accurately record immigrants' commitments to settle in the UK and engage with UK society (2008: 116). At the same time, Lord Goldsmith is adamant that Britain needs to better emphasize the relationship between those who already enjoy formal citizenship and the state (2008: 92) through the development of a statement of citizenship, rights and responsibilities. For Lord Goldsmith:

> One can imagine a number of circumstances in which such a statement could be of benefit, for example, as part of citizenship education or the coming of age ceremonies.[9] ... It could moreover make a much clearer statement of what we expect of citizens and what they can expect of their country.
>
> (Lord Goldsmith 2008: 92)

The one striking difference between the Dutch Charter of Responsible Citizenship and Lord Goldsmith's ideas for a statement or declaration of British citizenship is that the Goldsmith's review was not conducted under the auspices of 'doing something about Muslims'. Goldsmith's review and the recommendations in it consist of a systematic re-appraisal and an attempt to simplify and render coherent 'the history of legislation on citizenship and nationality' in the UK in order to provide 'a clear and self-contained statement of the rights and responsibilities' of all citizens in the UK (Lord Goldsmith, Ministry of Justice 2008: 1). Lord Goldsmith's report contains 'a range of proposals that touch every stage of an individual's life' with the intention of promoting 'the mean-ing and significance of citizenship within modern Britain' (in Ministry of Justice 2008: 1).

I will end this chapter with one final development, that is an exami-nation of the much delayed *Rights and Responsibilities: Developing our Constitutional Framework* Green Paper which was published in March 2009. Despite the JCHR's recommendations, Straw and Wills are still fix-ated on 'responsibilities' and 'citizenship' in this Green Paper. However, one significant difference is the shift in emphasis in security discourse, that is, there is a relative lack of reference to the threat from terrorism in the Green Paper; it emphasizes instead on the 'crisis in the world's finan-cial system' (Foreword, Ministry of Justice 2009: 3). A further develop-ment is the stipulation in the Green Paper of the government's position on the relationship between rights and responsibilities. For example, with regard to the contingency of rights on responsibilities, it was stipu-lated in the Green Paper, that

> [t]he government is clear that the rights in the European Convention cannot be legally contingent on the exercise of responsibilities. However, it may be that responsibilities can be given greater reso-nance in a way which does not necessarily link them to the adjudica-tion of particular rights.
>
> (Executive Summary, Ministry of Justice 2009: 8)

At the same time, there are a number of acknowledgements of the fact that the government has given a strong steer towards the relationship between rights and responsibilities not being legally enforceable:

> The government does not consider a general model of directly legally enforceable rights or responsibilities to be the most appropriate for a future Bill of Rights and Responsibilities ... the imposition of new

penalties is unlikely to be the best way to foster a sense of civic responsibility and encourage respect and tolerance for others and participation in the democratic process.

(Executive Summary, Ministry of Justice 2009: 10)

The result of these constraints is that the Green Paper, as predicted above, was less of a discussion paper on a Bill of Rights and responsibilities and more a discussion paper on what Straw and Wills describe as 'the constitutional question' of the relationship between the citizen and the state with a focus on 'how this relationship can best be defined to protect fundamental freedoms and foster mutual responsibility as the country is going through profound changes.' (Foreword, Ministry of Justice 2009: 3). Thus the Green Paper, in my opinion, becomes a discussion paper for providing a 'clearer and more explicit understanding' of the relationship between rights and responsibilities in order to 'articulate what we owe, as much as what we expect' in order to 'foster a stronger sense of shared citizenship among all those who live in the UK' (Ministry of Justice 2009: 17). The Green Paper is peppered with statement such as these, all of which are evidence of the shift in emphasis from the Bill of Rights and Responsibilities to something more akin to a British Statement of Responsible Citizenship.

This shift in emphasis to a non-legalistic declaration of responsible citizenship is evident in the Green Paper, for example, the creation of an 'accessible document' is mentioned on page 20, by page 26 other examples of 'national instruments' are listed including the plans in the Netherlands to draw up a Charter for Responsible citizenship. By the end of the Green Paper, 'a charter or declaration' of rights and responsibilities (2009: 52) is suggested before 'a non-justiciable declaration of rights and responsibilities' is plumped for, which would 'have the advantage over other options for legal effect' by including 'broad aspirations'[10] and focussing on 'cultural change' (2009: 53). Such a declaration, as noted earlier, in the discussion of the Dutch Charter for Responsible Citizenship and Lord Goldsmith's recommendations for 'a narrative, non-legalistic statement of the rights and responsibilities of citizenship', according to the Green Paper, 'would provide an opportunity to express rights and responsibilities in inspiring and motivating language, without the constraints placed by the careful drafting needed in legislative provision' (Ministry of Justice 2009: 53). At the same time, the British Declaration of Rights and Responsibilities will (as the British Bill of Rights and Responsibilities was supposed to) 'reflect the consensus which emerges from the development of the Statement of

Values on which the government will also be consulting' (Ministry of Justice 2009: 52). What we can deduce from this shift in emphasis from a Bill of Rights to a Declaration of Citizenship is that the government is considering attempting to better articulate rights and responsibilities and bolster British citizenship outside of the legalistic constraints of human rights frameworks. Furthermore, a British Statement of Values is presented as being a crucial component (in terms of underwriting), either a Bill of Rights or Statement of Responsible Citizenship.

4.5 Conclusion: Towards a British Declaration of Rights and Responsibilities

Gordon Brown, during his speech on Liberty on 25 October 2007, announced that Jack Straw had on that same day initiated 'a national consultation on the case for a new British Bill of Rights and Duties'. According to the Prime Minister:

> This will include a discussion of how we can entrench and enhance our liberties – building upon existing rights and freedoms but not diluting them – but also make more explicit the responsibilities that implicitly accompany rights. ... The debate on the Bill of Rights and Duties will be of fundamental importance to our liberties and to our constitutional settlement and opens a new chapter in the British story of liberty.
>
> (Brown 2007: 14)

However, this might not be the new chapter that the government wants to write. The future of the British Bill of Rights and Responsibilities is uncertain. According to an article in the *Monitor* (the Constitution Unit's newsletter), it was reported that 'amidst the gathering economic gloom the government's constitutional reform plans are being quietly shelved' (2009: 1). This, according to the *Monitor*, has impacted on plans for the Bill of Rights, which was to take centre stage in Gordon Brown's planned constitutional reform programme as introduced in the *Governance of Britain* Green Paper. According to this article in the *Monitor*, and numerous newspaper articles, the main problem with the Bill of Rights is the lack of enthusiasm among cabinet colleagues and the proposed link between the Bill of Rights and the British Statement of Values (Constitution Unit 2009: 1). According to Patrick Wintour, writing in the *Guardian*, the cabinet revolt on the Bill of Rights can be summed up as 'some cabinet ministers believe there is no demand for such a complex constitutional development and it will be regarded as irrelevant in times of economic stress or, at worst, be highly unpopular' (2008: 1). Wintour highlighted the potential clash between the Ministry of Justice and the Home Office around the proposed Bill of Rights. Far from building a consensus on security and human rights as alluded to in Chapter 2, Jacqui Smith has been described by Wintour as a leading opponent of the Bill of Rights; from the former Home Secretary's perspective the 'Bill of rights will strengthen the hand of the judiciary over parliament' which will lead to 'further public alienation from the concept of human rights' (Wintour 2008: 2). Wintour reports that Smith's opposition to the Bill of Rights is being backed by Home Office lawyers 'who feel that they have a hard enough time trying to protect their decisions from the impact of the Human Rights Act'.

Straw and Wills' response to such criticisms, according to Wintour, is to make 'the unpopular Human Rights Act' more palatable by balancing the existing emphasis on rights with a new emphasis on duties and responsibilities (2008: 3). However, this strategy of rebalancing rights and responsibilities, and the links between particularly 'British' values and the prefix 'British' in the Bill of Rights, have all been called into question and exposed as exclusive, counterproductive and feeding the very myths and misconceptions about human rights that they are setting out to challenge. More than that, the proposed Bill has become the repository for the clash of the domestic politics of citizenship and the politics of universal human rights. According to Melissa Kite, writing in the *Telegraph*, senior ministers are said to be unhappy with Straw's plans for the Bill of Rights as they fear they 'will be deeply unpopular with the public' and will become 'a charter for expensive lawsuits' especially if the proposed ECHR+ aspects of the proposed Bill of Rights and Responsibilities, which also features in the JCHR's UK Bill of Rights and Freedoms, such as social and economic rights, are included (Kite 2008: 2).[11]

In the context of these other sources of opposition, perhaps the greatest threat to the introduction of the Bill of Rights is the new rivalry between the Bill of Rights and the ideas for the informal (non-legalistic) Statement of Responsible British Citizenship. In many ways, the latter would, more than for example the JCHR's ideas for a UK Bill of Rights and Freedoms, do what the government (and arguably the opposition, under David Cameron) originally wanted the Bill of Rights and Responsibilities to do. That is, make the relationship between rights and responsibilities explicit and by so doing the statement or declaration would define 'British shared values' and include the injunction that citizens in the UK are expected to accept and share these British values.

In the next two chapters I will continue to examine the possibilities for the unfolding constitutional developments in the UK with regard to the place of a potential Statement of British values and Bill of Rights in contemporary Britain. Chapter 5 will examine the distinction between 'belonging together' (focusing on national identity) and projects that generate a sense of common belonging through emphasizing 'belonging to the polity'. In this chapter I will indulge in a more theoretical exercise in the form of exploring the potential for reconciling Mason and Parekh's theories of common belonging with Benhabib's observations with regard to the disaggregated citizenship, Taylor's writing of multiple belongings and Habermas' ideas for encouraging 'constitutional patriotism'. In Chapter 6 I will attempt to reconcile the theoretical exploration of multiple belongings, common belongings and constitutional patriotism (to be introduced in Chapter 5) with debates on the British Bill of Rights (and declaration of citizenship) with parallel debates surrounding the Equalities Bill of 2009 and the debates on the progressive realization of social and economic rights in a potential Bill of rights in the future.

5
Belonging Together or Belonging to the Polity? Shared Values, Britishness and Patriotism

5.1 Introduction

This chapter continues the examination of the questions of who 'we' are and what 'we' stand for, which were introduced in the last chapter. However, in this chapter I adopt a rather different approach in that the chapter explores these questions from a theoretical perspective. The theme of this chapter is belonging, with regard to how 'we' belong and what 'we' belong to. The context for the emergence of debates surrounding questions such as these is usually accredited to the intersecting discourses of shared values, national identities and the extent and variety of 'multiculturalism' operational in particular societies. In this chapter my primary focus will not be on 'multiculturalism'. Rather than focusing exclusively on multiculturalism or the shift from what Giddens describes as naïve to sophisticated multiculturalism (2009: xii),[1] this chapter will primarily focus on those discourses which attempt to tell 'us' who 'we' are and what 'we' stand for, derived from the government and normative political philosophy. I will examine the promotion of overarching, all-encompassing identities (for example, Britishness) and also the promotion of the shared values which are supposed to give expression to and facilitate 'our' being together as Britons. Therefore, the chapter will examine particular aspects of the contemporary promotion of Britishness in the context of a discourse of multiple, complex 'real world' identities gleaned from recent Prime Minister's speeches, government reports and government commissioned reports. I will suggest that the now numerous references to multiple and complex identities in a range of politician's speeches, policy documents and government-commissioned reports exist for a particular purpose. That is, the promotion of the idea that certain aspects of 'our' identities are more important than others and furthermore, that those aspects of 'our' identities in addition to the values 'we' are told 'we' share are to become the common ground that provides national 'unity in diversity'.

In this light, the chapter is in part a critical analysis of government-derived problematizations and solutions to what, for example, politicians perceive to be the deficiencies with regard to national identities and a sense of shared citizenship and common values in Britain. Here I will once again focus on the problems (and problematizations) associated with creating 'unity in diversity' through projects dedicated to forging a national identity all can adhere to (through demanding that all should accept and share British values). However, in the chapter I also begin to explore the possibilities associated with other ways of generating a sense of belonging at 'an institutional level'. By shifting the focus in this way, I attempt to bypass the circular arguments with regard to Britishness and 'British shared values' and the associated questions of who 'we' are and what 'we' stand for to explore other questions, namely what 'we' want to become and how might 'we' achieve this. It is in this chapter that my critical analysis of government discourses is supplemented with what could be described as a normative analysis in the form of an exploration of pertinent theoretical and philosophical literatures on different 'modes' of belonging in multicultural societies. Some could say that it is rather late in a book to be 'reviewing' literatures. However, these literatures should be viewed as a bridge which takes 'us' beyond the sense of belonging encouraged by the discourses of Britishness and British shared values to alternative and potential ways of belonging that could be facilitated through some of the promised yet unrealized constitutional develop-ments (under Gordon Brown), including the creation of a Bill of Rights.

In order to begin the process of exploring the latter I will examine the work of Miller, Mason, Parekh and Habermas with regard to how these government problematizations and solutions, with some imagi-nation and political courage, might be rescued from what I perceive to be inward looking and past orientated discourses of 'Britishness' to be replaced with something much more creative, future orientated and outward looking in the form of a variety of constitutional patriot-ism in and through a Bill of Rights. The argument that I will be mak-ing here (and in the next chapter) is that in order to promote a sense of belonging and strengthen citizenship the polity (symbolized, for example, by the potential Bill of Rights) should be perceived as being inclusive, constitutional and universal.

The chapter will include three main sections. The first section will examine the questions of who 'we' are and what 'we' stand for with regard to recent political discourses on Britishness, identities and what Nikolas Rose calls the ethno-political articulation of 'core' values.

The second section will examine what leading political philosophers (David Miller, Andrew Mason and Bhikhu Parekh) have to say with regard to questions of national identity, citizenship and belonging. In this section I will contrast Miller's theory of common belonging through 'belonging together' with those of Mason and Parekh who advocate common belonging through 'belonging to the polity'. The central question that will be explored here is do we need to 'belong together' in terms of having a national identity, or do we just need to feel that we 'belong to the polity' without recourse to a national identity?

The third section will come back to the question of a new constitutional settlement in the UK and the potential for the Bill of Rights (see Chapter 5) to generate what Habermas describes as a sense of constitutional patriotism. In this section I will contextualize Mason's and Parekh's theory of common belonging (to a polity) with Charles Taylor's theory of deep diversity to theorize the potential for developing a sense of constitutional patriotism in the UK.

5.2 Multiple identities, shared values and shared futures

There has been a great deal written and said about Britishness, citizenship and shared values in recent years. In Chapter 3, I examined David Blunkett's problematization of what he described as the weak sense of British citizenship and the necessity of the British people finding the common ground of shared citizenship in the aftermath of the disturbances in Oldham, Burnley and Bradford in 2001. For Blunkett, 'Citizenship means finding a common place for diverse cultures and beliefs, consistent with the core values we uphold' (Blunkett, 2001: 2).[2] In many ways Blair and Brown have followed Blunkett's lead on the questions of who 'we' are and what 'we' stand for. I will begin this section by examining some of Gordon Brown's speeches on Britishness, patriotism and values before moving on to examine his predecessor's rather more explicit, Muslim-focused 'duty to integrate' speeches. I will end the section by examining a parallel development in official government papers and government commissioned reports, for example, the Commission on Integration and Community Cohesion's (CICC) report of 2007 in relation to the use of a discourse of multiple identities as a means of promoting an overarching British identity that trumps all other 'competing' identities.

It was in his Managed Migration and Earned Citizenship speech delivered in February 2008 (see also Chapter 3) that Gordon Brown employed his civic nationalist definition of patriotism to promote his proposals for an earned citizenship contract, for example:

> Patriotism is the sense that 'all-of-us' matters more than 'any-of-us'. It defines a nation not by race or ethnicity, but by seeing us all as part of a covenant, in which we recognize that our destinies are inter-linked. For rights only exist where people recognize responsibilities; responsibilities only exist where people have a sense of shared fate; and shared fate only exists where there is a strong sense of collective belonging. So Britain is not just where we are but is an important part of who we are.
>
> (Brown 2008b: 1)

In this speech Brown is attempting to launch an ambitious 'twin' strategy of encouraging citizens to be 'virtuous' at the same time as promoting a type of nationalism based on a discourse of 'conscientious fellow nationals' (Tamir 1993: xxix) under the banner of Britishness. This speech echoes some of Brown's earlier speeches, for example, in his 'the Futures of Britishness' speech in 2006 in which the presentism and future flavour of the 'sense of shared fate' in the quotation above is complemented with what could be described as his 'backward looking' insistence that 'our' Britishness and 'our' British values are to be found in 'our' historically enduring institutions:

> British people should be able to gain great strength from celebrating British identity which is bigger than the sum of its parts and a union that is strong because of the values we share and because of the way these values are expressed through our history and our institutions.
>
> (Brown 2006: 2)

Gordon Brown, it seems, has attempted to answer these questions by appealing to 'our' British past, present and future. The problem being that he is asking everyone to subscribe to and pledge allegiance to, and thus assimilate to the established polity and its institutions. To date the new constitutional framework and the debate on British values that would inform and become the preamble to a potential Bill of Rights, as promised in *The Governance of Britain* Green Paper of 2007,[3] has not happened (as noted in the previous chapter). What we are left with in speeches such as these is only one side of the process, a promotion of hollow Britishness without the promised national debates on shared values and on the constitutional changes that were to accompany it. When it comes to the promotion of shared values as the cure-all solution to Britain's alleged citizenship, cohesion and integration deficits, Tony Blair has eclipsed all other British politicians. In the aftermath of 7/7, Blair (see also McGhee 2008a: 133) was very explicit about what he called the 'duty to integrate':

> Obedience to the rule of law, to democratic decision-making about who governs us, to freedom from violence and discrimination are not optional for British citizens. They are what being British is about. Being British carries rights. It also carries duties. And those duties take clear precedence over any cultural or religious practice.
>
> (Blair 2006: 3)

The 7/7 bombings and the characteristics of the 7/7 bombers in particular (that is, home grown, seemingly integrated members of settled communities) have initiated a new discourse of Britishness and integration in the UK. This new authoritarian discourse demands more from settled communities than just 'economic' integration. For example, according to Blair, the 7/7 bombers were 'integrated' at one level in that they were integrated in terms of lifestyle and work (2006: 2), but they were not integrated fully:

> Integration is not about culture or lifestyle. It is about values. It is about integrating at the point of shared, common unifying British values. It isn't about what defines us as people, but as citizens, the rights and duties that go with being a member of our society.
>
> (Blair 2006: 2)

Statements such as these expose the anxiety of politicians such as Tony Blair and their assumptions and fears with regard to, for example, the split or distorted loyalties among settled immigrant communities in the UK. In many ways the 'duty to integrate' discourse is part of a tradition which survives (as noted in Chapter 3) in a softened version in Brown and Smith's earned citizenship proposals, that has increasingly placed duty before rights in Britain. This tradition was established in Tony Blair's Labour Party Conference speech in 1997, where he stated that 'a decent society is not actually based on rights. It is based on duty. Our duty to each other' (Blair, in Klug 2000: 61). Blair's duty to integrate and Brown's requirement that immigrants earn their British citizenship display particular modes of governance which are being expressed in some of the most explicitly assimilationist and reflexive immigration and naturalization policies (and proposed policies) to be produced in the UK in recent decades in the form of the combined managed migration strategy and the earned citizenship proposals (see Chapter 3). What this amounts to is a circularity in political reasoning when it comes to the roles shared values are supposed to play. That is, where 'Britain's values' are presented as being articulated and expressed in Britain's enduring and historical institutions; however, simultaneously with this can be observed the ethno-political articulation of the shared values discourse. According to Nikolas Rose, the shared values discourse becomes 'the medium within which the self-government of the autonomous individual can be connected up with the imperatives of good government' (Rose, in Walters 2004: 254). In this context 'good government' amounts to the strategies deployed whereby the apparently different values of different communities become assimilated through the 'medium' of what Rose calls 'the shared common core' of values which, and this is what I will be examining here and in the next chapter, 'can be embraced and empowered within a common constitutional framework' (Rose 1999: 170). It is my contention that there are numerous ways of doing this in a continuum from authoritarian top-down demands that all accept and share 'core values' to a rather more inclusive invitation in the form of bottom-up processes dedicated to the creation of a statement of values through a national debate. Furthermore, it is also my contention that the purpose behind formulating a statement of shared values should be exclusively for the purpose of underwriting (and not undermining) Britain's human rights culture.

In many ways, the authoritarian ethno-political (governmental) assimilation in and through the demands that 'core' values that are articulated through 'our' historically enduring institutions should be accepted and shared by all should be contextualized in an emergent discourse of national identity. I have noted the emergence of a particular discourse of identity which promotes the idea that identities are multiple, fragmented or open-ended in a number of politicians' speeches, government papers and government commissioned reports (for example, the CICC report in 2007). It will be suggested here that these parallel discourses add another development in the government's strategies with regard to the questions being discussed in this chapter. For example, in *The Governance of Britain* Green Paper (which was one of the first Green Papers to be introduced under the new government led by Gordon Brown) multiple and complex identities were being promoted in an attempt to promote a variety of civic nationalism. It was in the last chapter of this Green Paper that a discourse of multiple identities was employed for the purpose of separating out the different weights between the different components of 'our' identities in order to promote 'our' meta-allegiance as citizens of the state:

> Each of us possess multiple identities because we define ourselves in different ways depending on the factors that matter most to us. Factors such as gender, race, ethnicity, age, disability, class and faith are shared with some and different from others. But in addition to these there is a national identity that we can all hold in common: the overarching factor – British citizenship – that brings the nation together.
>
> (Ministry of Justice 2007: 53)

Furthermore, the inclusion of the discourse of multiple identities in this Green Paper was employed as a means of articulating how 'our' other multiple allegiances and identities could be or should be trumped by 'our' overarching identity as British citizens:

> It is important to be clearer about what it means to be British, what it means to be part of British society and, crucially, to be resolute in making the point that what comes with that is a set of values which have not just to be shared but also accepted. There is room to celebrate multiple and different identities, but none of these identities should take precedence over the core democratic values that define what it means to be British.
>
> (Ministry of Justice 2007: 57)

When these passages from the Green Paper are read in conjunction with Tony Blair's Duty to Integrate speech it becomes evident that for both Blair and Brown their emphasis on 'shared values' seems to eclipse their insistence on 'shared identity'. However, at the same time, there is a reciprocal relationship between sharing values and sharing a British identity in their speeches if one considers that it is in the process of sharing and accepting British values that 'our' Britishness is to be expressed.

Another example of the strategic employment of the discourse of multiple identities to promote a common sense of belonging was employed by the CICC.[4] The CICC's final report titled *Our Shared*

Futures can be described as promoting a particular post-structuralist perspective on what they call 'real world' multiple identities, that is:

> People are moving away from single identities to multiple identities not just based on race or ethnicity, but differences in values, differences in life-style, consumption, social class, differences across generations, gender etc. People now have multiple identities and adjust these to the situation they are in – and this seems particularly true for the children or grandchildren of migrants.
>
> (2007: 34)

There is a particular purpose behind the CICC's promotion of these 'real' world multiple identities which have a particular bearing on the question of what 'we' stand for. This, following Rose, is an ethno-political articulation of the common core that exists behind or alongside 'our' multiple identities, that is:

> It seems at times that we have lost sight of the complexity of individual identity, its fluid nature, and the ability in the real world to identify with different things at the same time – to be a woman or a man, within a particular ethnic group, or a particular social class – and the ability to share hopes and fears with others who are not of your group.
>
> (CICC 2007: 46)

The CICC's shared futures discourse is a discourse of 'mutual interdependence' (2007: 46) which involves everyone 'moving forward together' as a result of different groups relinquishing their attachments to the past through moving away 'from narrow identities towards a vision of the future shared by different groups' (2007: 46). The CICC's ethno-political strategy in this report is to promote a particular perspective on identity that shifts, modifies and opens out identities, and how 'we' think about 'our' identities and hence 'our' place in a 'shared future' as a British person.

The CICC's approach can be said to be a fusion of social science critiques of reified 'cultures' associated with the 'naivety' of mosaic multiculturalism (Benhabib 2002: 8) with the 'new ethnicities' theory of identities. Modood describes the criticism of reified cultures associated with multiculturalism from social scientists as being anti-essentialist in that the central theoretical criticism against multiculturalism is that '"cultures" or "groups" do not exist in the ways presupposed by multiculturalism' (2007: 89). This is a perspective which views cultures as 'discrete, frozen in time, impervious to external influences, homogeneous and without internal dissent' (Modood 2007: 89). For Gilroy, these are both essentialist and reductive conceptions which feed into the belief in the insurmountable nature of ethnic categories (1992: 50) which, according to Yuval-Davis, have resulted in both multiculturalist and anti-racist strategies being accused of holding the autonomy of minority communities sacred (1992: 281). As noted earlier, this critique of cultural essentialism and what Parekh refers to as 'cultural conservatism' (2000: 79) is combined in the CICC with a theory of identities derived from new ethnicities theory associated with multiple, complex and fluid identities (Back 1996; Cohen 1999; Mac an Ghaill 1999).

The problem here is that the CICC has, like others (for example, the Community Cohesion Review Team) overemphasized cultural factors, for example, identity, culture and communication, over their material and structural context (McGhee 2003, 2008c). The government's and the CICC's promotion of multiple identities as the means to overcoming 'communal' tensions and competition is evidence of what Cohen describes as the hegemony of a one-sided new ethnicities theory of identity which instituted a new moral binarism between 'good, new' ethnicities which celebrated healthy, happy hybridity, and the 'bad, old' ethnicity mired in pathological purity (1999: 7). Cohen reminds us that the forerunner of the new ethnicities perspective was Stuart Hall. Hall urged us to recognize that we are composed of multiple social identities, not singular identities. However, Hall also urged us to be cognizant of the fact that our complex identities which were complexly constructed through different categories and different antagonisms may have the effect of locating some of us in multiple positions of marginality and subordination (1991: 57). According to Cohen, it is this aspect of the new ethnicities theory that has been lost. In the (academic and government) rush to celebrate multiple, fluid, diasporic, transnational, transracial and hybrid identities, social scientists and politicians alike have forgotten Hall's concerns with regard to the impact of, for example, structural and cultural racisms (Cohen 1999: 7). Multiple and complex identities are lived in particular socio-political contexts. Just because we celebrate multiple identities does not necessarily prevent the persistence of individuals also occupying multiple positions of marginalization and subordination. Thus class position, gender position and economic and political relations (Anthias 1998: 525), those 'structured forms of inequalities' (Bottero 2005: 102), are absent from much of the recent debates on 'new ethnicities' (Anthias 1998: 525). Blair, Brown and the

CICC's one-sided celebration of multiplicity perpetuates this marginalization of the multiple forms of structural inequalities. My intention here is merely to 'flag-up' this one-sided discourse of multiple identities. The questions of inequalities, equalities and discrimination will be explored in earnest in the next chapter in my examination of the unfolding debates on equality and the place of social and economic human rights in a potential Bill of Rights in the UK.

The point that I have been attempting to make in these examples is that the appreciation of complex 'real world' multiple identities in the Green Paper and in the CICC's report is to demonstrate a shift in official thinking with regard to who 'we' in Britain are supposed to be, which is part of a much larger project of trying to determine what 'we' stand for. The introduction of the debates on the British Bill of Rights and Responsibilities and the associated introduction of the possibility of developing a Statement or Declaration of Responsible Citizenship in Britain (as examined in the previous chapter) could potentially lead to a new discourse of British patriotism, beyond the rhetoric of the Britishness-inflected shared values discourse that has been articulated by Blair and Brown. There are, however, a few clues as to how this might emerge among Gordon Brown's attempts to underplay 'ethnic' in favour of 'civic' nationalisms. For example,

> [t]his British patriotism is, in my view, founded not on ethnicity nor race, not just on institutions we share and respect, but on enduring ideals which shape our view of ourselves and our communities – values which in turn influence the way our institutions evolve.
>
> (Brown 2006: 4)

It is the suggestions with regard to how (and the reasons why) 'we' in Britain are to have a national debate on 'shared values' and the supposed impact of this national debate on 'the way our institutions evolve' that will be examined in the next section (and will be further developed in Chapter 6). Before that, I will explore further the questions of 'who 'we' are and what 'we' stand for by examining the divergent views on belonging (together or to the polity) from leading British political philosophers.

5.3 Belonging together or belonging to the polity?

Britain is at a crossroads when it comes to the questions of who 'we' are and what 'we' stand for. In contemporary Britain politicians are looking both backwards and forwards to find our shared values, shared identity, shared futures, common horizons and the shared foundations of citizenship. The major challenge to be overcome and one of the major ambitions of the government is to foster a sense of common belonging which transcends differences. As noted earlier, there has been a great deal written and said about 'Britishness' in recent years, by government, opposition, media and academics. At the same time, the government has persistently championed 'shared British values' as the solution to many of our woes from counter-terrorism, to the lack of integration and community cohesion in the UK. In this section of the chapter I want to examine what political theorists, for example, David Miller, Andrew Mason and Bhikhu Parekh have to say about these in order to develop potential ways of rethinking and potentially reigniting progressive debates with regard to the constitutional developments promised in *The Governance of Britain* Green Paper (which could include a Bill of Rights).

According to David Miller, the 'encompassing identities' (2000: 76) that people have as a result of being members of a national community are important for a number of reasons. These overarching national identities offer the diverse peoples of a national territory a point of common identification in that 'they can bond citizens into a single community' (2000: 4). Encompassing identities are important for Miller for the following reasons: if citizens lack a sense of common identity that transcends the particularity of their group identities, the prospects of achieving social justice are very remote (Miller 2000: 79). That is, for Miller, overarching, encompassing national identities facilitate the process (which, according to Miller, would be eroded by the 'identity politics' associated with what he calls 'the politics of recognition'[5]) whereby 'disparate groups in a culturally plural society can work together to achieve social justice for all groups' (2000: 5). This is a very important point for Miller. His championing of overarching national identity (that is, distinctive national identities based on a shared public culture) is also a matter of achieving 'procedural justice' in a context of the institutionalization of deliberative democracy. The only hope 'minority groups' have, if we follow Miller's line of reasoning, is that by being part of the community of shared identity, what he calls 'majority groups' will identify with and be sympathetic towards them. This, according to Miller, 'minority groups' must 'rely on appeals to the majority's sense of justice and fairness' (2000: 5). Miller sums up his argument thus: 'If citizens lack a sense of common identity that transcends the particularity of their group identities, the prospects of achieving social justice are very remote' (2000: 79). In many ways this comes down to the practicalities with regard to Miller's conclusion that 'minority groups' have 'little bargaining power' and that their only opportunity for advantaging themselves is through, appealing to the majorities' generosity. For Miller, a shared sense of reciprocal citizenship translated into the obligations of fairness and justice is achieved in and through disparate groups (both powerful majorities and less powerful minorities) identifying with and being identified as members of an encompassing national identity. Therefore, for Liberal Nationalists such as Miller, 'national identity come first' and 'a particular political morality based on "fellow-feeling" is then in more or less direct ways supposed to "follow" from such an identity' (Müller 2007: 12).

Andrew Mason has other ideas about citizenship and identity. Mason calls into question the centrality of a national identity for the development of 'a sense of shared belonging together' (Mason 2000: 117) for the realization of various fundamental liberal values (for example, fairness and justice). For Miller, according to Mason, 'it is only if citizens have a shared sense of belonging together that they will value participating together politically' (2000: 118); this is based on what Mason describes as Miller's four assumptions: (1) a shared national identity is required in pluralistic societies to avoid certain groups from being alienated from their political institutions; (2) Miller maintains that liberal political institutions are unlikely to be stable or enduring unless citizens share a national identity; (3) that a shared national identity is the precondition for the existence of the kind of trust which makes compromise possible in the face of conflicting interests; and (4) that a shared national identity is a necessary condition for a politics of the common good, including widespread support for redistribution on grounds of social justice (Mason 2000: 118). Mason's question with regard to Miller's four assumptions is 'why should it be possible that this sense of belonging together is a necessary condition in practice for the realization of liberal values?' (2000: 118). Mason's major contribution to these debates is to suggest that belonging to a polity does not necessitate belonging together (2000: 127). A sense of belonging together among citizens is possible when they believe that there is some deep reason why they should live together (for example, shared first language, shared history and shared culture) other than that they (for a multiplicity of reason, for example, immigration) have ended up living in the same state. In the absence of the possibility of achieving this 'foundational' deep reason for belonging together, in, for example, the context of multicultural diversity, Mason suggests that it is the sense of belonging to the polity that is the necessary condition for the realization of liberal values, rather than the sense of belonging fostered by, for example, a shared national identity. But what does belonging to a polity entail? According to Mason,

> a person has a sense of belonging to a polity if and only if she identifies with most of its major institutions and some of its central practices, and feels at home in them. When a person identifies with those institutions and practices, she regards her flourishing as intimately linked to their flourishing. In order to be able to identify with something outside of herself, a person must be able to perceive it as valuable, at least on balance, and see her concerns reflected in it. When a person feels at home in a practice or institution, she's able to find her way around it, and experiences participation in it as natural. In order to be able to feel this way, she must not be excluded from the practice or institution or be marginalized in relation to it.
>
> (Mason 2000:127)

For Mason, common belonging in the polity is a matter of shared citizenship, which generates special obligations and 'good citizenship' generates special obligations. For Miller, the special obligations of citizenship derive from sharing a national identity. Mason makes a distinction, similar to that made by Schinkel (in the previous chapter) with regard to the Dutch Charter of Responsible Citizenship, that is, the distinction between the 'formal' and 'moral' aspects of citizenship; in other words, the difference between 'being a citizen and being a good citizen' (Mason 2000: 110). It is important, however, to distinguish between the processes of becoming a good citizen here, for Schinkel the process of creating 'moral citizens' in the Netherlands is a moralizing strategy introduced by the government which is associated with the inculcation of values deemed to be lacking in particular communities. For Mason, good citizenship emerges as a result of the process of feeling at home in a polity and all that comes with this, for example, being included, being encouraged to participate, not being discriminated against, and so on.

One of Britain's most renowned political theorists (who also sits in the House of Lords) Bhikhu Parekh has in turn taken up Mason's experiential sense of 'common belonging' and applied it in his assessment of government assimilation and integration policies. According to Parekh, rather than asking how immigrants can be assimilated or integrated, we should ask how they can become equal citizens and how they can be bound to those already established in the 'host community' by the ties of common belonging (2008: 87). Parekh elaborates on what common belonging to the polity would entail:

> Common belonging refers to a broadly shared feeling among the citizens that they form part of the same community, belong together, share common interests, are bound to each other by a common system of rights and obligations, depend on each other for their well-being, and wish to live together in peace for the foreseeable future.
>
> (Parekh 2008: 87)

For Parekh, common belonging is a two-way process, which involves 'the host' community being welcoming to immigrants and immigrants wanting to belong to it 'with all it entails' (2008: 87). Carens poses a similar challenge for 'the host' community. According to Carens, as well as considering the reasonable ways 'we' might ask immigrants to adapt to 'us' when they join 'our' community, he also asks 'in what ways might immigrants reasonably ask us to adapt to them?' (2009: 151). For Lœgaard, this model of reciprocity comes down in the end to a matter of toleration, in which the national culture needs not only to tolerate people with ethnic, cultural and religious backgrounds other than that of the majority but also to recognize them, positively, as contributing inhabitants of the nation (2009: xxiii). In many ways the contrast between Miller and Parekh comes down to different conceptions of toleration. Forst describes two conceptions of toleration; the permission conception and the respect conception (2007: 294). The permission conception is closer to the position that Miller adopts with regard to the relationship between 'majorities' and 'minorities' which involves minorities accepting their dependent position in relation to majorities (2007: 295). In contrast, Parekh adopts something akin to what Forst calls the respect conception of toleration whereby 'tolerating parties recognize each other in a reciprocal, "horizontal" way' (Forst 2007: 295). For Parekh, common belonging requires a broad consensus on what is expected by both parties and can only be achieved 'if each discharges its part of the moral covenant' (2008: 88).

Thus for Mason and Parekh, the sense of common belonging and the realization of shared values in response to the experience that one belongs 'or is at home' in a polity does not depend on what Mason describes as a 'deeper sense of belonging together, which a shared national identity would involve' (2000: 134). When it comes to recent government strategies and discourses on 'Britishness', citizenship, shared values and responsibilities (some of which have already been examined here and in previous chapters) one can say that these seem to demand that we all should belong together in prescribed ways through subscribing to a particular set of 'shared British values'. The result being that these strategies can come across as examples of what Mason describes as 'radical' and oppressive as opposed to 'moderate' and non-oppressive processes of assimilation (2000: 121). At the same time, in previous chapters (Chapter 2, and also in the discussion about Gordon Brown's speeches earlier in this chapter) a discourse of 'common fate' has also been employed to galvanize and unify the 'nation' under threat. Melissa Williams' theory of citizenship is pertinent here, not only because, like Andrew Mason, she attempts to find alternatives to the liberal nationalist 'identity-centric' theories of citizenship but also for what she has to say (like Gordon Brown) about the role of 'shared fate' in generating a sense of citizenship. For Williams citizenship should be conceived 'as membership in a community of shared fate' (1983: 8). As noted earlier, there are a number of parallels between Mason's and Williams' theories with regard to the reconstruction of the moral boundaries of citizenship and especially their search for alternative to citizenship as 'shared identity'. That being said, I consider the idea that citizenship should be reconceived as a product of 'common' or 'shared fate' as being too prone to securitizing tendencies associated with the reification of 'the public' or 'the citizenry' as 'victims' (or potential victims) whose safety and prosperity (see Chapters 1, 2, 3 and 4) must be protected above all others. I much prefer the reconceptualization of citizenship as common belonging through a shared sense of belonging to and investment in the polity, which, I will argue, is more prone to a politics of hope and conviviality. Furthermore, I consider the renowned Canadian political theorist Charles Taylor to have offered a way to further develop Mason's and Parekh's belonging to the polity as opposed to belonging together thesis which could inform debates on who 'we' are and what 'we' stand for in contemporary Britain.

According to Taylor, rather than asking the questions 'who are we?' and 'what do people cherish as good?' we should instead ask the question 'what is a country for?'(Taylor 1991: 54). This question, according to Taylor, remains in the realm of 'values in some broad sense' (1991: 54) but, for me this is a question that fits the purpose of facilitating and nurturing a common sense of belonging, as advocated by Mason and Parekh, in the context of diverse, pluralistic and multicultural societies. Taylor takes the debates on who 'we' are and what 'we' stand for to another 'dimension'. By using Charles Taylor to build on Mason and

Parekh we can begin to ask new questions such as what 'we' want to be and what we need to do to promote common belonging.

5.4 Belonging to an evolving polity?

As indicated earlier, this section of the chapter will be organized around the two questions: what 'we' want to be and what 'we' need to do to promote common belonging. The question of what 'we' want to be could also be put another way, to reflect the flavour of this section of the chapter, that is, what can 'we' become, which also results in the modification of the related question into how do 'we' achieve this outcome.

In answer to the question of what 'we' want to become, I am going to build on Mason's and Parekh's promotion of forging a sense of common belonging through belonging to the polity. I am going to do this through a journey which takes in Charles Taylor's work on multiple belongings and Jürgen Habermas' writings on constitutional patriotism. By so doing I hope to develop Mason's and Parekh's ideas with regard to belonging to the polity. However, before doing so 'we' must consider what 'the polity' is and what are the possible obstacles that could arise in a multicultural society with regard to nurturing a sense of belonging to it. Iris Marion Young offers a now familiar critique of the dominance of the public sphere, and hence the polity, in terms of the establishment of pre-existing majorities over newcomers. For Young, newcomers and minorities in this situation are being invited to come into a game that has already begun, after the rules and standards are already set and they then have to proceed to prove themselves according to those rules and standards (1990: 164).[6] Now I am with Andrew Mason when he suggests that the polity cannot be remade anew to incorporate every newcomer into infinity. What Mason advocates (as do Parekh and Carens) is some mutual adjustment on the part of 'host' and 'newcomer' (2000: 124). The purpose of exploring these issues in this section of the chapter is to attempt to shift debates beyond Britishness and the authoritarian ethno-political articulation of the 'shared values' discourse. At the same time I want to suggest that perhaps 'we' should also be thinking a little bigger than mere informal 'mutual adjustments' to facilitate this process, as suggested by Andrew Mason. What I have in mind is a much bigger gesture, which would necessitate the creation of what Parekh refers to as 'a broad consensus' through the process of remaking that aspect of the polity that we can all belong to through creating a new constitutional framework which would include the drawing up of a

Bill of Rights. What I am advocating here is that the process of introducing a Bill of Rights in the Britain[7] (as part of a new constitutional framework) has the potential for providing the opportunity of attempting to formalize much of what is 'informal' in Mason's and Parekh's conception of common belonging through belonging to the polity.

As noted earlier, one of the aspects of Mason's and Parekh's conception of common belonging through belonging to the polity is their attempts to distance their theory from the fixation on national identity by liberal nationalisms (such as David Miller). By so doing they suggest a model of multiple belongings, or multiple routes to belonging to the polity. This resonates with Charles Taylor's theory of deep diversity in his essay 'Shared and Divergent Values'. According to Taylor, in order to build a country for everyone, a country needs to acknowledge and accept a plurality of ways for citizens to belong to that country (1991: 75–6). This is a far cry from Tony Blair's ultimatum that Muslims should accept and share British values and from Gordon Brown's proposals with regard to demanding more of those undertaking the journey of citizenship (see Chapter 3). Taylor asks: is this utopian thinking? Could a people ever come to see their country in this way? (1991: 76). According to Taylor, Pessimists would say no, they would claim that 'the model of citizenship has to be uniform, or people would have no sense of belonging to the same polity' (1991: 76). However, Taylor also suggests that exploring the space of deep diversity might be an option 'instead of pushing ourselves to the point of breakup in the name of a uniform model' (1991: 76). Taylor is of course talking about the Canadian context in the late 1980s and early 1990s; citizenship in today's Britain is a very different context to say the least. However, in the same essay Taylor referred to what he described as the astonishing effect of the Canadian Charter of Rights as introducing a further point of unity and a common reference point of identity which rallied (in 'English Canada' at least) 'people from many diverse backgrounds and regions' (Taylor 1991: 58). The important point Taylor makes is that such Charters or Bills of Rights can rally people (under the right conditions with adequate preparation and wide consultation, see Chapter 6) through the process of becoming a common reference point for a diverse group of people who belong to the polity in non-uniform ways. By protecting the rights of individuals in a variety of ways and guaranteeing equal treatment of all citizens in a variety of respects (Taylor 1991: 66), the Canadian Charter of Rights can be described as introducing a forum, or perhaps more accurately a symbolic space hovering between the domestic politics of citizenship and the universal politics of human rights, where the diverse people in multicultural societies 'can transcend their differences' (Kymlicka 1995: 175).

Taylor's theory of deep diversity is more than just what Kymlicka describes as a theory of accommodation (1995: 189).[8] It can be read as breaking out of the preference model of toleration to embrace the respect conception of toleration (see Forst). Paul Gilroy suggests the following for achieving this type of toleration and promoting what he calls relations of conviviality:

> [W]e need to consider whether the scale upon which sameness and difference are calculated might be altered productively so that the strangeness of strangers goes out of focus and other dimensions of a basic sameness can be acknowledged and made significant.
>
> (Gilroy 2004: 3)

Gilroy and Parekh are advocating the same thing, namely, the recognition of common humanity, what Parekh calls a 'more coherent way to relate to other human beings' to see them not as generalized others, or in terms of abstract similarity, but rather to see them in their 'concrete particularity' (Parekh 2008: 237). The recognition of common humanity requires us to see everyone as 'being like us, who are just as keen as we are to lead fulfilling lives, care for their families and close relations just as much as we do, and grieve at their losses and delight in their successes' (Parekh 2008: 237). In many ways, Taylor's project and the project I am advocating for the UK is not an attempt to overcome pluralism but to deepen and foster pluralism (Chambers and Carver 2008: 4),[9] that is, to encourage a plurality of different ways of belonging to a polity reconceived as a 'common horizon' (Habermas 1994: 134). What I am advocating here is not a version of what Martha Nussbaum would describe as 'cosmopolitan citizenship' (1996), which is less concerned with political practice and becomes instead a moral attitude which involves not placing the affairs and concerns of one's immediate community ahead of others who may be stranger to us, residing in faraway lands (Benhabib 2001: 365). As laudable as this is I think this selfless turning out to 'the global other' through a process of what Beck would describe as cosmopolitanization (Beck 2002) is a couple of steps beyond the process being advocated here. What is being advocated here is what Raymond Williams called 'imaginative encouragement' (Williams 1983: 13) in the form of attempting to reconcile some of the tensions between (1) multicultural diversity within nation states and (2) the politics of citizenship and the conformity to the principles of human rights through the development of a variety of what Habermas calls 'constitutional patriotism' (Habermas 1997 and 1998).

There are a number of problems associated with the processes of encouraging a country to rethink who they are and to recognize and share a diverse array of ways of belonging to the polity. When this is added to the simultaneous processes associated with an evolving constitutional framework and the creation of a Bill of Rights, the difficulties are compounded. With regard to the first set of problems Kymlicka has suggested that a society that is founded on 'deep diversity' is unlikely to stay together unless people value deep diversity itself and want to live in a country with diverse forms of cultural and political membership (1995: 191). There are at least two developments in contemporary political theory through which the beginnings of possibilities with regard to making the transition to new ways of belonging to the polity can be imagined. These are (1) evidence of the demise of the 'unitary citizen' (and hence multiple ways of belonging) through the processes associated with what Seyla Benhabib calls the disaggregation of citizenship and (2) the synergy of the historically enduring institutions and the values of a particular polity with constitutional principles embodied in international human rights instruments.

There is an ever growing body of work which depicts what Melissa Williams describes as 'the globalization of citizenship' replete with a 'dizzying array' of the modifiers to the term citizenship, according to Williams, citizenship is now "cosmopolitan" (Nussbaum 1996), "global" (Held 1995), "world" (Thompson 1998), "postnational" or "denationalized" (Sassen 2004), "transnational" (Bauböck 1994; Soysal 2004) and "diasporic" (Laguerre 1998).[10] Williams suggests that despite the important differences among these diverse conceptions of citizenship 'they all emphasize the incapacity of territorial nations-states to contain the new structures of political power and the new forms of political engagement that we cluster under the broad heading of "globalization"' (Williams 2007: 237–8). Rather than the globalization of citizenship Benhabib prefers to examine what she refers to as the disaggregation of citizenship in certain states in the EU. According to Benhabib, what is beginning to be observable in the EU is a disaggregation effect between the constituents of citizenship, namely, collective identity, political membership and social rights and benefits (2001: 380). Benhabib cites numerous examples, for example, in Denmark and Sweden, where Third Country (that is, foreign, non-EU) nationals can participate in local and regional elections and can be candidates for these elections (Benhabib 2001: 380). In other countries such as in Norway, Finland

and the Netherlands these rights are granted to Third Country nationals at the local but not the regional level (Benhabib 2001: 380). In many instances this is the case of having one set of rights, for example, political rights without being a national; furthermore one can have social rights and the rights to benefits in virtue of being a 'foreign worker' without either sharing in collective identity or having the privileges of political membership (Benhabib 2001: 380). All of these processes for Benhabib are beginning to cause a degree of institutional separation between the three dimensions of constitutive citizenship: collective identity, political membership and social rights and entitlements which suggest that it is time to rethink the 'identity and virtues of citizens' from a normative point of view (Benhabib 2001: 381). What these processes could lead to according to Benhabib is the demise of the unitary citizen, that is:

> Despite the hold of this model upon our political and institutional imagination – and nowhere is this more evident than in practices governing naturalization, immigration, asylum and refugee rights – we have entered a world in which liberal democracies will have to come to grips with the end of the unitary citizen.
>
> (Benhabib 2002: 181)

From certain perspectives these developments would be viewed with some trepidation and would be grist to the mill of far right political organizations. However, politics cannot just be about responding to or 'heading off' the far right. Rather than playing the far right at their own game by embarking on a politics of fear with regard to immigrants, migrant workers and asylum seekers, perhaps our major political parties could open up their institutional imaginations and begin the process of encouraging the recognition and acceptance of all people in the UK in all their diverse and multiple ways of belonging to the polity and the many different ways they contribute (economically, culturally, civically and socially) to their 'communities'. Rather than being a threat, the disaggregation of citizenship and the complexity of belongings in all of 'our' multiplicity could be seen as an opportunity. In this light the recent appreciation of multiple, complex 'real world' identities by the government under Gordon Brown could lend itself to moving beyond the fixation with 'belonging together' to instead privilege common belonging as expressed, demonstrated and felt as 'belonging to the polity'. It is here that I would like to return to Kymlicka's words of caution with regard to Taylor's thesis of 'deep diversity' in the sense of multiple ways of belonging to the polity, for Kymlicka this is dependent upon people valuing it and wanting to live in a country with diverse forms of cultural and political membership (1995: 191). In the next section I want to spend some time musing on how this investment could be encouraged through a parallel process of constitutional reform. In order to do this I will examine Jürgen Habermas' thought experiments on constitutional evolution in the context of what some have called super diversity (Vertovec 2006).

Habermas extends the disaggregation of citizenship thesis by suggesting that in today's pluralistic societies characterized by a diversity of cultural forms of life, ethnic groups, religions and worldviews we can no longer depend on the suggestive unity of a more or less homogenous nation (1998: 117). The suggestive unity of the seemingly homogenous nation provided the context for the cultural embedding of a legally defined democratic citizenship status, which in turn became the focal point of the social ties of mutual responsibility (Habermas 1998: 117). Over time, as noted earlier, the 'majority culture' becomes fused with the general political culture which claims to be recognized and serve the needs of all citizens regardless of their cultural backgrounds (1998: 118). Habermas, in a similar vein to I. M. Young, suggests that this fusion must be resolved in order to make it possible for different cultural, ethnic and religious forms to co-exist and interact on equal terms within the same political community (1998: 118). This process is to be achieved, according to Habermas, by dissolving and displacing the limitations of restrictive 'nationalism' and the limitations of membership norms which insist on the permissive toleration of 'belonging together'. For Habermas 'multicultural societies can be held together by a political culture' but only 'if democratic citizenship pays off not only in terms of liberal individual rights and rights of political participation, but also in the enjoyment of social and cultural rights' (1998: 118). What Habermas calls 'solidarity between strangers' in the context of multicultural societies is only possible if democratic citizenship 'proves itself as a mechanism that actually realizes the material conditions of preferred forms of life' (1998: 119). In order to achieve this Habermas advocates a shift from the insistence (found in Tony Blair and Gordon Brown) on holding, for example, Britain (in all its diversity) together through a 'substantive consensus on values' (1998: 225). Habermas, in a similar vein to I. M. Young, recognizes that this arrangement merely reinforces the dominant cultural values of 'the majority'. Rather, Habermas advocates a consensus on the procedures for 'the legitimate enactment of laws and the legitimate exercise of power' (1998: 225).

For Habermas the universalism of legal principles manifest itself in the procedural consensus which must be embedded through a kind of constitutional patriotism in the context of a historically specific political culture (1998: 226). What this would entail is the development of a 'formal consensus' which ultimately rests upon the unity of procedure to which all consent (Habermas 1997: 496).

What Habermas is advocating is a formal consensus in pluralistic societies based on a constitutional settlement through encouraging 'relations of recognition' (1997: 499) which would engender 'supportive spirit' (1997: 499), this is what Parekh would call reciprocity and Gilroy would call conviviality. For Habermas, this is not a case of reinventing the wheel, 'the dynamic project of creating an association of free and equal persons' under constitutional patriotism must be anchored in the political culture of each country (1997: 499). That is, for constitutional principles to take shape in social practices and be the driving force for creating the political culture depicted earlier (and therefore, in Kymlicka's terms, be seen as being valuable) they must be 'situated in the historical context of a nation of citizens in such a way that they link up with those citizens' motives and attitudes' (Habermas 1997: 499). It is here that I think Habermas' emphasis on consensus through fair and equal procedures collapses and necessitates an appreciation of the 'shared' values in multicultural societies. This is not a defence of dominant values which have been 'spun' to 'us' by Tony Blair and Gordon Brown as 'our' 'shared British values'. The deployment of their discourse of shared British values fits with Cecile Laborde's depiction of ethnocentric and often coercive 'soft rules' which permeate public institutions (2008: 17).[11] These institutionalized soft rules can be the site of 'the experienced exclusion of minorities' especially in the formerly culturally homogenous Western European nation states (2008: 17–18). These soft rules can be coercive in terms of their exclusivity and marginalizing insistence on their relative superiority. Furthermore these soft rules 'are parties in a certain kind of power relationship where they are the socially constructed artefacts of the beliefs and perceptions of the majority' (Laborde 2008: 18).

Therefore, I am not advocating the adoption of the 'soft-rules' associated with the authoritarian top-down ethno-political articulation of Britain's shared values. Rather what I am suggesting is that the precursor (and necessary preparation) for the evolution of the polity as suggested by Habermas to embrace the procedures of constitutional forms, embodied in what he describes as 'popular sovereignty and human rights' (1998: 118), can only be accomplished through initiating wide-ranging debates on what the shared values of multicultural Britain actually are.[12] By so doing, the unique context of the country in terms of both historical and enduring characteristics and institutions (which includes the continuing respect for international institutions of human rights) and also equally in terms of its contemporary multicultural diversity could be included to underwrite the 'distinctive interpretation' (Habermas 1998: 118) of the constitutional principles that will ensure that all citizens experience 'the fair value of their rights' (Habermas 1998: 118–9).

In many ways these values would not necessarily deviate considerably from the universal values which have been repackaged as historically enduring and institutionalized 'British shared values'; furthermore, these values, especially those pertaining to, for example, tolerance, equality, anti-discrimination, would also include, what Habermas would describe as procedural fairness. What is important or distinctive about what I am describing with regard to values is the process of their constitutionalization, their relationship with established human rights conventions and their potential for underwriting what 'we' in Britain in all 'our' diversity stand for. It is in this process whereby the sense, and what Andrew Mason describes as the experiential and emotional feeling of common belonging to the polity, is to be encouraged in multicultural Britain, which I will turn to in the next chapter.

5.5 Conclusion

In this chapter I approached some of the central themes of this book from a slightly different angle, employing different analytical frameworks, namely a more normative philosophical approach to the questions of who 'we' are and what 'we' stand for. In previous chapters I have demonstrated that the government's attempts to establish who 'we' are and what 'we' are supposed to stand for in the context of particular policies and strategies, from counter-terrorism to immigration, are potentially counterproductive and obstructive to the task of uniting Britain in all its diversity. These ethno-political articulations of national identity and 'national' core values can be too exclusive, regressive and on the whole too 'established' and institutionalized in 'our' historically enduring institutions to generating a sense of common belonging on their own. The argument that I have begun to make here, and will continue to make in the next chapter, is that the ethno-political articulation of the authoritarian shared values and Britishness discourses are not 'our' only option in this country for generating a sense of common belonging. Our sense of belonging and 'our' sense of citizenship need not be remade and remoulded around, for example, public security and the other tendrils of the politics of fear. What I want to advocate here is that perhaps there are alternative, more inclusive, less fearful ways of remaking and remoulding 'our' sense of common belonging.

In this chapter I have examined the relationship between values, identities, citizenship and belonging in multicultural societies. I have explored what both political philosophers and politicians (namely recent Labour Prime Ministers, Blair and Brown) have had to say about this relationship with regard to identity, or more accurately, identities. I have begun to question whether what matters is that 'our' sense of 'belonging together' or 'our' sense of 'belonging to the polity' is fostered. In the chapter I plumped for the latter. At the same time, in this chapter I explored the concepts of multiple belongings (to a polity) and the disaggregation of citizenship (also referred to more broadly as the globalization of citizenship) as being parallel theoretical developments that could lead to ways of rethinking how 'we' belong to the polity in the context of an evolving polity. That is, I suggested here that for all of 'us' to belong to the polity and thus for a sense of common belonging to be fostered it is essential that the institutions of the polity itself should evolve with and accommodate and facilitate 'us' in all our diversity. What I am suggesting here, following Habermas, and perhaps even more so, Alisdair MacIntyre, is that 'the practice of patriotism' is in advanced societies 'no longer possible in the way that it once was' (MacIntyre 2007: 254). It is in this context that a variety of what Habermas calls constitutional patriotism could be the way of harnessing patriots of the present and the future rather than the inculcating patriotism associated with established and historically enduring institutions and the values assumed to be articulated in and through them. In the next chapter I will advocate such a process by returning to the proposals with regard to creating a Bill of Rights in the UK (previously examined in Chapter 4).

6
Patriots of the Present and the Future – Ethical Solidarity and Equalities in Uncertain Times

6.1 Introduction

This chapter follows on directly from Chapters 4 and 5 but I will also re-examine some of the earlier themes introduced in Chapters 1, 2 and 3. In this chapter I further explore the possibilities for the introduction of a variety of constitutional patriotism through the development of a potential Bill of Rights in the UK. As such this chapter will contain an examination of many of the suggestions and proposals with regard to introducing a national debate in the UK on shared values in the run-up to establishing a Bill of Rights. As noted in Chapter 4, Britain's human rights culture is facing an uncertain future with the shift in emphasis from a Bill of Rights to a declaration of 'responsible' British Citizenship in the *Rights and Responsibilities* Green Paper of 2009 and with David Cameron's plans to scrap the Human Rights Act and to replace it with his Modern Bill of Rights if the Conservatives are victorious in the next general election to be held in May 2010. The purpose of writing this chapter is to explore the potential in the processes of introducing a Bill of Rights for reinvigorating a sense of belonging to the polity in the UK which was introduced in the previous chapter. Here I will explore just two of the potential array of 'core values', namely equality and fairness in this context.

This chapter is very much a product of its time, that is, a product of the global financial crisis that has shaken the world. Whereas 9/11 introduced a significant tension between civil liberties and 'security' in Western democracies, the global financial crisis has, to say the least, unleashed a great deal of uncertainty. It remains to be seen whether this crisis in the world's financial systems might lead to new ways of 'us' living together which could include introducing new ways of thinking about equalities. Furthermore, this chapter is dedicated to exploring this potential through examining what 'we' in Britain and elsewhere in the world could do to rebuild the ethical framework of 'our' living together and for generating a new type of patriotism underwritten by practical, actualized human rights. This is a process associated with bringing the everyday substance of people's lives into the debates on human rights and 'shared values'. What I am referring to here is the potential positive side to the global financial crisis that might result in the opening up of the necessary space for reflection with regard to what 'we' aspire to be, what 'our' pertinent concerns and worries are and what 'we' can do to elevate them. It should be noted that this theme is not just 'wishful thinking' on my part. In this chapter I will examine existing debates found in the statements made by the government's Equalities Office, with regard to the new equalities agenda. Furthermore, these debates are also present in the JCHR's exploration of the feasibility of introducing a Bill of Rights in Britain and the place of social and economic human rights, rather than just, civil and political rights in this Bill of Rights. This theme will also be explored in the recommendations made by the Equalities Review. It is here that the 'new equalities agenda' is directly linked to 'biopolitical' themes explored in previous chapters with regard to public safety, social order and national prosperity.

I argue in this chapter that the economic downturn could become the context out of which, for example (1) the 'historic' separation of civil and political human rights from social and economic rights can be once again debated and perhaps re-addressed and (2) the attempted separation between statutory and constitutional discrimination legislation could also be addressed. The economic downturn and the new sense of financial vulnerability it has brought in its wake could become, in other words, a new opportunity to bring 'rights back home' into the ethical frameworks by which 'we' intend to live by.

This chapter comprises four sections. Section 6.2 will focus on the suggestions and proposals that exist in the public realm and the justifications for introducing a national debate to establish a statement of common or shared values and the UK today. In this section I will once again focus on the symbolic role the Bill of Rights (and Statement of Values) is supposed to play with regard to 'unifying' the nation. This section of the chapter will examine why, for politicians and commentators, this process of establishing values is important and will explore some of the suggestions for how a statement of contemporary values in Britain will be used, for example, in terms of underwriting a potential Bill of Rights. This section can be described as focusing on the initial process in the potential (and somewhat precarious) next step in Britain's human rights policy. However, in this section of the chapter, I will advocate (following Habermas) a slightly different emphasis to these processes, that is, from an emphasis on generating a list of abstract and general values (as suggested by politicians) to instead establishing a consensus on procedures (following on from Chapter 5) in the form of an ethical framework for the legitimate enactment of laws and the legitimate exercise of power (Habermas 1998: 225).

In section 6.3 my attention will shift away from exploring the symbolic, inspirational and participatory mechanisms for public involvement and investment in the process of developing a Statement of Values and a Bill of Rights to focus on the unfolding debates on 'equalities' in contemporary Britain. This section of the chapter will include an examination of (1) debates surrounding the inclusion of ECHR+ social and economic rights in the British Bill of Rights and Responsibilities led by the JCHR and (2) the recommendations in the Cabinet Office's Equalities Review of 2007 and in the Discrimination Law Review also of 2007 with regard to the introduction of a single Equality Act. This section of the chapter will examine both the moral and ethical components of the arguments in these documents with regard to harmonizing, simplifying and hybridizing (statutory and constitutional discrimination legislation) and for creating a 'holistic' definition of 'equality' (Cabinet Office 2007b: 5) and ultimately for facilitating the creation of a more equal society of the future.

Section 6.4 will connect the new equalities agenda and the emphasis on those communities experiencing 'persistent disadvantage' as yet another biopolitical discourse. In this section of the chapter I will demonstrate how the debates on contemporary equalities and inequalities especially found in the Equalities Review's recommendations have been linked directly to some of the biopolitical debates that have been examined in previous chapters on public security (Chapter 2) and social disorder and national prosperity (Chapter 3). In this section I will also briefly examine the government's recent targeted 'race equality' interventions with persistently disadvantaged social groups in the form of the Connecting Communities programme introduced in 2009 which some commentators have described as a programme employed by the government to attempt to woo those white working-class communities at the frontline of the economic downturn back (from the British National Party) in the run-up to the general election in 2010.

The theme of section 6.5 will be 'evolution versus revolution' with regard to the context for the emergence of a Bill of Rights. In the vast majority of cases Bills of Rights have been introduced after a cataclysmic event such as a revolution or civil war; this is not the case in contemporary Britain. The question which will be explored here is: does the global financial downturn and the unresolved debates in Britain with regard to who 'we' are and what 'we' stand for present a significant enough crisis to necessitate the emergence of a unifying constitutional statement?

6.2 Towards shared values?

In Chapters 4 and 5 I briefly mentioned the role that the Statement of Values was supposed to play in the overall creation of a Bill of Rights in the UK. In this section of the chapter I'm going to examine debates on the Statement of Values in terms of proposals leading to its creation and the role this statement is to play in the process of creating a potential Bill of Rights. According to Jack Straw,

> if a Bill of Rights and responsibilities ... is to be more than a legal document and become a mechanism for unifying the population, it is vital that it is owned by the British people and not just the lawyers ... for a Bill of Rights and Responsibilities to have real traction with the British people they must have an emotional stake in, and connection with it.
>
> (Straw 2008a: 7)

Generating the general public's emotional stake in the Bill of Rights was to be achieved, according to the *Governance of Britain* Green Paper, through the process of 'giving practical effect to our common values' (Ministry of Justice 2007: 61). Furthermore, it was stated in the Green Paper that 'the government believes that there is considerable merit in a fuller articulation of British values' and that a British Statement of Values, that will 'set out the ideals and principles that bind us together as a nation' will be established 'through an inclusive process of national debate' (2007: 58). The British people were promised in the Green Paper that 'over the next few months the government will release a series of discussion documents and materials to inform this national debate' which would include 'tapping into the wealth of knowledge amongst expert and representative groups in the country' and through using 'a range of engagement mechanism to support a national conversation and debate, suitable to the level of knowledge, interest, needs and characteristics of different groups' (2007: 59). The problem is this process has not started yet.

As noted in Chapter 4, the role that the Statement of Values was supposed to play with regard to the creation of the Bill of Rights was one of informing the preamble to the Bill of Rights. In a vein similar to Habermas' suggestions with regard to 'cultural' or 'national' particularity (see Chapter 5), the JCHR suggests that preambles to Bills of Rights and constitutions 'often reflect the unique nature of the particular historical moment in which those fundamental documents were born' (2008: 34). The JCHR suggests that the preamble to what they called the UK Bill of Rights and Freedoms 'could simply state that it is being adopted to give lasting effect to the values which are considered fundamental by the people of the United Kingdom, followed by a short list of values' (2008: 35). The JCHR informs us that this would include 'a strong interpretive clause requiring anybody interpreting the Bill of Rights to strive to achieve the purpose of the Bill of Rights and give practical effect to the fundamental values underpinning it as set out in the preamble' (2008: 35).

Thus the Statement of Values that would inform the preamble and which would also underwrite and guide those interpreting the rights in the Bill of Rights is extremely important for the success of the Bill of Rights. But what are these 'British values' and what is distinctly British about them? The House of Lords Constitution Committee asked Jack Straw this very question, namely, what would be distinctly British about the values included in the Statement of Values? In answer to this question Mr Straw attempted to differentiate between distinctive British values and exclusive British values:

> I cannot say what will be distinctive about this until the process is finished but I would like to suggest that personally I think one of the things that is distinctive about the United Kingdom – and is not exclusive, which is a different point, but is distinctive – is our tolerance.
>
> (Straw 2007b: 37)

I am not sure everyone would agree with Straw's summation of the extent and distinctiveness of British tolerance. I have suggested in Chapter 2 that 'our' so-called shared values (which includes tolerance and respect for law) on occasion have become relegated to second-order ideals that have been put in the shade relative to concerns over personal and public security. In typical authoritarian terms, Tony Blair, when Prime Minister, dictated a number of 'essential values' in his speeches on the themes of integration and multiculturalism in 2006 (see also McGhee 2008a: 133–4). According to Mr Blair,

> when it comes to our essential values – belief in democracy, the rule of law, tolerance, equal treatment for all, respect for this country and its

shared heritage – then that is where we come together, it is what we hold in common, it is what gives us the right to call ourselves British.

(Blair 2006: 6)

The Conservative leader David Cameron has cited the following as being distinctly British values: 'freedom of speech, respect for the rule of law, fairness and tolerance' (in BBC News 2006: 2). Also in 2006, Gordon Brown in his 'Futures of Britishness' speech described what he considers to be 'our enduring British values':

In addition to our qualities of creativity, inventiveness, enterprise and our internationalism, our central beliefs are a commitment to – liberty for all, responsibility by all and fairness to all.

(Brown 2006: 3)

All of these political leaders envisage the nation in these speeches as 'a community of equal, rights-bearing citizens, united in patriotic attachment to a shared set of political practices and values' (Ignatieff 1993: 6). The civic nationalistic flavour of especially Brown's statements on values is explicit, as is the role these values are supposed to play in turbulent times, that is, these values are supposed to protect, defend and unite us (see Chapters 2 and 3). That is a rather tall order for a list of abstract and general ideals and principles to perform. For example, for Blair, in a speech on Britishness and constitutional reform in 2000, establishing values and standing up for these values is essential if Britain is to survive 'the huge changes we are living through' (2000: 1); for Brown, shared purpose as a country is found through being 'more explicit about what we stand for' and as a result 'we will meet and master challenges best' (Brown 2006: 4). According to Brown (as noted in Chapter 3), it is the heated 'debates about immigration, asylum and multiculturalism in particular' that 'challenge us to be more explicit about Britishness' (2006: 2); at the same time, it is the events of 7 July 2005 that, according to Mr Brown, 'lead us to ask how successful we have been in balancing the need for diversity with the obvious requirements of integration in our society' (Brown 2006: 2). It is looking to the future, to Britain's ability to meet and master the challenges of the global economy, and also to the international, demographic, constitutional, social and security challenges ahead, according to Brown, 'that requires us to rediscover and build from our history and apply in our time the shared values that bind us together and give us common purpose' (2006: 3).

Therefore shared values are supposed to define what 'we' stand for and be a prophylactic against an array of both external (globalized) and internal threats and challenges (associated, it seems, with the by-products of non-integration, see Chapter 3). I suggest that the discourse of shared British values being articulated here as (1) a shield against danger and (2) the location of 'our' common ground from whence to meet present and future challenges is too closely associated with a politics of fear. This type of fear-mongering platform is hardly the premise for launching a progressive national debate on who 'we' are and what 'we' stand for. At the same time Gordon Brown's attempts to emphasize what is distinctive about these 'British' values results in them being anchored in the institutional past and established 'national identities' (see Chapter 5). In my opinion this makes the launching of a national debate to establish who 'we' are and what values 'we' stand for seem rather a wasted effort if 'we' are already being told what they are and how and where they are to be articulated.

But how do societies establish what their shared values are (when they are not being told what their 'our' values are by politicians)? And what role are these 'shared' values supposed to play in contemporary societies? Habermas is very clear in answering these questions. According to Habermas (as noted in Chapter 5), in complex societies the citizenry as a whole can no longer be held together by 'a substantive consensus on values', rather for Habermas the citizenry of complex, multicultural societies must be held together 'by a consensus on the procedures for the legitimate enactment of laws and the legitimate exercise of power' (1998: 225). Therefore, what Habermas advocates is 'a procedural consensus' embedded through a constitutional patriotism in the context of a historically specific political culture (1998: 226). Rather than integration at the level of shared values as advocated by Tony Blair (see Chapter 5), Habermas advocates political or civic integration at the level of the polity; by so doing, abstract values which have been depicted as something to be 'accepted and shared' under the government's moral authoritarianism are instead given 'practical effect' by giving them the 'ethical substance' (Habermas 1998: 225) of constitutional principles (Habermas 1997: 499). There is however, a great deal of work to be done to achieve this. For Habermas:

Constitutional principles can neither take shape in social practices nor become the driving force for the dynamic project of creating an association of free and equal persons until they are situated in the historical context of a nation of citizens[1] in such a way that they link up with those citizens' motives and attitudes.

(Habermas 1997: 499)

According to Habermas, legally guaranteed relations of equal recognition do not 'reproduce themselves of their own accord', they depend on 'the supportive spirit of a consonant background of legally non-coercible motives and attitudes of a citizenry oriented towards a common goal' (Habermas 1997: 499). A defensive politics of fear can only take 'us' a little way down the road to creating a sense of common belonging in contemporary Britain. A shift in the language of values and their relationship with potential new constitutional developments, especially the more formal Bill of Rights rather than the informal Declaration of Responsible British Citizenship (see Chapter 4), needs to be less regressive, defensive and exclusive. As Tamir notes, too much consensus on values can lead to exclusivity, enmity and marginalization, that is, 'when membership is based on an overlapping consensus of shared values, those outside the consensus can be marginalized, and their membership questioned to the point of turning them into outcasts' (1993: 90). What I am advocating is the promotion of membership norms through a sense of belonging which is made possible, not through adhering to a set of compulsory 'non-negotiable' values or a national identity (see Chapter 5); rather membership is to be achieved by having a stake (emotion, ethical and practical) in a living, evolving polity. Thus the ties that bind this process are both 'thin' in terms of being procedural, yet also 'thick' in terms of being relevant in peoples' 'practical' everyday realities; furthermore, they have the potential for facilitating 'ethical solidarity' in terms of the explicit obligations among co-nationals; and they are also emotive in terms of encouraging patriotic attachments (to the polity) as in Charles Taylor's example of the 'rallying effect' of the Canadian Charter of Rights (see Chapter 5).

As noted in Chapter 4, there is often a tension between domestic 'civic' politics and the universal politics of human rights. What is being advocated here is a variety of constitutional patriotism which although contextualized in the particular historical and political culture of the UK is ethical in orientation. For Habermas, ethical integration into a polity cannot always ensure 'ethical neutrality'[2] through the interpretation of constitutional principles from the perspective of the nations' historical experience (1994: 134). To ensure this process Habermas' recommendation is that ethical integration could take place through striving for a 'common horizon of interpretation' within which current issues give rise to public debates about the citizenries' political self-understanding (1994: 134). For Habermas, the process of shaping citizens' political opinions and wills cannot, as the communitarians suggest, be equated with a process by which citizens reach agreement about their ethical-political self-understanding (1994: 125). At the same time, this process does not depend on the moral stability that comes with a Rawlsian 'overlapping consensus' where support for the polity comes from each reasonable comprehensive view supporting 'the political conception for its own sake or on its own merits' (Rawls 1993: 148).[3] That is, this is not a matter of the quality of the endorsement of the rules and principles of our shared life together (Mills 2000: 198). Claudia Mills offers the following perspective on an example of an everyday ethical consensus, 'what is important is not why we endorse the rules that frame our lives together but that we truly endorse them' (2000: 198). What Mills is suggesting here is that political stability is not just a question of what Rawls calls the 'moral quality of public life' (Rawls 1993: 146–7) this is a potential end point to be striven for rather than being a place of departure. According to Mills, 'we may grow towards allegiance to principles because they allow us to live together and then, out of our shared experience of living together, develop into the kind of community that Rawls rightly believes we should cherish' (Mills 2000: 192). Habermas takes these ideas further by putting them into a constitutional framework. For Habermas, ethical integration and thus ethical stability involves the practical process of 'actualizing rights' (1994: 125). The process of actualizing rights should be embedded in contexts that require a discussion about a shared conception of the good and desired forms of life that are acknowledged to be authentic (Habermas 1994: 125). Habermas recommends what he calls a 'communicative praxis' (2005: 32) as a means of establishing ethical solidarity (rather than social solidarity) in the process of developing 'a nation's ethical self-understanding' (1994: 125) in the context of increasing the 'plurality of our cultural ways of life, our world views, and our religious convictions' (2005: 32).

How is all of this to be achieved? Can this be achieved through the creation of a Bill of Rights? According to Francesca Klug, the process of adopting a Bill of Rights can be as important as the rights themselves (2007a: 13). Klug suggests that if the objectives are clear and the process is inclusive then establishing a Bill of Rights is an opportunity for the UK to return to the unfinished project begun by the late Labour leader John Smith (see Chapter 4). This is a project John Smith referred to as 'a new deal' between the people and the state (Klug 2007a: 13). As a result of this process, according to Smith, 'the people' would be given new powers and a stronger voice in the affairs of the nation which would also restore a sense of cohesion and vitality to the nation (Smith, in Klug 2007a: 13). For Klug, a Bill of Rights can provide a unifying force in a diverse society, but it is easy to underestimate what is involved in a consultation process of this magnitude, she warns that such an undertaking can be a long and difficult process (Klug 2007c: 18). Michael Wills (Justice Minister) echoed Klug's wise words when he suggested that with regard to the British Statement of Values and the Bill of Rights 'the process of discussion and deliberation is as important as the outcome' (2008a: 3). For Wills the national debate on Britishness and British values will involve a number of innovative constitutional processes including a series of discussions, disseminated, printed and online material and fora on 'what it means to be British, what is best about it, and what best expresses what is best about it' (Wills 2008a: 3). Data from these discussions and forums will, according to Wills, be fed into what he describes as 'a citizens Summit' which will comprise of a representative sample of 500 people selected randomly from the population (Wills 2008a: 3). For Wills, the citizens summit will decide on four main questions: 'should there be such a statement, if so what it should be, how it should be expressed and finally what it should be used for' (2008a: 3) and their decisions on these answers will then go to parliament for a final decision (2008a: 3). Apart from the precarious final question in his list, that is, 'what should it be used for', Wills is not very clear about why this process is necessary (apart from getting in there first before the far right take over this debate, see Chapter 4) he hardly mentions the place of the British Statement of Values in relation to the Bill of Rights, which echoes the former Home Secretary Jacqui Smith's habitual uncoupling of the British Statement of Values from the process of establishing the Bill of Rights.

In my opinion, if the process of creating a British Statement of Values, which in Parekhian terms would ideally be a statement of society's 'operative public values' (Parekh 2000: 267) is uncoupled too much from the processes of introducing a Bill of Rights (which will give practical effect to these values), then a situation could arise, as already noted in Chapter 4, where the domestic politics of citizenship comes into tension with the universalism of human rights. If this process is to work then ethical integration (through actualizing human rights) has to be given priority over political integration (through making responsibilities explicit and establishing 'compulsory' values which 'we' are all supposed to accept and share) in the government's 'duty-centric' strategy of promoting 'civic identities' to bolster the thinness of British citizenship (Uberoi 2007: 147). There is a very real danger that the process of establishing a British Statement of Values could, as I. M. Young predicted, become a process of situating the specificity of 'the culturally dominant', that is, this could become a project of situating 'British' specificity through specifying what is particularly 'British' about 'British' values and the relationship between British rights and responsibilities which, despite Michael Wills' assertions of representativeness, might privilege 'the situation and experience of the dominant groups' who 'tend to define the norms of such a humanity in general' (Young 1990: 165). Rather than using this process to establish who 'we' are and what 'we' stand for (see Chapter 5), which could be too past orientated and inward looking I would prefer the emphasis to be on where 'we' are going and how 'we' are going to get there, which is both future orientated and outward looking. This could be achieved through establishing a Statement of Values in Britain which could take the form of a set of 'operative public values' which would form the preamble to a potential Bill of Rights in the UK. This process could enact a political culture infused with what Benhabib calls 'jurisgenerative processes' (2006: 49). For Benhabib, in jurisgenerative processes:

> A democratic people, which consider itself bound by certain guiding norms and principles engages in interactive acts by re-appropriating and reinterpreting these, thereby showing itself to be not only the subject but also the author of laws.
>
> (Benhabib 2006: 49)

For Benhabib these processes, in other words, permit us to think of creative interventions that mediate between universal norms and the will of democratic majorities (2006: 49). The potential of jurisgenerative processes therefore is that they promote ownership and following Habermas, ethical integration, through 'the augmentation of the meaning of rights claims and in the growth of political authorship by ordinary individuals, who thereby make these rights their own by democratically deploying them' (Benhabib 2006: 49). The facilitation of the jurisgenerative transformative processes that will be explored later is, following on from Chapter 5, an issue of political attachment and political mobilization. Rather than political attachment through exclusively belonging together, what is being advocated is the generation of an emotional, ethical and practical stake (and hence, sense of belonging to the polity) through 'institutional design' (Rothstein 1998).

6.3 Solidarity between strangers – 'equality' and 'integrative' citizenship

> Arguments about equality have gone on so long and have aroused such fierce feelings, that anyone venturing into this particular no-man's land needs to tiptoe. Much of the confusion is due to the assumption shared by many of the combatants that equality and inequality are simple and easily definable concepts.
>
> (Mount 2009: 193)

This section of the chapter will examine the unfolding debates in the UK with regard to equality and discrimination. In many ways, the emphasis on previous chapters (and section 6.2) on enhancing a sense of belonging to the polity, patriotism and the institutional modifications necessary for facilitating this process has been located in the 'recognition' side rather than the 'redistribution' side of what Benhabib describes as Nancy Fraser's 'mutually interconnected but distinct and irreducible paradigms of justice' (2002: 69; McGhee 2008a: 122–3).[4]

In order to explore the particular strategies with regard to UK discrimination law and the relationship between social and economic and civil and political human rights protections, I will rely more on David Miller and Michael Walzer than Nancy Fraser. The main reason for this is that in her most recent book (*Scales of Justice*) Fraser's arguments about justice and the scale of her analysis are at the level of what she calls 'the post-westphalian world' (2008: 9). For Fraser, globalization is driving a widening wedge between state territoriality and social effectivity (2008: 25) and therefore arguments about justice are no longer exclusively being 'played out within modern territorial states' (2008: 13). Although Fraser does concede that the westaphalian state 'remains undeniably relevant' (2008: 24), her recent book has little to offer contemporary scholars who are still attempting to analyse state-level debates, policies and strategies, such as those included in this chapter, with regards to justice, equality and fairness. In this chapter the emphasis will be mostly on top-down, government and parliamentary (for example, as recommended by the JCHR) derived strategies that are attempting to facilitate the emergence of a new, fairer, more equal society through attempting to change (or to progressively realize) what Miller calls 'the character of social relations' in societies (Miller 1995: 198). In Marshallian terms, what will be elaborated upon here is the 'three legged stool of citizenship' (Marshall 1950: 25) with regard to socio-economic, civil and political rights. In particular, I will be exploring the significance and evolution in debates with regard to what Marshall called social citizenship for developing a sense of common belonging through generating 'ethical solidarity', 'procedural fairness' and 'operative values' mentioned earlier and in the previous chapter. Marshall's concept of social citizenship accorded rights to basic standards of education, health and social care, housing and income maintenance (Marshall 1950). These social rights, according to McLaughlin and Baker, had been previously referred to by Tawney (1931 [1964]) in terms of 'practical equality', a platform on which meaningful equality of opportunity could be built (2007: 55).

A number of commentators have suggested the necessity of working on both the civil and political as well as the more 'material' (social and economic) aspects of 'life' in order to fully realize the 'integrative potential' of democratic citizenship. For example, Habermas suggests:

> Democratic citizenship can only realize its integrative potential – that is, it can only found solidarity between strangers – if it proves itself as a mechanism that actually realizes the material conditions of preferred forms of life.
>
> (Habermas 1998: 119)

Paul Gilroy gives a simpler (and perhaps more powerful) statement on this matter, that is, 'growing inequality makes recognition of common interests more difficult because people are actually becoming less alike in economic terms' (2004: 132). The arguments and strategies that will be examined here do not rehearse, repeat and regurgitate the now copious and familiar social theories of 'justice' and 'equality'. Rather, this part of the chapter is dedicated to examining government and parliamentary strategies associated with what David Miller and Michael Walzer refer to as 'complex equality' which is, for them, a political ideal, a vehicle of social change, and which, as will be revealed later, is not necessarily directly related to redistribution. Miller and Walzer in many ways follow Young's rejection of the material basis of equality associated with redistribution to instead focus more on what has been described as 'the equality of condition' which focuses on social relationships and in particular on 'non-material goods' such as mutual respect (McLaughlin and Baker 2007: 63). The precursor for the 'equality of condition' paradigm with its emphasis on non-material goods was R. H. Tawney's Christian socialism. Tawney, according to Wolff, had a particular understanding of the currency of egalitarian justice beyond material wealth which emphasized the non-material aspects of 'human flourishing' (Wolff 2001: 104). Following on from this rich tradition, according to Miller, a complex view of equality does not refer to the ways some identifiable good are distributed but describes the overall character of a set of social relationships (1995: 199). Whereas, the distributive notion of 'justice' comprises the various criteria that govern the allocation of social goods, 'equality' for Miller, 'is a predicate of the whole society within which many just distributions occur' (1995: 201). For Miller, it is by ensuring that justice is done within each particular sphere that we may achieve 'overall equality' (1995: 2001). Miller is building on Walzer's notion that 'equality' should be a free-standing concept that is empirically linked with but not conceptually reducible to the idea of 'distributive justice' (Miller 1995: 203). Miller therefore attempts to uncouple what he calls 'distributive justice' from what he calls 'egalitarian justice' associated with the notion of the political ideal of 'equality of status' or 'social equality' (Miller 2001: 231–2). Thus this notion of equality does not translate into simple, mechanical public policy strategies of redistribution, rather this ethos of equality is a matter of status, identification and socialization 'where each member of society regards himself as fundamentally the equal of all the others, and is regarded by the others as fundamentally their equal' (Miller, in Arneson 1995: 241). In other words, 'equality' becomes what Habermas would describe as being 'ethically grounded' through forging relationships of 'ethical solidarity'.

In this section of the chapter the focus will be on the political debates and strategies associated with two principles and ideals (in the armoury of what has been claimed as 'British' values), namely 'equality' and 'fairness'. In many ways these recent debates and strategies can be described as attempting to facilitate the development of social egalitarianism (Laborde 2008: 11) through the processes of encouraging British citizens to internalize values such as equality, but also to identify with the groups whose interests are associated with those values (Pettit 1999: 256). Following on from section 6.2, these processes are associated with concerns over 'the quality of relationships that citizens enjoy with one another, and about the way in which large inequalities of condition and difference in life experiences affect the common status of citizenship' (Laborde 2008: 11). Equality or equalities, as shall be revealed later, in this context, are a matter of 'ethical integration' (Habermas) and a crucial aspect of the 'jurisgenerative processes' (Benhabib) associated with the evolution of the institutions of the polity and the norms and values they articulate (Rothstein). Following Rothstein's thesis that 'just institutions matter', Uberoi lends weight to the idea of jurisgenerative institutional evolution when he urges 'us' to reflect on the fact that 'when new institutions and policies replace older ones and are given time to gain legitimacy, they shape the impressions that members of the nation have about what they share and in so doing so they change them also' (Uberoi 2008: 410). It is this potential relationship between the evolving polity and in turn the evolution of how 'we' belong to each other and how 'we' belong to the polity that is the focus of this chapter.

In this section of the chapter I will examine the arguments that are being made across a number of government and parliamentary bodies for changes to be made with regard to constitutional legislation, statutory legislation, public service provision and the attitudes of the general public with regard to equality. This section of the chapter will begin with a discussion of the arguments for and against the inclusion of what are referred to as ECHR+ rights, namely social and economic rights in the Bill of Rights and Responsibilities, which will be in turn contextualized within the JCHR's report on the International Covenant on Social, Economic and Cultural Rights (ICSECR) with regard to the introduction of social and economic rights in the UK. I will then move on to examine the debates on the Single Equality Bill in the Discrimination Law Review 2007 and Equalities Unit report of 2008 for harmonizing and simplifying UK discrimination law. This will be initially contextualized in my analysis of the recommendations, definitions and arguments for an 'equal' British society in the Cabinet Office's Equalities Review of 2007.

According to the Equalities Review's final report *Fairness and Freedom*, British society needs 'a new definition of equality that will be relevant to our society now and in the future' (2007b: 5). The following definition of 'an equal society' was put forward in this report:

> an equal society protects and promotes equal, real freedom and substantive opportunity to live in the ways people value and would chose, so that everyone can flourish. An equal society recognizes people's different needs, situations and goals and removes the barriers that limit what people can do and can be.
>
> (Cabinet Office 2007b: 6)

The Equalities Review team promoted their definition as a holistic approach which encompasses different and competing theories of equality (for example, equality of process, equality of outcome and equality of opportunity). By defining equality in this way, the Equalities Review's intention was to enable the government and the devolved institutions supported by the Equalities and Human Rights Commission (EHRC) (see McGhee 2008a: 108–10) 'to take these foundations and use them to build a consensus on the benefits of equality, at every level from the national to the local' (Cabinet Office 2007b: 109). In many ways this process of building a consensus on equality (for the purposes of enhancing ethical integration and in the process a sense of common belonging) is what this chapter is all about. The Equalities Review sums up the challenge of doing this:

> Our survey of public opinion shows that the British people intuitively place a high value on greater equality, but this belief is often undermined by prejudice towards particular groups and an aversion to misguided political correctness. Success will therefore mean reaching beyond the traditional institutions and ensuring that the real equalities agenda is placed centre stage with the public at large.
> (Cabinet Office 2007b: 123)

There are at least two proposed ways, as indicated earlier, in which this process may come to fruition: (1) through simplifying (streamlining) and mainstreaming 'equality' in UK discrimination law for the benefit of educating the 'general' public and (2) through introducing the consideration of the possibility of ECHR+ social and economic rights in the public debates on a potential Bill of Rights. In many ways both of these proposals are related and share a common tension in the form of the statutory and constitutional legislative 'separation' in the UK. With regard to Britain attempting to 'move on' the 'equalities' agenda, 2005 was a significant year. For example, the Labour government introduced a manifesto promise with regard to the implementation of the Single Equality Act in 2005; in the same year the Discrimination Law Review was launched to consider the opportunities for creating a clearer and more streamlined discrimination law framework (Discrimination Law Review 2007: 3). The justification for this review was later described as a matter of practicalities with regard to simplifying the UK's discrimination law which has developed for over 40 years and includes nine major pieces of discrimination legislation and around 100 statutory instruments setting out rules and regulations and more than 2500 pages of guidance and statutory codes of practice (Government Equalities Office 2009: 7). In many ways, the Equalities Review of 2007 sets the tone of the reports that came afterwards with regard to the combination of moral (principled) and ethical (practical) components in the justifications for the different 'equalities' proposals. That is:

> We believe that there is an irresistible case for accelerating our society's movement towards greater equality. We would not underplay the traditional moral arguments, but we think that it has never been more evident that greater equality will benefit everyone, and not

just those who are currently disadvantaged ... objectively we can also show that greater equality will make our society better off, our economy stronger, our social fabric more cohesive, and reassert the moral values which underpin the British tradition of fairness.

(Cabinet Office 2007b: 19)

In her foreword to the Government Equalities Office's report *A Fairer Future* (2009), Harriet Harman (Minister for Women and Equality) reiterated a number of the points made above in the process of building her case for recalibrating the relationship between the moral and the practical principles with regard to 'equality' and 'fairness' in Britain. For Harman, 'everyone has a stake in creating a fair society because fairness is the foundation for individual rights, a prosperous economy and a peaceful society' (in Equalities Office 2009: 1). The Discrimination Law Review offered a similar justification also including moral and ethical components:

Equality is a fundamental part of a fair society in which everyone can have the best possible chance to succeed in life. We want to live in a society where everyone's rights are properly respected. There is also a clear business case for equality. As a nation we need to make the most of the potential talent and skills of all individuals in our increasingly diverse society. We want a flourishing economy in which all have equal opportunities to thrive and contribute.

(Discrimination Law Review 2007: 5)

As well as the justifications with regard to simplifying and streamlining the complexities of discrimination law in the UK, the Single Equality Bill is being held up here as a site of biopolitical (see Chapters 2 and 3), security and multicultural significance. That is, by bringing equality to the centre stage of public policy in these reports and reviews, the security (in terms of potential social tensions and episodes of social order) and prosperity (in terms of economic flourishing) of 'the nation' becomes inextricably bound by individual flourishing understood in terms of removing what are seen as discriminatory barriers to opportunities, especially those experienced by minority groups (this will be examined in section 6.4).

Despite all the rhetoric there are problems with fully realizing 'this dream' of an equal society. The major source of tension is the government's attempts to separate constitutional and statutory discrimination law (Malik 2008: 9). According to Malik, the relationship between the Human Rights Act and discrimination law is complex, Article 14 of the ECHR, requires non-discrimination (on the grounds of race, sex, religion and sexual orientation) in the enjoyment of rights protected under other articles included in the ECHR (Malik 2008: 7). These constitutional human rights operate alongside a complex system of EU and statutory discrimination law which also prohibit discrimination on the grounds of race, sex, sexual orientation, religion or belief, disability and age in a number of sectors (Malik 2008: 8). Therefore, public authorities are required to safeguard the rights introduced in the Human Rights Act as well as complying with the standards of the EU and statutory discrimination law.

Increasingly there are blurred boundaries between these statutory and constitutional regimes in the form of the emergence of a body of 'constitutional discrimination law' (through the equality provision in the form of Article 14) which is now incorporated into domestic law in the UK through the Human Rights Act (Malik 2007: 76). However, the government has been resistant to what they see as the further constitutionalization of discrimination law (Malik 2007: 76); the government was also particularly resistant, according to Malik, to the proposals for the incorporation of a purpose clause (referred to earlier with regard to the preamble in the potential Bill of Rights as an interpretative clause) which would set out the goals of the Equality Act 'in terms which relate it to "constitutional" values such as equality and dignity' (Malik 2008: 8). The government's reason for refusing the adoption of a purpose clause which would connect statutory discrimination protections to constitutional human rights protections was the matter of clarity. In their response to the Discrimination Law Review the government stated that 'one of the main aims of the Bill is to set out the law in clear and unambiguous terms. A purpose clause would undermine that aim because there would be an inevitable tension between a general statement of purpose and the specific provisions of the Bill' (in Malik 2008: 8).

The government told the Discrimination Law Review that they would revisit the possibility of including a constitutional equality provision in the preamble of a potential Bill of Rights and Responsibilities and that this would be the potential correct place (rather than in the Single Equality Act) for 'reflecting the central place of equality in our society as one of the values which informs governmental and public authority decision-making' (in Malik 2008: 8). The problem is, as will be noted below, when it comes to the place of 'equality' in debates on the Bill of Rights and Responsibilities, and especially the inclusion of ECHR+ social and economic rights in this Bill of Rights, the separation of the statutory and the constitutional is replaced with arguments for the separation of judicial and parliamentary powers. There are therefore issues here, as also found in Chapter 4, with regard to the tension between the politics of citizenship and the politics of human rights. These tensions are evident in (1) the government's attempt to maintain administrative separation between statutory and constitutional discrimination legislation and (2) the government's perceptions of tensions between the judiciary and parliament with regard to the potential enforcement of social and economic human rights if ECHR+ rights are adopted. With regard to the latter tension, a brief contextualizing 'history' of the development of human rights covenants is required.

According to Costas Douzinas, the various generations of human rights can be colour coded. The first (blue) generation of rights are civil and political or 'negative' rights associated with liberalism; the second (red) generation of rights are 'positive' social, economic and cultural rights; and the third (green) generation of rights are 'group' or national sovereignty rights associated with the decolonization process and belatedly, environmental rights (Douzinas 2007: 22). According to Douzinas, the difference between blue and red rights became a central aspect of the ideological cold war conducted in the UN, international institutions, academic conferences and the world media in the second half of the twentieth century (2007: 22). These different groups of rights became emblematic of the different priorities of states in the capitalist, liberal West and Soviet Bloc socialism (Douzinas 2007: 22–3, Puta-Chekwe and Flood 2001: 41). In turn these ideological conflicts, described by Scott as 'the grand bifurcation' (2001: 7), made it impossible for the UN to draft a common international Bill of Rights, the result being that two separate covenants were drawn up and eventually adopted (Douzinas 2007: 23).[5] The existence of these separate covenants has in turn served to perpetuate the belief that economic, social and cultural rights are different both in value and in kind from civil and political rights (Puta-Chekwe and Flood 2001: 39). Thus this ideological conflict was reflected in the texts of the treaties, and following Western priorities, human rights were hierarchized in that the civil and political rights covenant which created a state duty 'to respect and to ensure to all' the listed rights. However, the economic and social rights treaty is much more flexible and equivocal in that member states 'take steps, individually and through international assistance and cooperation … with a view to achieving progressively the full realization' of convention rights (Douzinas 2007: 23). When it comes to the ECHR, it is civil and political rights that are enshrined, that is not to say that social and economic rights do not exist in the ECHR, but it is to say that they are relatively marginalized. However, as Merali and Oosterveld point out, more recent international human rights treaties, such as the Convention on the Rights of the Child and the Convention on the Elimination of All Forms of Discrimination Against Women, have rejected a division or hierarchy of rights, in that they give equal importance to economic, social and cultural rights, and civil and political rights (2001: 1).

There has been a great deal of debate in the UK with regard to the place of social and economic rights. Academics such as Peter Weir of Democratic Audit in the Human Rights Centre at Essex University have called for social and economic rights to be prioritized alongside protected civil and political rights (2006: ix). At the same time, the inclusion of ECHR+ social and economic rights has been a source of concern in the debates surrounding the Bill of Rights and Responsibilities. In this section of the chapter I will map out the process whereby the debates on the inclusion of social and economic rights in the Bill of Rights (and all the complications associated with (1) the separation of powers and (2) the distinction between intentions to progressively realize and duties to enforce rights) have become eclipsed by the government's attempts to generate 'an accessible and straightforward statement of equality' in order to 'secure equality's place at the highest levels of political principle' (Ministry of Justice 2009: 38). I think it is important to explore these issues thoroughly even though the government has indicated a curtailment of these debates.[6] It will be noted here that the incorporation of social and economic rights (either in the form of justiciable rights or rights to be progressively realized) has been replaced in the *Rights and Responsibilities* Green Paper with the promotion of the political principle of equality reflected in 'society's commitment to equality' (Ministry of Justice 2009: 38). What this means is that a hollow political ideal of 'equality' in political discourse has come to overshadow the process of 'actualizing' social and economic rights in the UK.

It was suggested in the *Governance of Britain* Green Paper 2007 that the incorporation of social and economic rights into British law would involve a significant shift from parliament to the judiciary in making decisions about public spending and levels of taxation. It was stated that

[i]f specifically British rights[7] were to be added to those we already enjoy by virtue of the European Convention, we would need to be certain that their addition would be of real benefit to the country as a whole and not restrict the ability of the democratically elected government to decide upon the way resources are to be deployed in the national interest.

(Ministry of Justice 2007: 61)

There is some disagreement with regard to whether the inclusion of social and economic rights would necessarily interfere with the separation of powers between parliament and the judiciary. For example, in the JCHR's Twenty-First Report published in 2004, the committee attempted to grapple with the UK's obligation with regard to the protection of social and economic rights under the UN's ICESCR.[8] As well as obligations under the ICESCR the UK is already party to a number of international agreements for the protection of economic, social and cultural rights.[9] Although social and economic rights were not formally included in the Human Rights Act of 1998, this does not mean that the substance of these rights is not protected. The JCHR informs us that under legislation relating to housing, healthcare, employment relations and discrimination, significant aspects of the ICESCR rights are the subject of obligations on public bodies which may be judicially reviewed in courts (2004: 6). The judicial review of statutory duties, however, does not equate to the constitutional level protection of the universally applicable civil and political human rights standards provided by the Human Rights Act. For the JCHR, there are problems with relying on this level of protection in that this could introduce inequalities and unfairness between social groups by leaving 'marginalized groups or individuals, who fall outside of the scope of the legislation' unprotected and therefore vulnerable (JCHR 2004: 6). The JCHR cites the EU Charter of Fundamental Rights as an example of a possible human rights mechanism that contains guarantees for the protection of what Douzinas (2007) would refer to as first-generation (civil and political), second-generation (social and economic) and third-generation rights to environmental protection (2004: 7). The EU Charter is therefore viewed by the JCHR as an example of a possibility for the simplification, streamlining and reconciling of especially first- and second-generation rights.

Peter Weir (2006), the Equalities Review (2007) and the JCHR (2004) all cited opinion poll and survey data that suggested significant public support for the greater prominence of social and economic rights.[10] Can we assume that in the current economic downturn the public support and social importance accorded to social and economic rights will increase? If indeed this is the case then the government's position could be increasingly out of kilter with 'public opinion'. The government, according to the JCHR and as noted *Governance of Britain* Green Paper of 2007, 'considers that the greater part of the provisions of the ICESCR[11] are statements of principle and objectives which do not lend themselves to specific incorporation into legislation or to justiciable processes'

(Joint Committee on Human Rights 2004: 16). The JCHR's intention is to move beyond the 'off-limits' stance the government has taken with regard to social and economic rights in the *Governance of Britain* Green Paper to examine the solutions that other countries, notably South Africa, have adopted. According to the JCHR:

> The South African Bill of Rights contains a number of social and economic rights, such as the rights to housing, health care, food, water and social security, but qualifies the justiciability of those rights by providing that 'the state must take reasonable legislative and other measures, within its available resources, to achieve the progressive realisation' of these rights. The South African Constitutional Court has used the English administrative concept of 'unreasonableness', which has a very high threshold, to ensure that the courts will only very rarely intervene to uphold social and economic rights. This model therefore gives *some* role to the courts, but not a very substantial one.
>
> (Joint Committee on Human Rights 2008: 48)[12]

This arrangement has a number of advantages: democratic processes remain independent, however; the role of the courts is not eliminated, but at the same time, judicial interference is confined within narrow parameters so as to allow the courts to respond only in the event of large-scale violations, especially when these pertain to vulnerable groups (2008: 48, 49). On this basis the JCHR urged the government to draw inspiration from the South African approach to social and economic rights which would ensure that parliament and the government would retain their primary responsibility for economic and social policy and would include built-in limitations with regard to the role of the courts (recognizing the judiciary's relative lack of substantial expertise with regard to social and economic policy). Another advantage is that the government could also be held accountable against ICESCR social, economic and cultural standards (JCHR 2004: 18).

Following on from the parallels drawn between the EU Charter of Fundamental Rights which combines first-, second- and third-generation rights and the introduction of the Single Equality Act (that would simplify and streamline in one act diverse discrimination legislation and duties), the government has recognized that 'a new Bill of Rights and responsibilities could present the opportunity to bring together in one place a range of welfare and other entitlements currently scattered across the UK's legal and political landscape' (Ministry of Justice

2009: 9). However, it was also stated in the *Rights and Responsibilities* Green Paper that the government believes it would be important to avoid opening up new areas of litigation, disrupting the ability of front-line service providers to deliver services effectively and displacing the current balance of power between parliament, the executive and the judiciary (Ministry of Justice 2009: 38). Rather than being, as Jack Straw suggests, an ethical framework which gives practical effect to shared values (Straw 2008a: 7), or being 'emblematic of the fair society we want to live in' (Straw 2009: 7), the government in their plans for the Bill of Rights (and Responsibilities) has prevented the establishment of a human rights culture which actualizes 'the core economic and social rights' that form 'the substance of people's everyday lives' (JCHR 2004: 8). Instead, as already noted, they have taken the opportunity to regurgitate a hollow, de-contextualized and non-actualized discourse of 'equality' as a political value:

> The government's overarching aim in this area would be to set out in any Bill of Rights and Responsibilities an accessible and straightforward statement of equality to embody its central place in UK society ... the government welcomes views on how a statement of equality in the Bill of Rights and Responsibilities might be framed in order to secure equality's place at the highest levels of political principle.
>
> (Ministry of Justice 2009: 38)

The Prime Minister, Gordon Brown has in his statement to the JCHR Liaison Committee stated that a debate on the inclusion of social and economic rights cannot 'be off-limits' because of the importance the people of Britain accord to them. According to Brown, some of 'the social changes that happened in the twentieth century' such as the introduction of the National Health Service 'are seen by people to be of such importance that they accord them the status of rights in the way they talk about them' (Brown in JCHR 2008: 46). The Prime Minister's main concern with regard to the inclusion of social and economic rights, as noted earlier, was described by the JCHR as being 'relatively narrow' in that his main objection was 'that social and economic rights ought not to be directly enforceable by individuals in the courts' (JCHR 2008: 46). The government, in the *Rights and Responsibilities* Green Paper, left the door open for further discussion on the place of social and economic rights, but curtailed the discussion by stating that they 'would not seek to create new and individually enforceable legal rights in addition to the array of legal protections already available' (2009: 43). The discussion they invite is to be on the issue as to:

> Whether there could be advantages in articulating constitutional principles which can be drawn from existing welfare provisions. It might be possible to distil the values which frame our welfare system in order to reflect, in one coherent document, certain social and economic guarantees and the responsibilities and conduct expected of individuals.
>
> (Ministry of Justice 2009: 43)

Thus in the arena of social, economic and 'welfare' rights the government is attempting to encourage a discussion of constitutional principles in the absence of constitutional protections in the name of reflecting 'economic guarantees' (and also the responsibilities and conduct expected of individuals). The Green Paper contains two main options for achieving this. The first is to include 'a general interpretative principle' in the potential Bill of Rights which would provide guidance to courts and public authorities 'as to how discretion could be exercised or the law developed and interpreted' (Ministry of Justice 2009: 55). This would give the Bill of Rights (even in this watered down form) more legal force than a Declaration of Citizenship (see Chapter 4), 'but without increasing litigation' (Ministry of Justice 2009: 55). The second option suggested the inclusion of a general interpretative principle, whereby a duty could be placed on public authorities[13] to have regard to relevant principles when exercising their functions and in making decisions (2009: 56). The government's thinking here was that this duty would add an extra degree of legal effect to the type of provisions or principles set out, thus ensuring that 'parliament could indicate directly to decision-makers the overarching principles which should inform the exercise of their functions' (Ministry of Justice 2009: 56).

So rather than giving practical effect to overarching values of equality and fairness by establishing a Bill of Rights that would combine first-, second- and some third-generation human rights following the EU Charter of Fundamental Rights and the South African Bill of Rights the proposed Bill of Rights and Responsibilities in the Green Paper has become less an 'epic journey' (Straw 2009: 1) and more a compromised circular route to how things have always been. At best what might be adopted is a 'purpose clause' containing 'the constitutional value of equality' to be adopted in the forthcoming Equality Act (Malik 2008: 9) and for a 'general interpretative principle' to be adopted in the potential Bill of Rights in order to bring a little more legal force to the arena of social and economic principles in the relative absence of constitutional protections. The question that needs to be resolved here is would these initiatives really deliver in terms of being an emblematic, unifying force in society?

6.4 (In)equalities, biopolitics and targeted interventions

In many ways what has emerged in the debates and discussions about 'equality' in the context of UK discrimination law and the place of social and economic constitutional protections is yet another contemporary incarnation of biopolitics. The examples of neo-biopolitics found in the new border controls (Chapter 1), counter-terrorism strategies (Chapter 2) and the managed migration system (Chapter 3) are all associated with a domestic politics of protection with regard to safeguarding the nation's future prosperity and safety from internal disorder and external threats. At the same time, these examples of biopolitics are associated with a regressive defensiveness in the form of a fortress mentality which has had a negative impact on Britain's standing with regard to European and international human rights standards. For example, the UK is on shaky ground in relation to: International Humanitarian Law when it comes to 'our' obligations to asylum seekers under the Geneva Convention (Chapter 1); 'our' human rights record in terms of derogations from the ECHR and the continuing calls for human rights to be rebalanced in the name of 'public security' (Chapter 2 and also see the Afterword) to interference with ECHR Article 8 associated with the right to a 'private' 'family life' when the government attempts to 'end chain migration' through restrictions on family reunification (see Chapter 3). Under this type of biopolitics human rights are reduced to being the rights citizens enjoy over non-citizens, as the rights the law abiding majority enjoys over 'undesirable' others, whether they be failed asylum seekers or foreign national terrorist suspects. I want to suggest here that the particular debates on 'equalities' in this chapter can be described as opening up a space for an alternative discourse of biopolitics. This biopolitical discourse does, as noted in Chapter 2, include some elements of securitization; however, the striking difference is that this does not lead to a fortress mentality, but rather, the objective here is to open up 'our' ethical obligations to one another in societies characterized by super diversity.

It was in the pages of the Equalities Review report that we find a securitization process of a different order, for example, in this report we find the construction of the threat in our midst, the identification of the particular social groups in which this threat is associated and the 'political' or policy solution to this threatening internal disequilibrium. The Equalities Review team attempted to draw our attention to the 'persistent disadvantage' experienced by certain social groups in the context of what they describe as 'rapid economic and technological change' (2007: 12). The Equalities Review team's primary concern with regard to the latter was that the economic forces of globalization would, 'if left to themselves', further 'entrench' the inequalities experienced by certain social groups as persistent disadvantage (Equalities Review 2007: 12). The persistent disadvantage of these communities is not the primary social threat being constructed here, the Equalities Review makes a conceptual link between the experience of persistent disadvantage and the social threat of escalating social disorder emanating from persistently disadvantaged communities. They support their assertion in the following terms: 'the links between equality and social cohesion are well documented. Violence, conflict, insecurity and political stability are all more likely to occur in more unequal societies' (2007: 21). The ontological threats constructed here are however for rather different purposes than the usual securitizing strategy of enemy construction with a view to introducing 'emergency' measures (see Chapter 2). This also introduces an alternative discourse of 'shared' or 'common fate' (see Chapter 5); however, it should be noted that the Equalities Review's intention here was to attempt to promote amity and facilitate, through a variant of what Habermas would describe as ethical solidarity, 'a consensus on the benefits of equality' (Equalities Review 2007: 109). Therefore the biopolitical strategy that the Equalities Review attempted to initiate in British society is associated with the mantra: 'a more equal Britain would be a better Britain' this type of society would be more prosperous, more humane, more cohesive and fairer (2007: 123). What this potentially leads 'us' to is thinking about 'equality' differently; not just as a matter of mechanical policies of redistribution[14] but as the ethical substance (Habermas) that characterizes social relationships (Miller). At the same time, for policymakers this new equalities agenda leads us back to 'class'. Whereas Nancy Fraser and other theorists of intersectionality (see McGhee 2008a: 115–17) have educated us to complex relationships between 'bivalent collectivities' such as gender and ethnicity,[15] class has (once again) become the social category to trump all other social categories. For example, in their promotion of a new public duty to consider reducing 'socio-economic inequalities' in the Equality Bill, the Government Equalities Office stated:

> We know that inequality does not just come from your gender or ethnicity; your sexual orientation or your disability; your age, or your religion or belief. Overarching and interwoven with these specific forms of disadvantage is the persistent inequality of social class – your family background or where you were born.
>
> (Government Equalities Office 2009: 9)

According to the Government Equalities Office, 'social class still holds a powerful grip on people's lives' (2009: 9). They stated the following:

> Class trumps ability – less academically able but better off children overtake more able poorer children at school by the age of six; and, class trumps gender when it comes to life expectancy – while women generally have longer life expectancy than men, since the early 1980s poorer women can now be expected to live less long than rich men.
>
> (Equalities Office 2009: 9)

It is difficult at this point to evaluate the impact of the re-emergence of class as the meta-social category through which other (intersectional) dimensions of disadvantage (for example, gender, 'race', disability, religion, age, sexual orientation) are to be calibrated is either a step forward or a step backward. I am sure many would view this as an example of the marginalization of particular sources of disadvantage, for example, structural racism and the emergence of new 'race equality' foci namely the white working class. What is certain however is that when these debates are brought into this historical moment, which seems (at the moment) to be less dominated by the fear associated with terrorism, which has been eclipsed by fears for the sustainability of 'our way of life' associated with the economic downturn (see Chapter 5), then perhaps the perils of socio-economic disadvantage as depicted by the Equalities Review is, when co-opted into the discourses of human security and public safety (see Chapter 2), the ultimate multifaceted 'trump card'. However, as suggested, it is important to note that the Equalities Review emphasized the potential social threats associated with persistent disadvantage not for the purposes of encouraging a fortress mentality and 'tough' emergency action but rather to encourage what Hannah Arendt described as an emphatic 'enlarged way of thinking' (1968: 220) which is associated with an evolution in the ethical substance of social relations which has revolutionary potential. There is the potential here, which would require a great deal of political will, to encourage the emergence of what Wolff refers to as an egalitarian social ethos (1998: 105). For Wolff an ethos comprises of three essential parts: (1) the presence of underlying (implicit or explicit) values; (2) that these values are interpreted into a set of maxims or principles; (3) which are then applied in practice (1998: 105). Thus values and principles become internalized by the members of a society and inform their behaviours. According to Wolff, an ethos becomes an ideology if the members of a society claim to adhere to certain values and principles, but these claims do not correspond to their practices (1998: 105). This distinction between 'an ethos' and 'an ideology' is useful for analysing the government's troubled discourse of shared values which have appeared in most chapters of this book. In the context of the relative weight given to socio-economic and civil and political rights in contemporary Britain, the shared values discourse could be categorized as being ideological because the much cited values of equality, fairness and anti-discrimination as yet (when viewed through the 'grand bifurcation' in human rights conventions) do not fully correspond in practice to justiciable or progressively realizable social and economic rights. The questions we are left with at this juncture are: (1) has the government done enough (to quote the Ministry of Justice, see above) to 'secure equality's place at the highest levels of political principle'? and (2) has the government done enough to promote social change? (see Chapter four) with regards to the facilitation of a greater sense of ethical solidarity and debate on the social, economic and political necessity of promoting 'equality' and 'fairness' as operative social values and progressively realizable aims in British society?

Ultimately, equality strategies in the UK have become a mixed bag of encouraging social egalitarian 'complex equality' thinking in terms of promoting the benefits of greater equality in the country as a whole, but falling shy of fully enshrining the constitutional value of equality; however, simultaneous with this process are strategies that attempt to address the complex disadvantages experienced by particular communities. The Communities and Local Government Department are following the Equalities Review's suggestions rather closely with regard to the necessity of developing targeted interventions to tackle persistent disadvantage in particular communities in 2009–10. For example, in their Connecting Communities programme the Communities and Local Government Department have explicitly set out to address the perceived and actual disadvantages of particular persistently disadvantaged communities namely the white working-class community. This focus is justified through the department insisting that the needs of this social group in particular have been neglected by 'the outdated ideology or assumptions' of 'the inequality agenda' (Denham, in Doyle 2009: 2).[16] Over 100 neighbourhoods across 75 local authorities are involved in the 12 million pound Connecting Communities programme (Department for Communities and Local Government 2009b: 1). Four factors are listed by the Department for Communities and Local Government which justify the development of the Connecting Communities programme: (1) the impact of the economic downturn on white working class communities; (2) the decline in 'traditional jobs in predominantly white areas'; (3) the perceived changes in these communities as a result of recent immigration (4) and concerns with regard to the popularity of the British National Party in the white working class (Communities and Local Government Department 2009a: 1, 2009b: 1). In many ways the projects funded under the Connecting Communities programme could be described as a Prevent programme (see Chapter 1) for the white working class in that just as the PVEF projects were dedicated to facilitating 'community resilience' to extremism in local Muslim areas, the Connecting Communities funded projects in local white working-class communities are also dedicated to creating 'community resilience' to far right influences by tackling head-on 'the real and perceived' issues concerning the members of local communities, 'which if left neglected can prove fertile territory for extremism' (Communities and Local Government Department 2009b: 2). The Connecting Communities programme is dedicated to heading-off the exploitation of 'dissatisfaction and insecurity' by the far right through 'myth-busting' activities and promoting 'visible social justice' that, among other things, will respond to the perceptions of preferential treatment of one group over other groups in local communities (following Cantle and the CICC, see Chapter 3 and McGhee 2008a: 102–5) by making sure that people have their 'fair say' with regard to 'the issues that matter' (Communities and Local Government Department 2009b: 1). As well as tackling 'the real and perceived sense of unfairness some people are feeling' (Communities and Local Government Department 2009a: 1), the Connecting Communities projects also attempt to offer practical support with regard to employment and training opportunities available in local areas for those affected by the economic downturn (Communities and Local Government Department 2009a: 1). I am inclined to agree with Jack Doyle who suggested in his article in the *Independent* that the Connecting Communities programme was rather opportunistic, in that the emphasis on white working-class concerns over recent immigration is 'the latest attempt by ministers to address fears over immigration in

Labour heartlands, and confront the threat from the British National Party' (Doyle 2009: 1). Furthermore, John Azah (chair of the British Federation of Racial Equality Councils) also commented on the particular focus of John Denham's Connecting Communities programme on the white working class as an electioneering strategy when he was quoted in the *Independent* as saying, 'I think it is important for the government and all parties to work with all communities rather than playing to a certain core voter' (in Doyle 2009: 2). It is clear that attempting to play to certain voters (and counter potential internal disequilibria in the form of the ascendance of the far right) through targeted 'race equality' interventions such as the Connecting Communities programme is, in the run up to the general election in 2010, more *en vogue* than attempting to promote equality as an actualized right in a potential Bill of Rights.

6.5 Evolutions, revolutions and a 'proper' human rights culture

I want to end the chapter with some further considerations on the development of a Bill of Rights in Britain. There has been a lot of talk about the correct or usual context from whence a Bill of Rights and/or foundational epochal constitutional statement is written. The introduction of these emblematic documents usually occurs, for example, after monumental events such as civil wars, revolutions or extreme regime changes (for example, the end of apartheid in South Africa). The UK, according to the JCHR, has not undergone such events in the run-up to the debates initiated by the government on the possibility of introducing a Bill of Rights (2008: 23). There are a few exceptions to Bill of Rights being introduced in the aftermath of monumental historical events such as those listed above. The Canadian Charter of Rights and Freedoms (also discussed in Chapter 5) is one such exception[17] and is, according to the JCHR, 'one of the best examples of a Bill of Rights adopted by a democracy which has attained the status of a constitutional document in the popular imagination' (2008: 24). How could such a process be introduced in Britain? In answer to this question we could take encouragement from Conor Gearty's project of promoting the 'upbeat dimension' of human rights which stresses the positive human potentialities of human rights in the form of emancipation and 'human flourishing' (Gearty 2007: 6–7). This positive side of human rights, according to Gearty, stresses growth and personal success, it sees human rights 'as radically pluralist in the hospitality towards others – rather than mere tolerance of them – that its underlying ethic demands'

(2007: 140). Therefore, Gearty encourages us to see human rights as a whole as 'an idea that both protects us as persons and enables us to grow at the same time' (Gearty 2007: 141). The full realization of Gearty's vision could ensure that the 'socially caused suffering' (Honneth 2003: 118) in the form of 'distributional injustices' experienced, according to Honneth, by those affected as 'social injury' in the context of the 'institutional expression of social disrespect' (2003: 114) are explicitly and constitutionally recognized as an infringement of human rights. This would be a step beyond the interventions focusing on the 'perceived and real' issues and concerns associated with particular disadvantaged social groups in the context of the economic downturn found in John Denham's Connecting Communities programme (see section 6.4).

I am left with some unresolved questions. Can the government, in the context of the global financial crisis, still maintain that 'the market is the superior, if not the only, mechanism of distribution' (Douzinas 2007: 23)? Will social and economic rights remain merely non-justiciable principles and objectives rather than constitutionally protected entitlements? Julia Unwin the chief executive of the Joseph Rowntree Foundation (JRF) suggests, following the publication of the JRF's *Contemporary Social Evils* collection:

> To respond to the financial crisis requires a new approach. A new set of values, a willingness to confront inequality and greed, and understand the value of mutual support, work that is economically productive, and at the same time shape an economy that can offer prosperity and security, without necessarily promising endless growth.
>
> (Unwin 2009: 27)

This is, as noted earlier with regard to the biopolitical language employed in the Equalities Review, a matter of the future prosperity, security (and sustainability) of Britain. Unwin poses the following provocative questions: what will the post-recession world look like? What will be its features? And how can we ensure that it is both sustainable and just? (2009: 27). These are important questions that must be grappled with. Nicholas Timmins, in the foreword to the JRF's *Contemporary Social Evils* collection states that 'there is nothing like a crisis to trigger, a rethink, both individually and collectively, about society's values, goals and directions ... difficult times may paradoxically, provide the best moment for framing difficult solutions' (2009: vi).[18] Furthermore, the historian, Jose Harris draws our attention to the parallels between Britain in the first decade of the twentieth century and Britain in our present context, the last year of the first decade of the twenty-first century. For Harris, the former was associated with 'a prolonged fiscal crisis and the after-effects of an expensive and unpopular war in South Africa, and international economic recession' (2009: 7). The result of these crises in the early twentieth century was widespread unemployment and the shrinkage of average real incomes in Britain (2009: 7). A further result, according to Harris, was that public attention became concentrated on 'certain longstanding social conditions' in terms of 'the dangers' they posed 'to the overall "health" of the body politic' (Harris 2009: 7–8). The parallels with our own time are uncanny; we too are experiencing fiscal crisis, we too are involved in expensive and unpopular foreign conflicts in Afghanistan and Iraq and are in the midst of a global recession. As a result of the early twentieth-century crises philanthropic and governmental mobilizations were set in motion that would eventually lead to the setting up of the welfare state, the National Health Service and compulsory education legislation. The question is what will be set in motion in response to the crises afflicting contemporary Britain? According to Straw and Wills in their foreword to the *Rights and Responsibilities* Green Paper, 'at all times, but especially in turbulent times of rapid and radical change, people need to feel secure' (2009: 3). They stated that

> [a]t the heart of this Green Paper is the key constitutional question of the relationship between the citizen and the state and how this relationship can best be defined to protect fundamental freedoms and foster mutual responsibility as this country is going through profound changes.
>
> (in Ministry of Justice 2009: 3)

It was suggested that the 'Bill of Rights and Responsibilities and the values which gives rise to them ... could act as an anchor for people in the UK as we enter a new age of anxiety and uncertainty' (Ministry of Justice 2009: 13). I consider this to be a rather negative premise for the enactment of a Bill of Rights, which is testament to the politics of fear that has gripped the government's policy making in recent years. In this chapter I have explored an alternative role for the Bill of Rights (my preference would be for the JCHR's ECHR+ UK Bill of Rights and Freedoms over the Ministry of Justice's British Bill of Rights and Responsibilities, see Chapter 4) to play in contemporary Britain based upon a new politics of belonging underwritten by a new 'ethical solidarity'. In this context a sense of belonging to the polity has the potential for being experienced, according to Bauman, in 'the daily realities of its members'

(2009: 114). In this context '"belonging" translates as trust in the benefits of human solidarity, and in the institutions that arise from that solidarity' (Bauman 2009: 149). By striving for a new balance between positive and negative human rights in this way, there is the potential for creating distance between the public's media-fuelled ambivalence towards human rights. This is one further bonus which would come with the balancing of rights in this way, in that the incorporation of, for example, social and economic rights would be outside of the popular misconceptions of human rights (and the Human Rights Act in particular, see Chapter 4) as a terrorists' or criminals' charter. Rather, according to the JCHR, such a constitutional document which stipulates the rights to adequate health care and education, to equal treatment in the workplace and to protection against the worst extremes of poverty could be seen as bringing rights 'home', that is, into the very 'substance of people's everyday lives' (JCHR 2004: 8). These everyday and practical rights, which are experienced in the daily realities of all citizens and residents could become the key jurisgenerative processes, perhaps alongside a more effective and independent EHRC,[19] for 'placing human rights and equality at the heart of policy making, decision making and service delivery' (JCHR 2004: 23) in proper human rights culture in a potential Britain of the near future.

Afterword

We all think about the future, but in very diverse ways
—*Raymond Williams 1983: 3*

The above is the opening sentence of Raymond Williams' book *Towards 2000*. Williams has much to say in his book which speaks to us today, with regard to hope and fear and in relation to politics, planning and even political manifesto writing. At the time of writing (late 2009) the prospect of a general election and frantic manifesto writing is in the air.

I was struck by what Williams had to say about two different ways of thinking about the future in his book. He talks about, for example, one way of orientating oneself to the future which is associated with 'intense concern about the future of industrial civilization and, beyond even that, about the future of the species and of the planet, under destructive forces that are already loose' (1983: 50). However, Williams also talks about an orientation to the future which is characterized by 'a kind of hope which has accepted the facts underlying these fears and which can see ways beyond them which are fully within our capacity' (1983: 5). Following on from the normative turn in the last chapter (and in Chapter 5), I am intrigued by the relationship between what might be called the politics of fear and the politics of hope and the impact of these on the discourse of shared values and debates on human rights in the UK. When it comes to the place of human rights in the fear versus hope 'camps' we are confronted with more than just political rhetoric; there is a chance that this rhetoric is symbolic of the shifts in the values which underwrite human rights, for example, in the worst case scenario, moving away from the universality and respect for common humanity (see Chapters 2 and 4).

I was struck by the stark contrast Francesca Klug makes between the political leadership of President Obama on human rights and Jack Straw and Tony Blair's leadership with regard to human rights. As already noted in previous chapters, the JCHR regarded Straw's human rights strategy as being in collusion with 'tabloid' hostility with regard to the Human Rights Act[1] (see Chapter 4) and Tony Blair was described by Klug as sometimes acting like a cheerleader for tabloid hostility to the Human Rights Act (also in Chapter 4). Furthermore, Blair was explicit about his willingness to change 'the rules of the game' which included 'if necessary amending the Human Rights Act' in his infamous media briefing on anti-terror measures a month after 7/7 (see Chapter 2). In contrast President Obama had the following to say in his Inauguration Speech, delivered in January 2009, when we 'stand up for human rights, by example at home and by effort abroad we also strengthen our security and well being' (in Klug 2009: 7). Rather than standing firm and standing up for human rights, political leadership in the UK in recent years, whether Labour or Conservative, has exhibited an explicit willingness to rethink, amend, derogate and rebalance human rights. President Obama has initiated what Williams called 'imaginative encouragement' (1983: 13) in what I would describe as a politics of hope underpinned by a form of utopianism that reminds Americans of their values and encourages them to re-embrace their traditions which were put aside temporarily when America lost its way under the Bush administration. The director of Liberty, Shami Chakrabarti hopes that what she describes as 'the electrifying effect Barack Obama has had on political discourse the world over' will have 'a positive side-effect in British domestic debates about the balance between liberty and security in the modern age' (Chakrabarti 2009: 1). To date there is little evidence of an 'Obama effect' in British domestic and foreign policies. There is, however, evidence of some small but significant changes, for example, the introduction of a desecuritizing logic by Gordon Brown and Jacqui Smith (see Chapter 2) and the Foreign Secretary David Miliband's post 'war on terror' rhetoric (see Chapter 1). When it comes to human rights, however, political leadership in the UK seems to be attempting to introduce a new rationale for human rights which places the 'will of the majority' (Klug 2009: 7) and public security (see Chapter 2) at the forefront of human rights thinking, thus displacing 'the individual', 'the vulnerable' and minority groups from the centre of our human rights culture, which also puts in jeopardy what we are told are 'our' historically enduring core values in Britain, for example, equality, tolerance, fairness and respect for the rule of law. What this implies is that rather than recognizing our shared vulnerability as humans 'as the common basis of human rights' (Taylor 2006: 1) as an expression of the value systems that emerged in response to the catastrophes associated with the Second World War, there is an emergent value system which is attempting to reinterpret and redefine 'vulnerability' in a move to modify, as noted earlier in the book, the application of human rights in the context of what Parekh calls a 'hierarchical view of rights' (2006: 22), which is a component of the attempt by recent British politicians to remake and remould citizenship around a discourse of 'public security' and personal safety (see Chapter 2).

A passage in the *Rights and Responsibilities* Green Paper of 2009 reminds us that the ambition associated with rebalancing human rights or for the modification of the application of ECHR rights to favour the interests of the wider community of citizens over the interests of particular individuals (see Chapter 2) is still part of the Labour government's agenda:

> The government wishes to explore whether a future Bill of Rights and Responsibilities ought to have more prominence to principles such as that under pending Article 17[2] of the Convention; and to the principles of fair balance and the doctrine of proportionality, both of which are inherent threads running throughout the Convention. Such expression would make these principles more transparent to all citizens, and, if enshrined in legislation, could help guide the courts when they come to balance individual rights against limitations necessary in the wider interests of the community.
>
> (Ministry of Justice 2009: 23)

There is little by way of explanation as to why Article 17 rather than Article 2 (the Right to Life, see Chapter 2) of the ECHR is now seen as the potential 'trump card' human right through which all other human rights are to be filtered in the name of 'public security'. The government attempted to contextualize their proposals for the prioritization of human rights in terms of their 'correct' application, by reminding us in the Green Paper that limitations on the exercise of individual rights in the context of specific duties and responsibilities are included in other Declarations and Charters of human rights. For example, the following were listed in the Green Paper: the American Declaration of the Rights and Duties of Man[3] and the African Charter on Human Peoples' Rights[4] (Ministry of Justice 2009: 24). But this move contradicts how some of our leading academics view human rights and the ECHR in contemporary Britain. For Conor Gearty, human rights are the Esperanto of the virtuous, 'they should always be on the side of the underdog' (2006: 157). For Francesca Klug, there is no point in pretending that the purpose of human rights is to replicate what the democratic process can do anyway – which is to give voice to the 'will of the majority' (2009: 7). For Klug, human rights 'are there to defend individuals and minorities, of all kinds, whose voices will never be given equal weight through the ballot box' (2009: 7). It is in the context of this confusion, or complexity with regard to human rights protections, as either giving prominence to the protection of individuals from the state or as giving prominence to the protection of the state and the wider public from 'dangerous individuals', that Britain's human rights culture will unfold in the future.

The government is not alone in their rebalancing discourse on human rights. In 2009 'the finding the right balance' discourse with regard to human rights was also central to Conservative and Liberal Democrat campaigns. In February 2009, in a written statement for the Convention on Modern Liberty, David Cameron reiterated (see Chapter 4) his plans to scrap the Human Rights Act and replace it with a British Bill of Rights which would 'better tailor, but also strengthen, the protection of our core rights' (Cameron, in Travis 2009c: 1). Nick Clegg (leader of the Liberal Democrats) has also released statements in support of his party's 'Freedom Bill'[5] which was launched in February 2009. Clegg has stated in this context that 'for decades, our historic British liberties have been eaten away by governments determined to take more and more control over what we do' (in Travis 2009c: 1); the Liberal Democrats clearly view their Freedom Bill as a corrective against the government's excesses.

Britain, as Conor Gearty has suggested, is at a crossroads with regard to human rights, however, the nature of the alleged threats and dangers that assail the UK are also shifting. As noted in the previous chapter, the global economic downturn is a universal source of uncertainty. I could go as far to say that there is a possibility that the debates with regard to the striking of an appropriate balance between civil liberties and 'security' in terms of civil and political rights might be somewhat overshadowed, if the effects of the economic downturn continues, by debates on the necessity of striking the correct balance between social and economic rights and civil and political rights. There is some evidence that, as Gordon Brown suggested (see Chapter 6), some social and economic rights pertaining to 'health' might not remain 'off limits'. According to Travis, the current Home Secretary Alan Johnson in a speech made in September 2009 to coincide with Liberty's

'Common Values – Common Sense' campaign,[6] gave 'a thoughtful defence of the Human Rights Act'; furthermore in this speech Johnson 'defended Labour's proposals to extend the scope of the Human Rights Act to rights to healthcare access and other issues' (Travis 2009b: 1). By starting the process of incrementally incorporating more social and economic rights and thus extending the scope of the Human Rights Act, the government in this instance is working towards completing Marshall's vision of the three-legged stool of citizenship.

It remains to be seen whether Johnson represents the views of the rest of his cabinet colleagues and whether the government, if successful in the general election, will continue to be restricted by the simultaneous yet contradictory human rights rebalancing projects.[7] One thing is certain that without sustained support for the Human Rights Act the potential next step in Britain's human rights policy (for example, in the form of a Bill of Rights) could lead the country into uncharted waters.

It seems likely, given the government and the opposition's rhetoric on the subject, that after the general election some rebalancing of human rights (in terms of their application) or further calls for the Human Rights Act to be scrapped, will continue. Perhaps these developments, if they happen, could be described as a regressive variant of the jurisgenerative processes described in Chapters 5 and 6. These processes, if they happen, could be understood as being associated with the hierarchical view of rights underwritten by a new version of citizenship, articulated in particularly authoritarian discourses of Britishness and British shared values born out of the politics of fear.

Notes

Introduction: Value Trouble

1. Joppke suggests that what has been described as the essential values of Britishness are in fact the 'nationally anonymous' values of applied political liberalism (2008: 538).
2. A *dispositif* is according to Nikolas Rose, 'a family way of thinking and acting, involving calculations about probable futures in the present followed by interventions into the present in order to control that potential future' (in Aradau and van Munster 2008: 25)
3. That is shared in terms of them being the set of what Parekh calls the 'operative social values' (see Chapter 5) that are established through a wide-ranging and national debate in the process of developing a Statement of Values. It should be noted that the only purpose this author considers that this process should be undertaken is when it is for the purposes of underwriting what the Joint Commission on Human Rights calls the UK Bill of Rights and Freedoms (see Chapter 5).

1   Pre-Emptive Securities – Border Controls and Preventative Counter-Terrorism

1. Please see McGhee (2008a and 2008b) for a more direct exploration of the UK's recent counter-terrorism legislation.
2. According to the House of Lords European Union Committee (2008: 25), Frontex has six statutory tasks to:

    (1) co-ordinate operational cooperation between member states in the field of management of external borders;
    (2) assist member states on the training of national border guards, including the establishment of common training standards;
    (3) carry out risk analyses;
    (4) follow-up on the development of research relevant for the control and surveillance of external borders;
    (5) assist member states in circumstances requiring increased technical and operational assistance at external borders;
    (6) provide member states with the necessary support in organizing joint return operations.

3. According to House of Lords European Union Committee, the Schengen Implementing Committee took effect in 1995 for ten of the member states. Germany, France and the Benelux countries were the five original Schengen states; they were later joined by Spain, Portugal, Italy, Austria and Greece. In 2001 the convention took effect for Denmark, Sweden and Finland (and also for Norway and Iceland, the other two members of the Nordic passport

union). Since December 2007, it has additionally been in force for all ten member states which acceded in 2004 (except Cyprus) – a total of 24 states (House of Lords European Union Committee 2008: 9).

4. The Identity Card Act received Royal Assent in March 2006; the first 'Identity Commissioner', Sir Joseph Pilling, was appointed on 14 September 2009 to be the 'public's independent watchdog for the national ID card scheme' (Travis 2009a: 1).

5. The first major policy announcement made by the new Home Secretary Alan Johnson (who replaced Jacqui Smith in 2009) was, according to Tom Whitehead writing in the *Telegraph*, that ID cards would not be made compulsory for British citizens in the future (2009: 2). According to the new Home Secretary, 'holding an ID card should be a personal choice for British citizens – just as it is now to obtain a passport' (in Whitehead 2009: 2).

6. Britain has allegedly entered into a post-'war on terror' phase. This was marked by an article ('"War on Terror" was Wrong') by David Miliband (Foreign Secretary) in the *Guardian* in January 2009. According to Miliband, the notion of a 'war on terror' was not only wrong but was also 'misleading and mistaken' (2009: 1).

7. This is a comment on the potential 'corruption' of aspects of the data 'on individuals' held in some of these integrated databases. One just has to consider, for example, President Barak Obama's calls for further investigations into the CIA's role with regard to intelligence gathered through the use of augmented intelligence techniques and torture during the Bush administrations' 'war on terrorism' to consider just how 'tainted' and potentially unreliable some aspects of these risk-profiling technologies, which are reliant on integrated databases, could be. Bringing this closer to home, in the UK, at the time of writing, the Foreign Secretary, David Miliband, was attempting to prevent the High Court (in the name of protecting national security) from releasing evidence relevant to the case of Binyam Mohamed which would reveal that the Labour government knew of the illegal treatment of Mr Mohamed by the CIA in a secret prison in Pakistan (Norton-Taylor 2009: 4). It was reported in the *Guardian* that two senior judges (Lord Justice Thomas and Mr Justice Lloyd Jones) have criticized the Foreign Secretary's actions suggesting that 'the suppression of reports of wrongdoing by officials' is tantamount to subverting the rule of law which is 'the cornerstone of democracy' (Norton-Taylor 2009: 4). The High Court has ordered the release of a seven-paragraph summary of the CIA-derived intelligence (which was shared with British officials and perhaps even government ministers) which was gleaned from Mr Mohamed through 'ill-treatment' while in CIA custody (Norton-Taylor 2009: 4).

8. According to Vaughan-Williams, the Frontex strategies Hera I and Hera II can be described as 'pre-border surveillance' and intercept strategies that were introduced in response to unprecedented numbers of African would-be migrants who were attempting to enter the EEA (2008: 67). Hera I (which involved Frontex personnel from France, Portugal, Italy, Germany, the Netherlands, Norway and the UK) attempted to support the Spanish authorities in dealing with an unprecedented number of Africans who had arrived on the Canary Islands in an attempt to enter the EU in 2006 (Vaughan-Williams 2008: 67). Whereas Hera I involved 'conventional border work', Hera II was a strategy dedicated to deterrence in that surveillance planes from Finland and

Italy were flown along the coast and deeper into African territory and patrol boats were mobilized by Italy and Portugal off the West African coast with the intention of deterring 'would be immigrants from making the journey to the EU' (Bailey, in Vaughan-Williams 2008: 68).

9. Jacqui Smith's list of 'Muslim' grievances included grievances about foreign policy, grievances about socio-economic deprivation and grievances based on perceptions/misperceptions of police and law enforcement activity (2007: 15). On Blair government's refusal to recognize the relationship between these grievances and extremism see McGhee (2008a: 61–70).

10. See speeches made by Brown when he was the Chancellor of the Exchequer in McGhee (2008: 70–1).

11. The government reported that they have put in place what they call the Channel Programme which will be co-ordinated by police and local authorities with the aims of identifying those at risk from violent extremism and provide help to them, primarily through community-based interventions (HM Government 2009: 90).

12. According to the DCLG the strategic objectives for the programme (including national, regional and local dimension) are to develop a community in which Muslims identify themselves as a welcome part of a wider British society and are accepted as such by the wider community, reject violent extremist ideology and actively condemn violent extremism, isolate violent extremist activity and support and co-operate with the police and security services and develop their own capacity to deal with problems where they arise and support diversionary activity for those at risk (DCLG 2007a: 7).

13. One could suggest that this process of increasing the representativeness and reaching deep into Muslim communities is the end point of the recommendations made previously by the then Home Office Faith Communities unit in their 2004 report (see McGhee 2008a: 76–8).

2 Building a Consensus on 'National Security': Terrorism, Human Rights and 'Core Values'

1. It should be noted that many aspects of the Blair administration post-9/11 counter-terrorism emergency measures, as noted by Tony Blair in the media briefing on 5 August 2005 (to follow), have been challenged and overturned in the House of Lords and in the Courts including detention without charge of foreign national terrorist suspects introduced in the Anti-Terrorism, Crime and Security Act of 2001 and the initial restrictiveness of control orders introduced in the Prevention of Terrorism Act of 2005 (McGhee 2008a: 18–19).

2. The government has been prevented from deporting foreign nationals if they were at risk of ill-treatment (including torture) in their 'home' or designated receiving country; this was highly likely if the individual in question was deemed a terrorist suspect in their home country or deported as a 'terrorist' or 'terrorist suspect' from the UK (McGhee 2008a and 2008b). See also Chapter 4.

3. According to Roe, the Giddensian concept of ontological security refers to the individual's ability to act and to exist with a stable identity; ontological security, therefore, allows individuals to go on with everyday activities (2005: 782). For Giddens, ontological security concerns 'a person's

fundamental sense of safety in the world and includes basic trust of other people. Obtaining such trust becomes necessary in order for a person to maintain a sense of psychological well-being and avoid existential anxiety' (Giddens, in Roe 2005: 782).

4. At the time that the National Security Strategy was launched Gordon Brown stated that of these other threats 'terrorism is the most dramatic new threat' (2008: 1). However, later in the book, in Chapter 6 and in the Afterword I suggest that the global economic downturn has eclipsed the threat from terrorism, for example, in the *Rights and Responsibilities* Green Paper of 2009, the threat from terrorism was marginalized (in fact terrorism was mentioned only twice) compared to the overwhelming emphasis on the global economic crisis.

5. According to Buzan et al.'s typology, the military sector is about relationships of forceful coercion; the political sector is about relationships of authority, governing status and recognition; the economic sector is about relationships of trade, production and finance; the societal sector is about relationships of collective identity; and the environmental sector is about relationships between human activity and the planetary biosphere (1996: 7).

6. Article 2 of the ECHR is an absolute right. According to Freeden, the absoluteness of a right can only apply when all claimable rights are compatible with all others (1991: 36). According to Freeden, the right to life has been historically extended from protection against arbitrary killing, through including the servicing of attributes without which human existence is impossible (food, shelter, clothing), to encompass dignified human life (by means of work and adequate remuneration, without which human life is substandard) and finally, to full human expression and development (without which human life is impoverished or unrealized (1991: 103)). It is in this extension of the right to life from protection against arbitrary killing to include the wider protections of 'human security' that Jacqui Smith's discourse of protecting 'human welfare' should be located.

7. This is not to say that all of our 'freedoms' have not been constrained since 9/11, this is rather to bring some perspective to the material consequences of securitization and its impact on routine social practices, for example, international travel, see Chapter 1. On the whole, when 'we' travel as international passengers 'we' are reassured by and therefore pleased to be the object of ubiquitous forms of mostly unobtrusive but nonetheless all-pervasive tracking and surveillance practices (van der Ploeg 2006) if it means that 'we' are protected against 'danger' (Bigo 2006). 'We' seem to acceptance what Lyon (2003, 2006) describes as 'surveillant sorting' practices with their divergent effects on different types of 'travellers'.

8. Lord Falconer in his introduction to the Department for Constitutional Affairs *Review of the Implementation of the Human Rights Act* (2006) stated that two cases in particular (A and others v. the Home Secretary in the House of Lords and the Chahal v. United Kingdom case in the European Court of Human Rights in 1996, both examined in McGhee 2008a and 2008b) highlight the impact which human rights have had upon the UK law (Falconer, in Department for Constitutional Affairs 2006: 3). The analysis of the overall effects of human rights on the activities of security agencies according to the Department for Constitutional Affairs' review is that it is the Strasbourg Court (in cases such as Chahal) rather than the Human Rights Act that has had an impact on the

government's ability to deal with 'dangerous terrorist suspects' (Department for Constitutional Affairs 2006: 35). In Chapter 4 I will examine how the Chahal ruling is also central to the Conservative leader David Cameron's calls for the Human Rights Act to be replaced with his version of a Modern British Bill of Rights.

9. This is also suggested by the Department for Constitutional Affairs review in 2006. The public, media and politicians' hostility to human rights will be further explored in Chapter 4.

10. It should be noted that later in 2009, the Foreign Secretary, David Miliband, distanced himself (and by so doing the government) in a high-profile article in the *Guardian* newspaper (see Chapter 1) from 'the war on terror' and the 'new terrorism' thesis associated with it. According to Miliband, the phrase the 'war on terror' was mistaken and misleading because it 'gives a false idea of a unified global enemy, and encourages a primarily military reply' (2009: 1). Miliband is therefore disputing the impression that the 'war on terror' encouraged fighting 'a unified, transnational enemy, embodied in the figure of Osama bin Laden and al-Qaida' (Miliband 2009: 1). Miliband's salutary warning with regard to the effect of 'new terrorism' thinking is that 'the more we lump terrorist groups together and draw the battle lines as a simple binary struggle between moderates and extremists, or good and evil, the more we play into the hands of those seeking to unify groups with little in common' (2009: 1).

11. The 42 day-extension was presented by Gordon Brown as a pre-emptive provision allowing early intervention and a practical provision that will give police the extra time to unravel the complexity of cases (Brown 2008). According to Jacqui Smith, this extra time will allow the police to 'get to the bottom of who and what is involved and then build a case on the basis of the evidence that is admissible in court' (Smith, Hansard [Commons] 11 June 2008: 318).

12. It should be noted that this emergency positive duty of the state to safeguard the lives of those within its jurisdiction was introduced in the clarifications between 'intentional inflictions' and 'negligent failures' in the context of the violations of the right to life caused by the activities of industry before the European Court of Human Rights, especially in the case of Öneryildiz v. Turkey in 2004 (Xenos 2007: 2). According to Xenos, following James Fawcett in his book, *The Application of the European Convention on Human Right* (1987), when considering the European Court of Human Rights judgement in Öneryildiz v. Turkey, one should distinguish between what is the issue in this judgement; for Xenos it is not 'life' that is to be protected in this judgement, this judgement protects 'the right to life' (Xenos 2007: 4).

13. To 'personal safety' should be added other aspects of what 'we' stand for and what 'we' stand to lose, for example 'our' achieved standard of living and 'our' subjective and objective standards of well-being in the UK (see section 2.3).

3   Restoring Public Confidence – Managed Migration, Racialization and Earned Citizenship

1. Graham Watson MEP represents the South-West of England and Gibraltar; he is also the president of the Alliance of Liberals and Democrats for Europe.

2. According to Fekete, over the last two decades, the EU, while encouraging member states to harmonize asylum policy, has also slowly been introducing measures to control 'migratory movements' which in recent years has coalesced into an overall philosophy of 'global migration management' (Fekete 2009: 20). However, that being said, although particular European Commission directives have indicated 'an awareness of the need to co-ordinate immigration matters' they have mostly focused on the entry and stay of third country nationals in the European Union covering employment, family reunification and long-term residence (Home Office 2002: 26). These developments have resulted in what Balibar has described as the development of a 'European apartheid' (2004: x) between those deemed 'foreigners' and those deemed 'citizens' in Europe (2004: 33). Recently, according to Watson, the European Commission has introduced some directives that could be described as examples of 'managed migration' (which will come into force post-2010) which are restricted to the sectors of highly skilled workers, paid trainees, seasonal workers and transfers within multinational corporations (2008b: 76).

3. The civic integration strategy adopted in the Netherlands is rather unusual. According to Joppke, the Dutch government has refused to publish the contents of the citizenship exams and they have not published study guides (like the 'Life in the UK' citizenship test guides) which would offer those taking the citizenship exam the opportunity to prepare (2007: 45). The argument that the Dutch government has put forward to justify this is, 'one cannot study to be Dutch, one has to feel Dutch' (in Joppke 2007: 45). Another unusual development in the Netherlands is the introduction of the Integration Abroad Act 2006, which includes a pre-arrival civic integration test 'to prove assimilability' (Fekete 2009: 80). According to Fekete, this act is directed principally at applicants for family reunification and would-be spouses, mostly Moroccans and Turks (2009: 80). For these tests some course content/materials has been developed. However, aspects of the syllabus of this pre-arrival test have been described as being designed to be offensive to Muslims. According to Fekete, the 'syllabus' for this 'off-shore' test (which must be sat at a Dutch embassy or consulate) includes a DVD titled 'To the Netherlands' which illustrates Dutch life by showing gay men kissing in a meadow and topless women on the beach (Fekete 2009: 80).

4. In the previous chapters I traced the similarities and differences between Blair and Brown with regard to their approach generating a consensus on counter-terrorism legislation.

5. Section 3.2 of this chapter offers a summary of some of these earlier works for the purpose of providing the context for the analysis of the new material to be explored in the next two sections.

6. For example, The Independent Review in Oldham 2001, the Task Force Review in Burnley 2001, the District Race Review in Bradford 2001, The Cantle Report: Community Cohesion Review 2001, Guidance on Community Cohesion Report 2002, The Denham Report: Building Cohesive Communities 2002. For a more detailed analysis of this archive of reports, see McGhee 2005a.

7. Subsequently the Life in the United Kingdom Advisory Group (chaired by Sir Bernard Crick), in their report *The New and the Old* (2003) has proposed that after living in Britain for 3 years applicants for British citizenship will be set

English language and citizenship tests based on their knowledge 'of life in the UK'; as noted earlier, these were introduced in the Nationality, Immigration and Asylum Act 2002. The first ever citizenship ceremonies were held on the 26 February 2004.

8. According to the Home Office, the points-based system will consolidate more than 80 existing work and study routes into five tiers:

   tier 1 – highly skilled, e.g. scientists or entrepreneurs
   tier 2 – skilled workers with a job offer, e.g. nurses, teachers, engineers
   tier 3 – low skilled workers filling specific temporary labour shortages, e.g. construction workers for a particular project
   tier 4 – students
   tier 5 – youth mobility and temporary workers, e.g. working holiday makers or musicians coming to play a concert.

   (Home Office 2006b: 1)

9. In many ways this is an example of the central paradox of neoliberal globalization in migration policies, in that economic globalization both unites and integrates at the same time as it fragments and marginalizes, this paradox is perhaps most noticeable in the fragmentation of 'labour mobility' (Öniş 2000: 283). According to Öniş,

   mobility applies largely to a sub-group of highly skilled employees. Unskilled or semi-skilled workers are usually confined to their national territories and look to their respective governments to improve their living conditions.

   (Öniş 2000: 283)

10. It is difficult to distinguish the government's discourse with regard to the consequences of immigration from the far right propaganda on immigration and its consequences which has been produced by the British National Party.

11. These 'racial' and cultural (especially religious) assumptions are complicated by non-white, non-Christian EU citizens deciding to settle in the UK under the free movement provisions after previously being granted citizenship in another EU state.

12. Just to put these British policies in an European context; as well as the 'off-shore' civic integration test introduced in the Dutch Integration Abroad Act 2006 which targets family reunification in the Netherlands the Danes have introduced the strictest family reunification measures in Europe (Fekete 2009: 83). The Danish Aliens Act 2002, according to Fekete, removed the statutory right to family reunification on the grounds of wanting to secure 'the best possible base for integration' (2009: 83). The Netherlands and Denmark are not alone, France imposed limitations on family reunification and marriage rights after the disturbances of October and November 2005 (Fekete 2009: 83). These restrictions on family reunification and the marriage of spouses from abroad, including the UK's attempts to delay family reunification, are yet another example of the stratification associated with what Arendt called 'the right to have rights' (see Chapter 4) in which some families and individuals have the right to a private, family life under Article 8 of the ECHR and others rights to a private, family life are restricted in the name of increasing integration and reducing 'racial' tensions.

13. The views and concerns of the public were solicited through what are described in the Green Paper as a number of 'public listening sessions held across the UK (in Aberdeen, Birmingham, Cardiff, Croydon, Leeds, Newcastle, Nottingham and Portsmouth). These sessions were hosted by the Central Office for Information on behalf of the Home Office's Border and Immigration Agency. The aim of these events was to engage with the public on key immigration issues including successful integration, how potential citizens should demonstrate their commitment to Britain and celebrating citizenship (Home Office 2008: 11).

14. In a similar vein Lord Goldsmith in his Citizenship Review of 2008 actually called for a 'more rigorous access to citizenship' and that the status of permanent residence should be abolished to ensure that all people who live permanently in the UK share a common sense of belonging 'with the rights and responsibilities that go along with that' (Lord Goldsmith 2008: 77). The theme of rights and responsibilities will be explored in Chapter 4.

15. The latter can be categorized as an example of what Dean describes as the renewed use of sovereign power in advanced liberal democracies (2007: 104) which following on from Chapter 1 is characterized by territorial exclusions, deportations, removals and repatriations of 'undesirable' migrants and foreign nationals.

16. At the time of writing (late 2009) Gordon Brown in his Speech on Immigration at Ealing Town Hall on 12 November 2009 suggested that the managed migration points system for entry would be matched with a points system for citizenship (2009b: 6). It seems that the points based test for citizenship will be part of the temporary migrants application (after living in the UK for five years) for probationary citizenship. According to Brown, at the point of the application to probationary citizenship 'they will pass a points-based test, with evidence of continuing economic contribution, of skills, of progress in English and knowledge of life in Britain' (2009b: 6). In this speech Brown still refers to the 'final test' or more accurately 'meet the final test' when he states the following: 'if after a number of years as a probationary citizen – a minimum of one year but a maximum of five – someone wants to stay in this country, they will have to meet the test of full citizenship or permanent residence – or go home.' (Brown 2009b: 6). In this speech, as noted earlier in the chapter with regard to Brown's speech launching the *Path to Citizenship* Green Paper, there is still no detail as to what the content of this final test will be, or whether there will be a final test at all.

17. For example in the *Secure Borders – Safe Haven* White Paper of 2002 the following was stated: 'the first challenge migration poses is to our concepts of national identity and citizenship. Migration has increased the diversity of advanced democracies, leading to changes in national culture and identity' (Home Office 2002: 9).

18. In this chapter the emphasis has been on the inculcation and assessment of the commitment (acceptance and sharing) of British values in newcomers. In Chapter 4 I will examine developments in the UK and in the Netherlands with regard to extending this inculcation process to all citizens, including established or settled 'immigrant' communities and their descendants.

19. See McGhee 2008a and especially Blackledge's (2006a and 2006b) excellent analysis of the gendered nature of recent 'integration' discourses.

4 Security, Citizenship and Responsibilities – Debates on a Bill of Rights in the UK

1. These questions were partially inspired by Alston who suggested that a meaningful appreciation of the role played by a particular Bill of Rights can only be gained by seeing it in its broader constitutional, social and cultural context (1999: 4).
2. It has been suggested that the New Equalities and Human Rights Commission, headed by the former head of the Commission for Racial Equality, Trevor Phillips, will among other duties, take on the role of exploding the myths and misunderstandings about the Human Rights Act and promoting the constitutional value of the post-war human rights framework (Russell 2007: 6–7), thus helping to prepare the way for the new Bill of Rights (Wildbore 2008: 2).
3. The legal foundations (or lack of them) of Cameron's Human Rights Act scrapping policy have been called into question. According to Klug, Cameron is incorrect when he states that the replacement of the Human Rights Act with a British Bill of Rights and Responsibilities would 'somehow allow the UK government to ignore European Court of Human Rights rulings it does not agree with ... if anything the reverse applies' (Klug 2009: 3).
4. The Chahal ruling is at the epicentre of Labour government and Conservative parties' post-9/11 ambivalence towards human rights in the UK. For many the Chahal ruling has been perceived as protecting the human rights of a suspected terrorist (through preventing him from being deported back to India because he claimed that his deportation would result in him being tortured by the Indian authorities because of his membership of a Sikh separatist organization) over the rights of the general public to security in that the UK was prevented from deporting Chahal. In my previous book *The End of Multiculturalism? Terrorism, Integration and Human Rights*, I have devoted a chapter to the questions of torture, deportation and 'the right to have rights' and the government's attempts to navigate the constraints of the ECHR and the perceived constraints imposed by the Chahal ruling through developing memoranda of understanding with countries for the purpose of deporting foreign national terror suspects (please see McGhee 2008a for more details).
5. There has been some confusion with regard to the role of the Human Rights Act in cases such as Chahal. For one, the Human Rights Act had not been implemented at the time of the Chahal ruling. The analysis of the overall effects of the human rights on the activities of security agencies, according to the Department for Constitutional Affairs' review is that it is the Strasbourg Court (in cases such as Chahal) rather than the Human Rights Act that has had an impact on the ability of states to deal with 'dangerous terrorist suspects' (Department for Constitutional Affairs 2006: 35).
6. For more on the Department for Constitutional Affairs' (2006) Review of the Implementation of the Human Rights Act, see Chapter 2.
7. The JCHR reminds us that some legal rights are explicitly linked with citizenship, for example, the right to vote, the right to passport and the right to consular access abroad. There are also certain rights in any Bill of Rights

which may all apply to citizens, for example, the so-called democratic rights such as the aforementioned right to vote and also the right to stand for election. However, according to the JCHR the place occupied by the category of rights related to citizenship in any Bill of Rights would be relatively small (Joint Committee on Human Rights 2008: 26).

8. Honig describes Arendt's right to have rights as 'a polemical political call' which directs our attention repeatedly to the need for a politics whereby to express and address the paradox (that is, of human rights protections being based on membership and citizenship) 'as it is experienced by minorities, the stateless, the powerless, and the hapless' (Honig 2006: 108).

9. Lord Goldsmith recommended further consideration to be given to extending citizenship ceremonies to all young people and not just new citizens (2008: 97). These 'coming of age ceremonies', according to Lord Goldsmith, 'would emphasise what they had in common; confer a sense of achievement for what they had learned and done as part of citizenship education at school; as well as provide them with a spur to continue to be active citizens' (2008: 97).

10. What they have in mind under 'broad aspirations' is the resolution of disputes by peaceful means, the toleration and respect for others, and the safeguarding of the environment for future generations (Ministry of Justice 2009: 53). These are 'aspirations' for encouraging responsible behaviour in citizens, they would not be legally enforceable.

11. Kite is referring to the inclusion of economic welfare and environmental rights, such as the rights to welfare payments as well as rights to live in a clean environment (2008: 2). It should be noted that the inclusion of these rights (which do not feature in the ECHR) in the Bill of Rights is a departure from the *Governance of Britain* stipulation that economic and social rights would not be included in the Bill of Rights and Duties because their incorporation 'would involve a significant shift from parliament to the judiciary in making decisions about public spending, at least implicitly, levels of taxation' (Ministry of Justice 2007: 61). According to Kite, the suggestion that economic and social rights might be included in the Bill of Rights 'has caused particular concern' (Kite 2008: 2); furthermore, 'a cabinet insider' told the *Telegraph* that 'You can't legislate to say everyone has the right to a job. We are a free market economy' (Kite 2008: 2). It should be noted that the JCHR's response to concerns such as these is to recommend a 'progressive realisation' approach to the new ECHR+ proposed social and economic rights (inspired by the South African Approach to social and economic rights) which imposes a duty on the government to achieve the progressive realization of the relevant rights, by legislative or other measures, within available resources (JCHR 2008: 53). I will explore the inclusion of especially social and economic human rights in a potential Bill of Rights in the UK in Chapter 6.

5   Belonging Together or Belonging to the Polity? Shared Values, Britishness and Patriotism

1. For Giddens, naïve multiculturalism is viewed as encouraging 'people to live as they choose' (Giddens 2009: xii); however, sophisticated multiculturalism encourages all groups in society to recognize the obligations they

have to accept the common framework of law and citizenship (2009: xii). Giddens suggests that the Labour government has 'moved fairly far in the direction of sophisticated multiculturalism' (2009: xii). See also my previous book, *The End of Multiculturalism? Terrorism, Integration and Human Rights*.

2. See a fuller version of this quotation in Chapter 3.

3. The final chapter of this Green Paper can be described as an advertisement for the now postponed, see Chapter 6 debates on British citizenship and 'common British values' which were to take the form of a series of discussion documents and materials to inform this national debate (Ministry of Justice 2007: 59). As noted in the previous chapter, this was to a be 'a process of developing a British statement of values' through 'a range of engagement methods' that were intended to promote 'dialogue with the people of Britain and between the people of Britain' in order to facilitate 'a fuller articulation of British values' (Ministry of Justice 2007: 59).

4. The research and reports produced by the CICC was commissioned by the Communities and Local Government Department in 2007.

5. According to Miller, advocates of the 'politics of recognition' 'argue that a primary aim of democratic politics should be to endorse and promote, both symbolically and materially, the group identities of historically disadvantaged groups, such as women and ethnic minorities' (2000: 4). For Miller this would result in the development of new styles of politics 'in which groups are given formal recognition', for Miller this politics is problematic on a number of fronts, for example, (1) it misconceives the nature of group identities in contemporary society, and could result in 'fixing and privileging some identities at the expense of others' and (2) in the long run this would prove to be damaging to the interest of the minority groups it is supposed to serve (Miller 2000: 4).

6. As a result of this, according to Modood and Kastoryano (2006: 170), the public sphere is not morally neutral, the public order is not culturally, religiously or ethnically blind. 'The game', as I. M. Young refers to it privileges the position of the historically integrated 'majority' cultures at the expense of the historically subordinated or newly migrated folk (Modood and Kastoryano 2006: 170).

7. Preferably in the form of the JCHR's UK Bill of Rights and Freedoms, rather than Jack Straw's British Bill of Rights and Responsibilities and the informal or non-legalistic compromise in the form of the proposed British Declaration of Responsible Citizenship (see Chapter 4).

8. In Kymlicka's theory, he describes the accommodation of not only the diversity of cultural groups but also the accommodation of the diverse ways in which the members of these groups are encouraged to belong to the polity (1995: 189).

9. In this passage Chambers and Carver are referring to William Connolly's project of deep diversity, however, I think this 'project' also describes Taylor's inspirational project in his essay 'Shared and Divergent Values'.

10. All of these were listed in Williams (2007: 237).

11. In this passage Laborde cites Elisabetta Galeotti's theory of liberal recognition and the role of dominating social norms.

12. Thus distancing the process from the employment of British shared values by politicians as a political weapon against minorities who are deemed to be living 'outwith' them, the most striking example being Tony Blair's post-7/7 speeches in which the acts of Muslims accepting and sharing 'British values' became the ultimate measure of 'integration'.

6 Patriots of the Present and the Future – Ethical Solidarity and Equalities in Uncertain Times

1. There is an unresolved tension in Habermas' constitutional patriotism with regard to its contextualization within national cultures. Habermas does allow 'supplements of particularity' (Müller 2007: 10) as noted here (see also Chapter 5) in order for constitutional patriotism to become effective as a form of political attachment. However, at the same time, constitutional patriotism is seen as a 'purification' of the public sphere and political culture more widely associated with a highly critical attitude to national culture (Müller 2007: 38). Perhaps, this is a case that 'national culture' and national institutions of state seem to be a 'necessary evil' for the purpose of a polity's transformation under constitutional patriotism. Müller's understanding of the relationship between 'the national culture' and constitutional patriotism is 'constitutional patriotism does not make the nation-character die; it merely relegates him (or her) to a supporting role' (2007: 42).
2. By 'ethical' Habermas means all questions that relate to conception of the good life, or a life that is not misspent (1994: 122).
3. According to Habermas, it is through the instituting of 'overlapping consensus' in a Rawlsian sense that the constituents of different convictions can have a 'civilized debate' 'in which one party can recognize the other parties as co-combatants in the search for authentic truths' without sacrificing their own claims to validity (Habermas 1994: 133). Rawls describes reasonable comprehensive doctrines, as those doctrines which contribute to the constitution of an 'overlapping consensus' of comprehensive doctrines, in that all these doctrines, both religious and non-religious, support a political conception of justice underwriting a constitutional democratic society whose principles, ideals and standards satisfy the criterion of reciprocity (2005: 482–3). Thus, for Rawls, all reasonable doctrines affirm such a society with its corresponding political institutions: equal basic rights and liberties for all citizens, including liberty of conscience and freedom of religion. Comprehensive doctrines that cannot support such a democratic society, in Rawls' view 'are not reasonable' (2005: 483).
4. Whereas Fraser's recognition paradigm focuses on injustices understood as 'cultural', which are assumed to be rooted in social patterns of representation, interpretation and communication (Benhabib 2002: 69), the redistribution paradigm focuses on those interrelated injustices defined as socio-economic with regard to exploitation, economic marginalization and discrimination (Benhabib 2002: 69). According to Nancy Fraser, over time, the analysis of and struggles for 'justice' around recognition and redistribution had become uncoupled. It was Fraser who took up the challenge of attempting to connect a cultural politics of identity and difference (what she calls a politics of recognition) to a social politics of justice and equality (what she calls a politics of redistribution) by developing a 'credible model' of radical democracy adequate to our time (Fraser 1997: 186–7). This was to be achieved through re-coupling 'cultural politics' with 'social politics', that is, the politics of difference with the politics of equality (Fraser 2003: 8).
5. That is the United Nation's International Covenant on Civil and Political Rights (ICCPR) and the ICESCR. These covenants give the rights proclaimed in the Universal Declaration of Human Rights in 1948 binding legal force.

Both covenants were adopted in 1966 and entered into force in 1976 and have bound the UK in international law since that date (JCHR 2004: 1).

6. This curtailment is evident in statements made in the *Rights and Responsibilities* Green Paper in 2009; however, in a speech made in September 2009, Alan Johnson, the new Home Secretary, referred to proposals to extend the scope of the Human Rights Act to include 'rights to healthcare access and other issues' (Travis 2009b: 1). This will be discussed in the Afterword.

7. That is, ECHR+ social and economic rights.

8. The rights the ICESCR protects are: equality between men and women (Article 3), the right to work (Article 6); the right to fair conditions of employment (Article 7); the right to form and join a trade union (Article 8), the right to social security (Article 9); the right to protection of the family (Article 10); the right to an adequate standard of living, including the right to food, clothing and housing (Article 11); the right to health (Article 12); the right to education (Article 13); and the right to culture (Article 15) (JCHR 2004: 2).

9. For example, the European Social Charter 1961, the Council of Europe Treaty which complements the civil and political right guarantees of the ECHR, the Revised European Social Charter (when ratified) and a number of international treatises which also contain guarantees of economic and social rights including the International Labour Organization, the UN Convention of the Rights of the Child, The UN Convention on the Elimination of all forms of Discrimination against Women and the UN Convention on the Elimination of All Forms of Racial Discrimination.

10. According to Peter Weir, a series of opinion polls conducted between 1991 and 2004 for the Joseph Rowntree Reform Trust suggests that the public wants to secure economic and social rights alongside civil and political rights (2006: ix). The JCHR reported that according to the ICM 'State of the Nation' poll of 2000, which surveyed respondents on what rights they thought should be protected in a Bill of Rights, social and economic rights, many directly related to ICESCR rights, ranked highly (2004: 8). In the 2008 report the JCHR cites the Northern Ireland Human Rights opinion poll of 2001 and the more recent Joseph Rowntree 'State of the Nation' poll of 2006 as an indication of public support for the incorporation of social and economic rights: 'it seems that the rights which have been gradually conferred over the last 60 years or so by the welfare state, such as the right to health, housing and education, are now seen in the popular imagination as being just as fundamental as what are perceived to be the ancient rights of the *Magna Carta*' (JCHR 2008: 43).

11. Many elements of the ICESCR which do not require allocation of resources for their protection are recognized as imposing immediate obligations, for example, obligations of non-discrimination, the right to join a trade union, the right to strike, right to protection against forced labour, the right not to be forcibly evicted without due process of law and the right to be protected against forced marriage (JCHR 2004: 16).

12. The JCHR also states that the broad scheme of the social and economic provisions in the South African Bill of Rights 'is to impose a duty on the government to achieve a progressive realisation of the relevant rights, by legislation or other measures, within available resources, and to report to parliament on the progress made' (2008: 53).

13. The Discrimination Law Review recommended something similar; they suggested that in order to effectively address entrenched discrimination and disadvantage, public sector duties could be simplified by replacing them with a single duty to tackle disadvantage. This would also extend the coverage of public sector equality duties to ensure that public authorities take account of equality issues in procurement, ways to improve equality practice in the public sector and to improve the resolution of discrimination disputes outside of the workplace (Discrimination Law Review 2007: 8).

14. The Equalities Review's ultimate policy objective is targeted redistribution in the form of focusing on those groups deemed to be experiencing persistent disadvantage 'because of factors outside of their control' in order to use scarce resources efficiently (Equalities Review 2007: 6) rather than holding out for a fundamental shift in social relations in line with a new equalities agenda. I will develop this theme with regard to the targeted 'race equality' interventions found in the Community and Local Government Department's Connecting Communities programme under John Denham.

15. The strength of Nancy Fraser's paradigm, for example, is that she exposes certain categories, for example, race and gender, as being 'bivalent collectivities' that cut across the redistribution and recognition spectrum (Benhabib 2002: 69). These intersectional social categories necessitate the recognition 'that being a woman and a member of an oppressed "race" will have consequences for one's standing both in the redistributive scheme and in the recognition scheme' (Benhabib 2002: 69).

16. This statement contains aspects of the CICC's recommendations for moving beyond the habitual modes of thinking and policymaking under an ethos of multiculturalism (see McGhee 2008a: 99–102). In turn, by insisting that the inequality agenda should focus on 'need' and not on outdated ideologies and assumptions, John Denham is reiterating his predecessor's (Hazel Blears) insistence that 'one size fits all' approaches to achieving race equality need to adapt to the reality that different ethnic groups experience disadvantage in different ways (Blears, in Communities and Local Government Department 2009c: 1).

17. Other examples are state-level Bills of Rights adopted in a number of states in Australia which came about through process of consultation and political debate on the role Bills of Rights can play in modern democracies, rather than through particular political upheavals (JCHR 2008: 24).

18. There are many parallels between what these commentators are saying and what Ruth Lister describes as the 'poverty politics' engaged in by 'poverty activists' who frame their politics within a discourse of human rights and citizenship which represents their struggle as a matter of recognition and respect and not just a politics of redistribution (2007: 53). For Lister, poverty politics advocates a human rights conceptualization of citizenship which translates into concrete citizenship claims based upon 'the idea that rights are indivisible or interdependent so that socio-economic and cultural rights are not separate from civil and political rights' (Lister 2007: 53).

19. The intention is that the new Equality Bill will continue to cover race, gender and disability but will be extended to cover age, sexual orientation, religion, or belief, pregnancy and maternity and gender reassignment (Government Equalities Office 2009a: 11). One could say that this amounts to the near

completion of the process which was begun when the Commission for Racial Equality and other statutory bodies were incorporated into the Equalities and Human Rights Commission (EHRC) and new 'discrimination streams', such as sexual orientation, were introduced (see McGhee 2008a: 108–18). There are concerns however that the EHRC which functions as a human rights and 'minority protection agency' is subject to political control over its appointments and its budget (Malik 2007: 77) and is not institutionally independent enough from government to have a significant impact on society. The role of the EHRC could be strengthened by enhancing its independence by making it accountable to parliament through the parliamentary select committee structure under the supervision of the JCHR (Malik 2007: 44). This could lead to the annual review of the operation of the single Equality Act and thus discrimination legislation by the JCHR rather than the 'once in a lifetime' reviews like the recent Discrimination Law Review of 2007 (Malik 2007: 44). At the same time, Barbara Von Tigerstrom has suggested that national non-judicial human rights commission such as the EHRC (rather than the courts) have a crucial role to play in the advancement and implementation of social and economic rights (2001: 141).

Afterword

1. For example, Jack Straw's strategy in an interview in the *Daily Mail* on 8 December 2008 (see Brogan 2009), according to Klug, was an attempt to 'douse fears' regarding the impact of the Human Rights Act, by empathizing with the average *Daily Mail* readers' perspective that the act is 'a villains' charter or that it stops terrorists being deported' (Straw, in Klug 2009: 7).
2. The European Convention on Human Rights states, in Article 17, that

   [n]othing in this Convention may be interpreted as implying for any State, group or person any right to engage in any activity or perform any act aimed at the destruction of any of the rights or freedoms set forth herein or at their limitation to a greater extent than is provided in the Convention.

3. For example,

   [e]very person has responsibilities to his family, community, and mankind. The rights of each person are limited by the rights of others, by the security of all, and by the just demands of the general welfare, in a Democratic society.

4. For example,

   Article 27:

   1. Every individual shall have duties towards his family and society, the state and other legally recognized communities and the international community.
   2. The rights and freedoms of each individual shall be exercised with due regard to the rights of others, collective security, morality and common interest.

5. The Liberal Democrats' Freedom Bill proposes that pre-charge detention should be cut to 14 days, they want to scrap the ID card scheme and remove 'the innocent' from the DNA database (Travis 2009c: 2).
6. For more on Liberty's Common Values – Common Sense (in defence of the Human Rights Act) see http://www.liberty-human-rights.org.uk/issues/human-rights-act/index.shtml.
7. That is, rebalancing project 1, associated with 'the correct' application of human rights (for example, deciding whose rights come first), and with rebalancing project 2 with regard to proposals for extending human rights through incorporating more social and economic rights.

Bibliography

Alexander, C., Edwards, R. & Temple, B. (2007) 'Contesting Cultural Communities: Language, Ethnicity and Citizenship in Britain', *Journal of Ethnic and Migration Studies*, vol. 33 (5), 783–800.

Alkire, S. (2003) A Conceptual Framework for Human Security. CRISE Working Paper, http://www.crise.ox.ac.uk/pubs/workingpaper2.pdf

Alston, P. (1999) *Promoting Human Rights through Bills of Rights: Comparative Perspectives*, Oxford: Oxford University Press.

Amoore, L. & de Goede, M. (2008) 'Introduction: Governing by Risk in the War on Terror', in L. Amoore & M. de Goede (eds) *Risk and the War on Terror*, New York and London: Routledge, 5–20.

Amoore, L. (2006) 'Biometric Borders: Governing Mobilities in the War Terror', *Political Geography*, 25, 336–51.

Amoore, L. (2007) 'Vigilant Visualities: The Watchful Politics of the War on Terror', *Security & Dialogue*, vol. 38 (2), 215–32.

Amoore, L. (2008) 'Governing by Identity', in C. J. Bennett & D. Lyon (eds) *Playing the Identity Card*, London and New York: Routledge, 21–36.

Anderson, B. (1991) *Imagined Communities: Reflections on the Origin and Spread of Nationalism*, revised edition, London: Verso.

Anthias, F. (1998) Rethinking Social Divisions: Some notes towards a theoretical framework, *Sociological Review*, 46: 506–535.

Anthias, F. & Yuval-Davis, N. (1992) *Racialized Boundaries: Race, Nation, Gender, Colour and Class and the Anti-Racist Struggle*, New York and London: Routledge.

Appiah, K. A. (1998) 'Cosmopolitan Patsocial Disorder', in P. Cheah and B. Robbins (eds), *Cosmopolitics: Thinking and Feeling beyond the Nation, Cultural Politics*, 14, 91–114.

Appiah, K. A. (2006) *Cosmopolitanism: Ethics in a World of Strangers*, New York and London: W. W. Norton & Company.

Aradau, C. & van Munster, R. (2008) 'Taming the Future: The *Dispositif* of Risk in the War on Terror', in L. Amoore & M. de Goede (eds) *Risk and the War on Terror*, New York & London: Routledge, 23–40.

Aradau, C. (2004) 'Security and the Democratic Scene: Desecuritization and Emancipation', *Journal on International Relations and Development*, vol. 7, 388–413.

Aradau, C. (2006) 'Limits of Security, Limits of Politics? A Response', *Journal on International Relations and Development*, vol. 9, 81–90.

Arendt, H. (1968) *Between Past and Future*, New York: Viking Press.

Arendt, H [1951] (1979) *The Origins of Totalitarianism*, New York: Harcourt, Brace and Jovanvich.

Arneson, R. (1995) 'Against "Complex" Equality', in D. Miller & M. Walzer (eds) *Pluralism, Justice, and Equality*, Oxford: Oxford University Press, 226–52.

Ashby Wilson, R. (2005) 'Human Rights in the "War on Terror"', in R. Ashby Wilson (ed.) *Human Rights in the 'War on Terror'*, Cambridge: Cambridge University Press, 1–36.

Audit Commission (2003) *Human Rights: Improving Public Services*, www.audit-commission.gov.uk.

Axworthy, L. (2001) 'Human Security and Global Governance: Putting People First', *Global Governance*, vol. 17 (1), 19–23.

Back, L. (1996) *New Ethnicities and Urban Culture: Racisms and Multiculture in Young Lives*, Routledge: London.

Baker, C. R., Graham, E. L. & Scott, P. M. (2009) 'Introduction', in P. M. Scott, R. B. Baker & E. L. Graham (eds) *Remoralizing Britain? Political, Ethical and Theological Perspectives on New Labour*, London: Continuum, xv–xx.

Balibar, E. (2002) *Politics and the Other Scene*, London: Verso.

Balibar, E. (2003) 'Europe and an Unimagined Frontier of Democracy', *Diacritics*, 33 (3), 344.

Balibar, E. (2004) *We, the People of Europe*, New Jersey: Princeton University Press.

Bauböck, R. (1994) *Transnational Citizenship: Membership and Rights in International Migration*, Aldershot: Edward Elgar.

Bauman, Z. (1998) *Globalization: The Human Consequences*, Cambridge: Polity Press.

Bauman, Z. (2004) *Identity: Conversations with Benedetto Vecchi*, Cambridge: Polity Press.

Bauman, Z. (2006) *Liquid Fear*, Cambridge: Polity Press.

Bauman, Z. (2007) *Liquid Times: Living in an Age of Uncertainty*, Cambridge: Polity Press.

Bauman, Z. (2009) 'The Absence of Society', in D. Utting (ed.) *Contemporary Social Evils*, Bristol: Joseph Rowntree Foundation and The Policy Press, 147–58.

BBC News (2006) 'Cameron Speaks Out on Patriotism', 27 January, http://news.bbc.co.uk/go/pr/fr/-/1/hi/uk_politics/4650144.stm.

BBC News (2007) 'Support for Liberties 'Declining', http://news.bbc.co.uk/1/hi/uk/6290867.stm.

Beck, U. (1997) *The Reinvention of Politics: Rethinking Modernity in the Global Social Order*, Cambridge: Polity Press.

Beck, U. (2002) 'The Cosmopolitan Society and its Enemies', *Theory, Culture & Society*, vol. 19 (1–2), 17–44.

Beck, U. (2006) *The Cosmopolitan Vision*, Cambridge: Polity Press.

Benhabib, S. (2001) 'Of Guests, Aliens, and Citizens: Re-Reading Kant's Cosmopolitan Rights', in W. Rehg & J. Boham (eds), *Pluralism and the Pragmatic Turn*, Cambridge, MA: The MIT Press, 361–87.

Benhabib, S. (2002) *The Claims of Culture: Equality and Diversity in the Global Era*, Princeton and Oxford: Princeton University Press.

Benhabib, S. (2006) 'Democratic Iterations: The Local, the National, and the Global', in R. Post (ed.), *Seyla Benhabib: Another Cosmopolitanism*, Oxford: Oxford University Press, 45–82.

Berman, P. (2003) *Terror and Liberalism*, New York: W. W. Norton & Company.

Betts, A. & Eagleton-Pierce, A. (2005) 'Editorial Introduction: "Human Security"', *STAIR*, vol. 1 (2), 5–10.

Bigo, D. (1994) 'The European Internal Security Field: Stakes and Rivalries in a Newly Developing Area of Police Intervention', in A. Anderson & M. den Boer (eds) *Policing Across National Boundaries*, London and New York: Pinter Publishers, 161–73.

Bigo, D. (2001) 'The Möbius Ribbon of Internal and External Security(ies)', in M. Albert, D. Jacobson & Y. Lapid (eds) *Indentities, Borders, Orders: Rethinking International Relations Theory*, University of Minnesota Press: Minneapolis and London, 91–116.

Bigo, D. (2002) 'Security and Immigration: Toward a Critique of the Govern-mentality of Unease', *Alternatives*, vol. 27, http://www.accessmylibrary.com/coms2/summary_0286-25208777_ITM.

Bigo, D. (2006a) 'Globalized-in-Security: The Field and the Ban-opticon', in J. Solomos & N. Sakai (eds) *Translation, Philosophy & Colonial Difference*, Hong Kong: Hong Kong University Press, 72–97.

Bigo, D. (2006b) 'Security, Exception, Ban and Surveillance', in D. Lyon (ed.) *Theorizing Surveillance: The Panopticon and Beyond*, Devon: Willan Publishing, 46–68.

Bigo, D. & Tsoukala, A. (2008) 'Understanding (In)security', in D. Bigo & A. Tsoukala (eds) *Terror, Insecurity and Liberty*, London and New York: Routledge, 1–9.

Billig, M., Downey, J., Richardson, J., Deacon, D. and Golding, P. (2006) *'Britishness' in the Last Three General Elections: From Ethnic to Civic Nationalism*, report for the Commission for Racial Equality, http://www.CRE.gov.uk/downloads/britishness_elections.pdf.

Blackledge, A. (2006a) 'The Magical Frontier Between the Dominant and the Dominated: Sociolinguistics and Social Justice in a Multilingual World', *Journal of Multilingual and Multicultural Development*, vol. 27 (1), 22–41.

Blackledge, A. (2006b) 'The Men Say "They Don't Need It": Gender and the Extension of Language Testing for British Citizenship', *Studies in Language and Capitalism*, vol. 1, 143–61.

Blair, T. (2005) PM's Press Conference, 10 Downing Street, 5 August, http://www.number10.gov.uk/Page8041.

Blair, T. (2006) 'The Duty to Integrate: Shared British Values', Downing Street, http://www.number10.gov.uk/Page10563.

Blick, A., Choudhury, T. & Weir, S. (2006) *The Rules of the Game: Terrorism, Community and Human Rights*, a report by the democratic unit, Human Rights Centre, University of Essex for the Joseph Rowntree Trust, www.jrrt.org.

Blunkett, D. (2001) 'Blunkett Calls for Honest and Open Debate on Citizenship and Community', 10 Downing Street Newsroom, http://www.number-10.gov.uk/news.asp?newsID=3255, 17/12/01.

Blunkett, D. (2002) 'Integration with Diversity: Globalization and the Renewal of Democracy and Civil Society, Foreign Policy Centre', http://www.fpc.org.uk/articles/182.

Blunkett, D. (2004) 'New Challenges for Race Equality and Community Cohesion in the 21st Century', The Institute of Public Policy Research, 7 July 2004, http://www.homeoffice.gov.uk/comrace.

Booth, K. (2007) *Theory of World Security*, Cambridge: Cambridge University Press.

Borders and Immigration Agency (2008) 'The Path to Citizenship: Next Steps in Reforming the Immigration System', http://www.bia.homeoffice.gov.uk/sitecontent/documents/aboutus/consultations/pathtocitizenship/pathtocitizenship?view=Binary

Bottero, W. (2005) *Stratification: Social Division and Inequality*, Routledge: London & New York.

Bourdieu, P. (1998) *Acts of Resistance: Against the New Myths of Our Time*, Cambridge: Polity Press.

Brogan, B. (2008) 'Jack Straw Reveals: Why I Want to Change The Law: The Justice Secretary Opens Up On Greedy Lawyers, Privacy, Human Rights and Responsibilities', *The Daily Mail*, 8 December, http://www.dailymail.co.uk/news/article-1092695/Jack-Straw-reveals-Why-I-want-change-law.html.

Brown, G (2009a) 'Introduction', in M. d'Ancona (ed.) *Being British: The Search for Values that Bind the Nation*, Edinburgh and London: Mainstream Publishing, 20–5.

Brown, G. (2009b) Speech on Migration, Ealing Town Hall, 12 November, http://www.number10.gov.uk/Page21298.

Brown, G. (2008a) 'Security and Liberty can be Protected', 17 June, http://www.number10.gov.uk/Page15786.

Brown, G. (2008b) 'Managed Migration and Earned Citizenship', 20 February, Camden Centre, London, http://www.number10.gov.uk/output/Page14624.asp.

Brown, G. (2007) 'On Liberty, Westminster University', 25 October, http://www.number10.gov.uk/output/Page13630.asp.

Brown, G. (2006) The Future of Britishness, Speech at Fabian Britishness Conference, 14 January, http://www.fabian-society.org.uk/press_office/news_latest_all.asp?pressid=520.

Burnett, J. & Whyte, D. (2005) 'Embedded Expertise and the New Terrorism', *Journal of Crime, Conflict and the Media*, vol. 1 (4), 1–18.

Burnley Task Force (2001) *Burnley Speaks, Who Listens?* Burnley Task Force Report, http://resources.cohesioninstitute.org.uk/Publications/Documents/Document/DownloadDocumentsFile.aspx?recordId=95&file=PDFversion.

Butler, J. (2006) *Precarious Life: The Powers of Mourning and Violence*, London: Verso.

Buzan, B. (1983) *People, States and Fear: The National Security Problem in International Relations*, Harvester Wheatsheaf: London.

Buzan, B. (1991) *People, States and Fear: An Agenda for International Security Studies in the Post-Cold War Era*, London: Harvester Wheatsheaf.

Buzan, B., Wæver, O. & de Wilde, J. (1998) *Security: A New Framework for Analysis*, Boulder and London: Lynne Reinner Publishers.

Byrne, L. (2007) Proposal for Strengthening Visitors Visas, 18 December, http://www.direct.gov.uk/en/Nl1/Newsroom/DG_071924.

Byrne, L. (2008) Border Security and Immigration: Our Deal for Delivery in 2008, 14 January, http://www.ukba.homeoffice.gov.uk/sitecontent/documents/news/Milestones_final_speech_14.1.pdf.

Cabinet Office (2007a) Security in a Global Hub; Establishing the UK's New Border Arrangements, HMSO, http://www.cabinetoffice.gov.uk/~/media/assets/www.cabinetoffice.gov.uk/publications/reports/border_review%20pdf.ashx.

Cabinet Office (2007b) *Fairness and Freedom: The Final Report of the Equalities Review*, http://archive.cabinetoffice.gov.uk/equalitiesreview/upload/assets/www.theequalitiesreview.org.uk/equality_review.pdf.

Cabinet Office (2008) The National Security Strategy of the United Kingdom, HMSO, http://interactive.cabinetoffice.gov.uk/documents/security/national_security_strategy.pdf.

Cameron, D. (2006) 'Balancing Freedoms and Security – A Modern British Bill of Rights', *Centre for Policy Studies*, http://www.guardian.co.uk/politics/2006/jun/26/conservatives.constitution.

Campbell, D. (1998) *Writing Security: United States Foreign Policy and the Politics of Identity*, Manchester: Manchester University Press.

Cantle, T. (2001) 'Community Cohesion: A Report of the Independent Review Team', Home Office, http://www.homeoffice.gov.uk/comrace.

Cantle, T. (2008) *Community Cohesion: A New Framework for Race and Diversity*, revised and updated version, Basingstoke: Palgrave Macmillan.

Carens, J. (2009) 'Fear Versus Fairness: Migration, Citizenship and the Transformation of Political Community', in N. Holtug, K. Lippert-Rasmussen & S. Laegaard (eds) *Nationalism and Multiculturalism in a World of Immigration*, London: Palgrave Macmillan, 151–73.

Carmichael, S. & Hamilton, C. V. (1968) *Black Power: The Politics of Liberation in America*, Jonathan Cape: London.

Carter, S. Jordan, T. and Watson, S. (2008) 'Introduction', in S. Carter, T. Jordan and S. Watson (eds) *Security: Sociology and Social Worlds*, Milton Keynes: The Open University Press, 1–16.

Chakrabarti, S. & Crossman, G. (2007) *The First Victim of War ... Compromising Civil Liberties*, http://www.liberty-human-rights.org.uk/publications/pdfs/the-first-victim-of-war-smith-institute.pdf.

Chakrabarti, S. (2009) 'In 2009, the Fight for Liberty is about to Go Up a Gear', *The Guardian*, 22 January, http://www.guardian.co.uk/commentisfree/2009/jan/22/shami-chakrabarti-modern-liberty.

Chambers, S. A. & Carver, T. (2008) *William E. Connolly: Democracy, Pluralism and Political Theory*, New York and London: Routledge.

Cleverly, J. (2006) 'My Britishness Article in Full', 17 January, http:///jamescleverly.blogspot.com/2006/01/my-britishness-article-in-full.html.

Cohen, P. (1999) Through a Glass Darkly: Intellectuals on Race, in P. Cohen (ed.) *New Ethnicities, Old Racisms*, Zed Books: London, 1–17.

Commission on British Muslims and Islamophobia (2004) *Islamophobia: Issues, Challenges and Action*, Stoke on Trent: Trentham Books.

Commission on Integration and Community Cohesion (2007) *Our Shared Futures*, www.integrationandcohesion.org.

Communities & Local Government Department (2009a) John Denham – Connecting Communities, 14 October, 1–5, http://www.communities.gov.uk/news/corporate/1357214.

Communities & Local Government Department (2009b) Connecting Communities programme Triples in Size – John Denham, 14 December, 1–4, http://www.communities.gov.uk/news/corporate/1412643.

Communities & Local Government Department (2009c) Government Outlines New Plans for Achieving Race Equality in the UK, 24 February, 1–5, http://www.communities.gov.uk/news/corporate/1155518.

Constitution Unit (2009) Constitutional Reform Put on Hold, *Monitor*, Issue 41, http://www.ucl.ac.uk/constitution-unit/files/publications/monitor/Monitor 41_Jan_2009.pdf.

Crossman, G. (2007) *Overlooked: Surveillance and Personal Privacy in Modern Britain*, Liberty, http://www.liberty-human-rights.org.uk/issues/3-privacy/pdfs/liberty-privacy-report.pdf.

Davis, T. (2007) 'Do Terrorists have Human Rights?' keynote address, First International Conference on Radicalization & Political; Violence, King's College, http://www.icsr.info/files/ICSR%20Remarks%20by%20Terry%20Davis.pdf.

Dean, M. (1999) *Governmentality: Power and Rule in Modern Society*, London: Sage Publications.

Dean, M. (2007) *Governing Societies: Political Perspectives on Domestic and International Rule*, Berkshire: Open University Press and McGraw-Hill Education.

Democracy and Civil Society, Foreign Policy Centre, http://www.fpc.org.uk/articles/182.

DEMOS (2006) *Bringing it Home: Community-based Approaches to Counter-Terrorism*, www.demos.co.uk.

Denham, J. (2002) *Building Cohesive Communities: A Report of the Ministerial Group on Public Order*, HMSO, http://www.communities.gov.uk/documents/communities/pdf/buildingcohesivecommunities.

Department for Communities and Local Government (2007a) *Preventing Violent Extremism Pathfinder Fund*, http://www.communities.gov.uk/documents/communities/pdf/320330.

Department for Communities and Local Government (2007b) *Preventing Violent Extremism Pathfinder Fund 2007/08 Case Studies*, http://www.communities.gov.uk/documents/communities/pdf/324967.

Department for Communities and Local Government (2007c) *Preventing Violent Extremism – Winning Hearts & Minds*, http://www.communities.gov.uk/documents/communities/pdf/320752.

Department for Communities and Local Government (2007d) *The New Performance Framework for Local Authorities & Local Authority Partnerships*, http://www.communities.gov.uk/documents/localgovernment/pdf/505713.

Department for Constitutional Affairs (2006) Review of the Implementation of the Human Rights Act, http://www.dca.gov.uk/peoples-rights/human-rights/pdf/full_review.pdf.

Dillon, M. (2007) 'Governing Terror: The State of Emergency of Biopolitical Emergence', *International Political Sociology*, 1 (1), 2–27, http://www.hull.ac.uk/socsci/downloads/governingterror.pdf.

Discrimination Law Review (2007) *A Framework for Fairness: Proposals for a Single Equality Bill for Great Britain*, Communities & Local Government, http://www.communities.gov.uk/documents/corporate/pdf/325332.pdf.

Dodd, V. (2009) 'Communities Fear Project is Not What it Seems', *The Guardian*, 17 October, 4.

Donohue, K. (2008) *The Cost of Counterterrorism: Power, Politics and Liberty*, Cambridge: Cambridge University Press.

Douzinas, C. (2007) *Human Rights and Empire: The Political Philosophy of Cosmopolitanism*, New York: Routledge-Cavendish.

Doyle, J. (2009) 'Minister Accuses Councils over Poor White Communities', *The Independent*, 30 November, 1–3, http://www.independent.co.uk/news/uk/politics/minister-accuses-councils-over-poor-white-communities-1831578.html.

Driver, S. & Martell, L. (1997) 'New Labour's Communitarianisms', *Critical Social Policy*, 17 (3), 27–46.

Driver, S. & Martell, L. (1998) *New Labour: Politics after Thatcher*, Cambridge: Polity Press.

Dworkin, R. (2003) 'Terror & the Attack on Civil Liberties', *The New York Review of Books*, vol. 50 (17), 1–20, http://www.nybooks.com/articles/16738.

Equalities Office (2009) 'A Fairer Future: The Equality Bill and other Action to Make Equality a Reality, Government Equalities Office', http://www.equalities.

gov.uk/PDF/GEO_A%20Fairer%20Future-%20The%20Equality%20Bill%20an
d%20other%20action%20to%20make%20equality%20a%20reality.pdf.

Ericson, R. V. (2008) 'The State of Preemption: Managing Terrorism through Counter Law', in L. Amoore & M. de Goede (eds) *Risk and the War on Terror*, New York and London: Routledge, 57–76.

Etzioni, A. (1997) *The New Golden Rule: Community and Morality in a Democratic Society*, London: Profile Books.

Falk, R. A. (2004) *The Declining World Order: America's Imperial Geopolitics*, New York and London: Routledge.

Fawcett, J. (1987) *The Application of the European Convention on Human Rights*, Oxford: Clarendon Press.

Fekete, L. (2009) *A Suitable Enemy: Racism, Migration and Islamophobia in Europe*, London: Pluto Press.

Fekete, L (2008) *Integration, Islamophobia and Civil Rights in Europe*, London: Institute of Race Relations.

Fekete, L. (2005) *The Deportation Machine: Europe, Asylum and Human Rights*, London: Institute of Race Relations.

Fekete, L. (2004) 'Anti-Muslim Racism and the European Security State', *Race & Class*, Vol. 46 (3), 3–29.

Fenwick, H. (2002) 'The Anti-Terrorism, Crime and Security Act 2001: A Proportionate Response to 11 September', *Modern Law Review*, 65, 724–62.

Fenwick, H. & Baker, A. (2007) 'Constructing the Terrorist Suspect', *New Delhi Law Journal Golden Jubilee Celebrations*, 541–672.

Forst, R. (2007) 'A Critical Theory of Multicultural Toleration', in A. S. Laden & D. Owen (eds) *Multiculturalism and Political Theory*, Cambridge: Cambridge University Press, 292–313.

Fraser, N. (1997) *Justice Interruptus: Critical Reflections on the 'Postsocialist' Condition*, New York and London: Routledge.

Fraser, N. (2003) Social Justice in the Age of Identity Politics: Redistribution, Recognition and Participation, in N. Fraser & A. Honneth *Redistribution or Recognition? A Political-Philosophical Exchange*, Verso: London & New York.

Fraser, N. (2008) *Scales of Justice: Reimagining Political Space in a Globalizing World*, Polity Press: Cambridge.

Freeden, M. (1991) *Rights*, Milton Keynes: Open University Press.

Gearty, C. (2006) *Can Human Rights Survive?* Cambridge: Cambridge University Press.

Gibney, M. J. (2006) '"A Thousand little Guantanamos": Western States and Measures to Prevent the Arrival of Refugees', in K. E. Tunstall (ed.) *Displacement, Asylum, Migration*, Oxford: Oxford University Press, 139–69.

Giddens, A. (1993) *Modernity and Self-Identity: Self and Society in the Late Modern Age*, Cambridge: Polity Press.

Giddens, A. (1994) 'Risk, Trust, Reflexivity', in U. Beck, A. Giddens & S. Lash (eds) *Reflexive Modernization: Politics, Tradition and Aesthetics in the Modern Social Order*, Cambridge: Polity Press, 184–97.

Gilroy, P. (2004) *After Empire: Melancholia or Convivial Culture*, London and New York: Routledge.

Guild, E. (2003) 'The Border Abroad: Visas and Border Controls', in K. Groenendijk, E. Gould & P. Minderhoud (eds) *In Search of Europe's Borders*, The Hague: Kulwer Law International, 87–104.

Gutman, A. (1994) 'Introduction', in A. Gutman (ed.) *Multiculturalism: Examining the Politics of Recognition*, New Jersey: Princeton University Press, 3–24.

Habermas, J. (1994) 'Struggle for Recognition in the Democratic Constitutional State', in A. Gutman (ed.) *Multiculturalism: Examining the Politics of Recognition*, New Jersey: Princeton University Press, 107–48.

Habermas, J. (1997) *Between Facts and Norms: Contributions to a Discourse Theory of Law & Democracy*, Cambridge: Polity Press.

Habermas, J. (1998) *The Inclusion of the Other: Studies in Political Theory*, Cambridge: Polity Press.

Habermas, J. (2005) Pre-political Foundations of the Democratic Constitutional State?, in J. Habermas & J. Cardinal Ratzinger *Dialectics of Secularization: On reason and religion*, Ignatius Press: San Francisco, 19–52.

Hall, S. (1991) Old and New Identities, Old and New Ethnicities, in A.D. King (ed.) *Culture, Globalization and the World System*, Basingstoke: Macmillan, 51–65.

Hampshire Constabulary (2007) *HMIC Inspection Report Hampshire Constabulary October 2007*, http://inspectorates.homeoffice.gov.uk/hmic/Inspections/phase_1_reports_20071/hampshire_2007?view=Binary.

Hampshire Police Authority & Hampshire Constabulary (2007) *Local Policing Plan 2007/2008*, http://www.hantspa.org/lpp_final_290607_june_version.doc.

Hampshire Police Authority Community Affairs Committee (2007) *Safer Neighbourhoods – Counter-Terrorism and Domestic Extremism – Report of the Chief Constable*, http://www3.hants.gov.uk/item_6_-_safer_neighbourhoods_-_counter_terrorism_and_domestic_extremism.doc.

Harris, J. (2009) '"Social Evils" and "Social Problems" in Britain Since 1904', in D. Utting (ed.) *Contemporary Social Evils*, Bristol: Joseph Rowntree Foundation/ The Policy Press, 5–26.

Hayward, A. (2006) 'On Securitization Politics as Contexted Texts and Talk', *Journal of International Relations and Development*, vol. 9, 70–80.

Held, D. (1995) *Democracy and the Global Order*, California: Stanford University Press.

Hillyard, P. (2006) The 'War on Terrorism': Lessons from Ireland' in T. Bunyan (ed.) *The War on Freedom and Democracy: Essays on Civil Liberties in Europe*, Spokesman Books: Nottingham, 5–10.

HM Government (2006) 'Countering International Terrorism: The United Kingdom's Strategy', The Stationery Office: Norwich, Cm 6888, http://www.intelligence.gov.uk/upload/assets/www.intelligence.gov.uk/countering.pdf.

HM Government (2009) 'The United Kingdom's Strategy for Countering International Terrorism', The Stationery Office: Norwich, Cm 7547, http://security.homeoffice.gov.uk/news-publications/publication-search/general/HO_Contest_strategy.pdf?view=Binary.

Home Office (2001) 'Community Cohesion: A Report of the Independent Review Team', Home Office, http://www.homeoffice.gov.uk/comrace.

Home Office (2002) 'Secure Borders, Safe Haven: Integration with Diversity in Modern Britain', Home Office, CM 5387.

Home Office (2004a) 'Counter-Terrorism Powers: Reconciling Security and Liberty in an Open Society', Cm 6147, The Stationery Office: London.

Home Office (2004b) 'Strength in Diversity: Towards a Community Cohesion and Race Equality Strategy', Home Office Communication Directorate. http://www.homeoffice.gov.uk/comrace.

Home Office (2005a) 'Preventing Extremism Together Working Groups', http://www.aml.org.uk/pdf_files/PET_Report.pdf.

Home Office (2005b) 'Controlling Our Borders: Making Migration Work for Britain', http://www.archive2.official-documents.co.uk/document/cm64/6472/6472.pdf.

Home Office (2005c) 'Improving Opportunities, Strengthening Society: The Government's Strategy to Increase Race Equality and Community Cohesion', Home Office, http://www.homeoffice.gov.uk/documents/improving-opportunity-strat?view=Binary.

Home Office (2006a) 'Counter-Terrorism Policy & Human Rights: Prosecution and Pre-Charge Detention (The Government Reply to the 24th Report of the Joint Committee on Human Rights', HMSO, Cm 6920, http://www.official-documents.gov.uk/document/cm69/6920/6920.pdf.

Home Office (2006b) 'Points-based Migration System is Announced', 7 March, http://www.homeoffice.gov.uk/about-us/news/points-based-system-announced.

Home Office (2007) 'Securing the UK Border: Our Vision and Strategy for the Future', HMSO, http://www.homeoffice.gov.uk/documents/securing-the-border?view=Binary.

Home Office Faith Communities Unit (2004) 'Working Together: Co-operation between Government and Faith Communities', Home Office, http://www.communities.gov.uk/index.asp?id=1502454.

Honig, B. (1996) 'Difference, Dilemmas and the Political Home', in S. Benhabib (ed.) *Democracy and Difference: Contesting the Boundaries of the Political*, Princeton, NJ: Princeton University Press, 257–77.

Honneth, A. (2003) 'Redistribution as Recognition: A Response to Nancy Fraser', in N. Fraser & A. Honneth (eds) *Redistribution or Recognition? A Political-Philosophical Exchange*, London and New York: Verso, 110–97.

Hope, C. & Gammell, C. (2007) 'David Cameron: Scrap the Human Rights Act', *The Telegraph*, http://www.telegraph.co.uk/news/uknews/1560975/David-Cameron-Scrap-the-Human-Rights-Act.html.

House of Common (Hansard), 24 May 2007, Column 1428–33.

House of Commons Home Affairs Committee (2005) *Terrorism and Community Relations*, London: House of Commons, HC 156-1.

House of Lords European Union Committee (2008) 'Frontex: The EU External Borders Agency', Report with Evidence, 9th Report, HL Paper 60, http://www.parliament.the-stationery-office.co.uk/pa/ld200708/ldselect/ldeucom/60/6002.htm.

Huntington, S. P. (1993) 'The Clash of Civilizations?' *Foreign Affairs*, vol. 72 (4), 22–49.

Huysmans, J. (2006) *The Politics of Security: Fear, Migration and Asylum in the EU*, London and New York: Routledge.

ICESCR (1966) International Covenant on Economic, Social and Cultural Rights, Office of the United Nation's High Commissioner for Human Rights, http://www.unhchr.ch/html/menu3/b/a_cescr.htm.

Ignatieff, M. (2005) *The Lesser Evil: Political Ethics in an Age of Terror*, Edinburgh: Edinburgh University Press.

Ignatieff, M. (1996) 'Nationalism and Toleration', in R. Caplan and J. Feffer (eds) *Europe's New Nationalism: States and Minorities in Conflict*, Oxford: Oxford University Press, 213–32.

Ignatieff, M. (1993) *Blood and Belonging: Journeys into the New Nationalism*, New York: Farrar, Straus and Giroux.

Joint Committee of Human Rights (2004) *The International Covenant on Economic, Social & Cultural Rights*, Twenty-First Report, 2003–4, http://www.publications. parliament.uk/pa/jt200304/jtselect/jtrights/183/183.pdf.

Joint Committee on Human Rights (2006) *The Human Rights Act: The DCA and Home Office Reviews*, Thirty-second Report, http://www.publications.parliament. uk/pa/jt200506/jtselect/jtrights/278/27802.htm.

Joint Committee on Human Rights (2008) *A Bill of Rights for the UK?* Twenty-ninth Report of Session 2007–8, http://www.parliament.the-stationery-office. com/pa/jt200708/jtselect/jtrights/165/165i.pdf.

Joppke, C. (2004) 'The Retreat of Multiculturalism in the Liberal State: Theory and Policy', *British Journal of Sociology*, 55 (2), 241–50.

Joppke, C. (2007) 'The Transformation of Citizenship: Status, Rights, Identity', *Citizenship Studies*, 11 (1), 37–48.

Joppke, C. (2008) 'Immigration and the Identity of Citizenship: The Paradox of Universalism', *Citizenship Studies*, vol. 12 (6), 533–46.

Kalra, V. S. (2002) 'Riots, Race and Reports: Denham, Cantle, Oldham and Burnley, Inquiries', *Sage Race Relations Abstracts*, 27 (4), 20–30.

Kelly, R. (2006) 'Britain: Our Values, Our Responsibilities', Speech to Muslim Organizations on Working Together to Tackle Extremism Together, 11th October, http://www.communities.gov.uk/index.asp?id=1503690.

Kite, M. (2008) 'Gordon Brown's Advisor Denounces Bill of Rights as "Unworkable"', *Telegraph*, 9 November, http://www.telegraph.co.uk/news/ newstopics/politics/labour/3405947/Gordon-Browns-advisor-denounces-Bill-of-Rights-as-unworkable.html.

Klug, F. (2000) *Values in a Godless Age: The Story of the United Kingdom's New Bill of Rights*, London: Penguin Books.

Klug, F. (2007a) 'A Bill of Rights: What for?' *The Smith Institute*, http://www.lse.ac.uk/ collections/humanRights/articlesAndTranscripts/FK_SmithInstitute_07.pdf.

Klug, F. (2007b) 'The Future: A Constitutional Settlement for Modern Britain?', Smith Institute/Harvard Society Seminar, RUSI, http://www.lse.ac.uk/collections/ humanRights/articlesAndTranscripts/FK_SmithHansardJuly07.pdf.

Klug, F. (2007c) 'A Bill of Rights: Do We Need One or Do We Already Have One?' Irvine Human Rights Lecture 2007, University of Durham, http:// www.lse.ac.uk/collections/humanRights/articlesAndTranscripts/Durham07_ Klug.pdf.

Klug, F. (2009) '"Solidity or wind?" What's on the Menu in the Bill of Rights Debate?' Open Democracy, http://www.opendemocracy.net/article/solidity-or-wind-what-s-on-the-menu-in-the-bill-of-rights-debate.

Kostakopoulou, D. (2006) 'Thick, Thin and Thinner Patriotism: Is This All There Is?' *Oxford Journal of Legal Studies*, 26 (1), 73–106.

Kundnani, A. (2001a) 'From Oldham to Bradford: The Violence of the Violated', *Race & Class*, 43 (2), 105–31.

Kundnani, A. (2001b) 'In a Foreign Land: The New Popular Racism', *Race & Class*, vol. 43 (2), 41–60.

Kundnani, A. (2007) *The End of Tolerance: Racism in 21st Century Britain*, London: Pluto Press.

Kymlicka, W. (1995) *Multicultural Citizenship*, Oxford: Clarendon Press.

Laborde, C. (2008) *Critical Republicanism: The Hijab Controversy and Political Philosophy*, Oxford: Oxford University Press.

Laguerre, M. (1998) *Diasporic Citizenship: Haitain Americans in Transnational America*, New York: St Martin's Press.

Larner, W. (2008) 'Spatial Imaginaries: Economic Globalisation and the War on Terror', in L. Amoore & M. de Goede (eds) *Risk and the War on Terror*, London: Routledge, 41–56.

Lash, S. (1994) 'Reflexivity and its Doubles: Structure, Aesthetics, Community', in U. Beck, A. Giddens & S. Lash (eds) *Reflexive Modernization: Politics, Tradition and Aesthetics in the Modern Social Order*, Cambridge: Polity Press, 110–73.

Life in the United Kingdom Advisory Group (2003) *The New and the Old: Report of the Life in the United Kingdom Advisory Group*, Home Office, http://www.ind.homeoffice.gov.uk/6353/aboutus/thenewandtheold.pdf.

Lister, R. (2007) 'Inclusive Citizenship: Realizing the Potential', *Citizenship Studies*, vol. 11 (1), 49–61.

Lœgaard, S. (2009) 'Introduction', in N. Holtug, K. Lippert-Rasmussen & S. Laegaard (eds) *Nationalism and Multiculturalism in a World of Immigration*, London: Palgrave Macmillan, viii–xxiv.

Lord Falconer (2007) 'Human Rights and Terrorism', Speech to Royal United Services Institute, 14 February, http://www.rusi.org/events/ref:E45740BC85792E/info:public/infoID:E45D3093433F92/.

Lord Goldsmith (2008) 'Citizenship: Our Common Bond', Citizenship Review, Ministry of Justice, http://webarchive.nationalarchives.gov.uk/+/http://www.justice.gov.uk/docs/citizenship-report-full.pdf.

Lord Phillips (2006) Terrorism & Human Rights, University of Hertfordshire Law Lecturer, 19th October, http://www.judiciary.gov.uk/publications_media/speeches/2006/sp191006.htm.

Lyon, D. (2003a) *Surveillance After September 11*, England: Polity Press.

Lyon, D. (2003b) *Surveillance as Social Sorting: Privacy, Risk and Digital Discrimination*, New York and London: Routledge.

Lyon, D. (2006) 'Why Where You are Matters: Mundane Mobilities, Transparent Technologies and Digital Discrimination', in T. Monahan (ed.) *Surveillance and Society: Technological Politics and Power in Everyday Life*, London and New York: Routledge, 209–24.

Lyon, D. (2008) 'Filtering Flows, Friends, and Foes: Global Surveillance', in M. B. Salter (ed.) *Politics at the Airport*, Minneapolis: University of Minnesota Press, 29–50.

Lyon, D. & Bennett, C. J. (2008) 'Playing the ID Card: Understanding the Significance of Identity Card Systems', in C. J. Bennett & D. Lyon (eds) *Playing the Identity Card*, London and New York: Routledge, 3–20.

Mac an Ghail, M. (1999) *Contemporary Racisms and Ethnicities*, Buckingham: Open University Press.

McDonald, M. (2008) 'Global Security after 11 September 2001', in S. Carter, T. Jordan and S. Watson (eds) *Security: Sociology and Social Worlds*, Milton Keynes: The Open University Press, 47–80.

MacIntyre, A. (2007) *After Virtue*, third edition, London: Duckworth Publishers.

Malik, M. (2007) '"Modernising Discrimination Law": Proposals for a Single Equality Act for Great Britain', *International Journal of Discrimination Law*, vol. 9, 73–94.

Malik, M. (2008) '"From Conflict to Cohesion": Competing Interests in Equality', *Law & Policy: A Paper for the Equality & Diversity Forum*, http://www.edf.org.uk/blog/wp-content/uploads/2009/02/competing-rigts-report_web.pdf.

Malmvig, H. (2005) 'Security through Intercultural Dialogue? Implications of the Securitization of Euro-Mediterranean Dialogue Between Cultures', *Mediterranean Politics*, 10 (3), 349–64.

Mamdani, M. (2005) *Good Muslim, Bad Muslim: America, the Cold War and the Roots of Terror*, New York: Three Leaves Press.

Marranci, G. (2006) *Jihad Beyond Islam*, London: Berg.

Marshall, T. H. (1950) *Citizenship and Social Class*, Cambridge: Cambridge University Press.

Mason, A. (2000) *Community, Solidarity & Belonging*, Cambridge University Press: Cambridge.

Massumi, B. (1993) 'Preface', in B. Massumi (ed.) *The Politics of Everyday Fear*, Minneapolis: University of Minnesota Press, vii–x.

McGhee, D. (2003) 'Moving to "our" Common Ground – a Critical Examination of Community Cohesion Discourse in Twenty-First Century Britain', *Sociological Review*, vol. 51 issue 3, 383–411.

McGhee, D. (2005) *Intolerant Britain? Hate, Citizenship and Difference*, Maidenhead: Open University Press & McGraw-Hill.

McGhee, D. (2008a) *The End of Multiculturalism? Terrorism, Integration and Human Rights*, Maidenhead: Open University Press & McGraw-Hill Education.

McGhee, D. (2008b) 'Deportation, Detention & Torture by Proxy: Foreign National Terror Suspects in the UK', *Liverpool Law Review* (Special Issue on Violence), 29 (1), 99–115.

McGhee, D. (2008c) '"A Past Built on Difference, a Future which is Shared" – A Critical Exploration of the Recommendation made by the Commission on Integration and Community Cohesion', *People, Place & Policy*, 2 (2), 49–64.

McLaughlin, E. & Baker, J. (2007) 'Equality, Social Justice and Social Welfare: A Road Map to the New Egalitarians', *Social Policy and Society*, vol. 6 (1), 53–68.

McSweeney, B. (1996) 'Identity and Security: Buzan and the Copenhagen School', *Review of International Studies*, 22, 81–93.

Meer, N. & Noorani, T. (2008) 'A Sociological Comparison of Anti-Semitism and Anti-Muslim Sentiment in Britain, *The Sociological Review*, 56: 2, 195–219.

Merali, I. & Oosterveld, V. (2001) 'Introduction', in I. Merali and V. Oosrterveld (eds) *Giving Meaning to Economic, Social and Cultural Rights*, Philadelphia: University of Pennsylvannia Press, 1–6.

Miles, R. (1989) *Racism*, London and New York: Routledge.

Miliband, D. (2009) '"War on Terror" was Wrong', *The Guardian*, 15 January, http://www.guardian.co.uk/commentisfree/2009/jan/15/david-miliband-war-terror.

Miller, D. (1995) 'Complex Equality', in D. Miller & M. Walzer (eds) *Pluralism, Justice, and Equality*, Oxford: Oxford University Press, 197–225.

Miller, D. (1999) *Principles of Social Justice*, Cambridge, MA: Harvard University Press.

Miller, D. (2000) *Citizenship and National Identity*, Cambridge: Polity Press.

Miller, P. (1997) 'Accounting and Objectivity: The Invention of Calculating Selves and Calculable Spaces', in A. Megill (ed.) *Rethinking Objectivity*, Durham and London: Duke University Press, 239–64.

Mills, C. (2000) '"Not a Mere *Modus Vivendi*": The Bases for Allegiance to the Just State', in V. Davion & C. Wolf (eds) *The Idea of a Political Liberalism*, Oxford: Rowman & Littlefield Publishers, 190–203.

Ministry of Justice (2007) 'The Governance of Britain', CM 7170, http://www.official-documents.gov.uk/document/cm71/7170/7170.pdf.

Ministry of Justice (2008) 'Lord Goldsmith Recommends New Emphasis on the Common Bond of Citizenship', 11 March, http://www.justice.gov.uk/news/newsrelease110308b.htm.

Ministry of Justice (2009) *Rights and Responsibilities: Developing Our Constitutional Framework*, http://www.justice.gov.uk/publications/docs/rights-responsibilities.pdf.

Modood, T. & Kastoryano, R. (2006) 'Secularism and the Accommodation of Muslims in Europe', in T. Modood, A. Triandafyllidou & R. Zapata-Barrero (eds) *Multiculturalism, Muslims and Citizenship: A European Approach*, London: Routledge, 162–78.

Modood, T. (2005) *Multicultural Politics: Racism, Ethnicity and Muslims in Britain*, Bodmin: Edinburgh University Press and University of Minnesota.

Modood, T. (2007) *Multiculturalism* (Themes for the 21st Century), Cambridge: Polity Press.

Monahan, T. (2006) 'Preface', in T. Monahan (ed.) *Surveillance and Security: Technological Politics and Power in Everyday Life*, New York and London: Routledge, ix–xi.

Morris, L. (ed.) (2006) *Rights: Sociological Perspectives*, London and New York: Routledge.

Morton, S. & Bygrave, S. (2008) 'Introduction', in S. Morton & S. Bygrave (eds) *Foucault in the Age of Terror: Essays on Biopolitics and the Defence of Society*, London: Palgrave Macmillan, 1–13.

Mount, F. (2009) 'Five Types of Inequalities', in D. Utting (ed.) *Contemporary Social Evils*, Bristol: Joseph Rowntree Foundation/The Policy Press, 193–202.

Müller, J. W. (2007) '*Constitutional Patriotism*', Princeton: Princeton University Press.

Murji, K. & Solomos, J. (2005) 'Introduction: Racialization in Theory & Practice', in K. Murji & J. Solomos (eds) *Racialization: Studies in Theory & Practice*, Oxford University Press: Oxford, 1–28.

Mythen, G. & Walklate, S. (2009) '"I'm A Muslim, But I'm Not a Terrorist": Vicitimization, Risky Identities and the Performance of Safety', *British Journal of Criminology Advanced Access*, 3 June, 1–18.

Neal, A. (2007) 'Discourse of Liberty and Security since 9/11', Kings College London, http://www.psa.ac.uk/2007/pps/Neal.pdf.

Norton-Taylor, R. (2009) 'Miliband's Actions Harm the Rule of Law, Says High Court', *The Guardian*, 17 October, 4.

Nussbaum, M. (1996) 'Patriotism and Cosmopolitanism', in J. Cohen (ed.) *For Love & Country: Debating the Limits of Patriotism*, Boston, MA: Beacon Press, 9–23.

O'Malley, P. (2004) *Risk, Uncertainty and Government*, London and Sydney: Glasshouse Press.

Oldham Independent Review (2001) 'One Oldham One Future', Oldham Independent Review, http://resources.cohesioninstitute.org.uk/Publications/Documents/Document/DownloadDocumentsFile.aspx?recordId=97&file=PDF version.

Oliver, M. (2005) 'Blair Calls for Task Force to Combat "Evil Ideology"', 19 July, *The Guardian*, http://www.guardian.co.uk/attackonlondon/story/0,16132,1531798,00. html??gusrc=rss.

Ong, A. (2006) *Flexible Citizenship: The Cultural Logics of Transnationality*, Durham and London: Duke University Press.

Öniş, Z. (2000) 'Neoliberal Globalization and the Democracy Paradox: The Turkish General Elections of 1999', *Journal of International Affairs*, 54 (1), 283–306.

Parekh, B. (2000) *Rethinking Multiculturalism: Cultural Diversity and Cultural Theory*, Basingstoke: Palgrave Macmillan.

Parekh, B. (2006) 'Finding a Proper Place for Human Rights', in K. E. Tunstall (ed.) *Displacement, Asylum, Migration*, Oxford: Oxford University Press, 17–43.

Parekh, B. (2008) *A New Politics of Identity: Political Principles for an Interdependent World*, Basingstoke: Palgrave Macmillan.

Paris, R. (2001) 'Human Security: Paradigm Shift or Hot Air?' *International Security*, 26 (2), 87–102.

Peck, J. & Tickell, A. (2002) 'Neo-was Liberalizing Space', *Antipode*, 34 (3), 380–404.

Pettit, P. (1999) *Republicanism: A Theory of Freedom & Government*, Oxford: Oxford University Press.

Portes, A. & Zhou, M. (1993) 'The New Second Generation: Segmented Assimilation and its Variants', *ANNALS, AAPSS*, 530, 74–96.

Privy Counsellor Review Committee (2003) *Anti-Terrorism, Crime & Security Act 2001 Review: Report*, HC 100, London: The Stationery Office.

Puta-Chekwe, C. & Flood, N. (2001) 'From Division to Integration: Economic, Social and Cultural Rights as Basic Human Rights', in I. Merali and V. Oosrterveld (eds) *Giving Meaning to Economic, Social and Cultural Rights*, Philadelphia: University of Pennsylvannia Press, 39–51.

Rattansi, A. (2005) 'The Uses of Racialization: The Time-Spaces and Subject-Objects of the Raced Body', in K. Murji & J. Solomos (eds) *Racialization: Studies in Theory & Practice*, Oxford: Oxford University Press, 271–302.

Rattansi, A. (2007) *Racism: A Very Short Introduction*, Oxford University Press: Oxford.

Rawls, J. (1993) *Political Liberalism*, New York: Columbia University Press.

Rawls, J. (1997) 'The Idea of Public Reason Revisited', *University of Chicago Law Review*, 64 (3), 765–807.

Rawls, J. (2005) *Political Liberalism*, expanded edition, New York: Columbia University Press.

Roe, P. (2005) 'The "Value" of Positive Security', *Review of International Studies*, 34, 777–94.

Rose, N. (1994) 'Expertise and the Government of Conduct', *Studies in Law, Politics and Society*, vol. 24, 359–67.

Rose, N. (1999) *The Powers of Freedom: Reframing Political Thought*, Cambridge: Cambridge University Press.

Rose, N. (2007) *The Politics of Life Itself*, Princeton and Oxford: Princeton University Press.

Rothstein, B. (1998) *Just Institutions Matter*, Cambridge: Cambridge University Press.

Rumford, C. (2006) 'Border and Re-Bordering', in G. Delanty (ed.) *Europe and Asia: Beyond East and West*, London: Routledge, 181–92.

Rumford, C. (2007) 'Does Europe have Cosmopolitan Borders?' *Globalisations*, 4 (3), 1–13.

Rumford, C. (2008) 'Citizens and Borderwork in Europe', *Space & Policy*, 12 (1), 1–12.

Russell, J. (2007) 'Liberty's Response to the Joint Committee on Human Rights: A British Bill of Rights', http://www.liberty-human-rights.org.uk/pdfs/policy07/response-to-jchr-re-british-bill-of-rights.pdf.

Sassen, S. (2004) 'The Repositioning of Citizenship: Towards New Types of Subjects and Spaces for Politics', paper read at 'Transforming Citizenship? Transnational membership, Participation and Governance', at Campbell Public Affairs Institute, Syracuse, New York.

Schinkel, W. (2008) 'The Moralization of Citizenship in Dutch Integration Discourse', *Amsterdam Law Forum*, 1 (1), 15–26, http://ojs.ubvu.vu.nl/alf/article/viewFile/56/78.

Scott, C. (2001) 'Towards the Institutional Integration of Core Human Rights Treaties', in I. Merali and V. Oosrterveld (eds) *Giving Meaning to Economic, Social and Cultural Rights*, Philadelphia: University of Pennsylvannia Press, 7–38.

Sivanandan, A. (2001) 'Poverty is the New Black', *Race & Class*, 43 (2), 1–6.

Smith, J. (2007) 'Our Shared Values – A Shared Responsibility', keynote address, First International Conference on Radicalization & Political; Violence, King's College, http://www.icsr.info/files/ICSR%20Remarks%20by%20Jacqui%20Smith.pdf.

Smith, J. (2008) Counter-Terrorism Bill, House of Commons Hansard Debates, 11 June, http://www.publications.parliament.uk/pa/cm200708/cmhansrd/cm080611/debtext/80611-0004.htm.

Solana, J. (2004) *A Human Security for Europe: The Barcelona Report of the Study Group on Europe's Security Capabilities*, 15 September, http://www.centrodirittiumani.unipd.it/a_laurea/esami/ppsuenu/HSDoctrineEurope.pdf.

Solomos, J. (2003) *Race and Racism in Britain*, third edition, Palgrave Macmillan: Basingstoke.

Soyal, Y. N. (1994) *Limits of Citizenship: Migrants and Postnational Membership in Europe*, Chicago: University of Chicago Press.

Soysal, Y. N. (2004) Postnational Citizenship: Reconfiguring the Familiar Terrain. Paper read at 'Transforming Citizenship? Transnational Membership. Participation, and Governance', Campbell Public Affairs Institute, Syracuse, New York.

Spalek, B. & Imtoual, A. (2007) 'Muslim Communities and Counter-Terrorism Responses: "Hard" Approaches to Community Engagement in the UK and Australia', *Journal of Muslim Minority Affairs*, vol. 27 (2), 185–202.

Steel, D. (1969) *No Entry: The Background and Implications of the Commonwealth Immigrants Act 1968*, London: C. Hurst & Co.

Straw, J. (1999) Building a Human Rights Culture, address to the Civil Service College Seminar, 9 December, http://www.nationalarchives.gov.uk/ERO/records/ho415/1/hract/cscape.htm.

Straw, J. (2007a) Mackenzie-Stuart Lecture, University of Cambridge, Faculty of Law, 25 October, http://www.justice.gov.uk/news/sp251007a.htm.

Straw, J. (2007b) House of Lords Constitution Committee, Meeting with Rt Hon. Jack Straw MP, Lord Chancellor and Secretary of State for Justice, Session 2006–7, http://www.publications.parliament.uk/pa/ld/lduncorr/const231007.pdf.

Straw, J. (2008a) 'Towards a Bill of Rights and Responsibilities', Ministry of Justice, http://www.justice.gov.uk/news/sp210108.htm.

Straw, J. (2008b) Modernising the Magna Carta, Ministry of Justice, http://www.justice.gov.uk/news/sp130208.htm.

Straw, J. (2009) 'Changing the Face of Human Rights', Ministry of Justice, http://www.justice.gov.uk/news/sp280109.htm.

Tamir, Y. (1993) *Liberal Nationalism*, New Jersey: Princeton University Press.

Taureck, R. (2006) 'Securitization Theory and Securitization Studies', *Journal of International Relations and Development*, 9 (1), 53–61.

Tawney, R. H. (1931[1964]) *Equality*, London: Allen and Unwin.

Taylor, B. S. (2006) *Vulnerability and Human Rights*, Pennsylvania: The Pennsylvania State University Press.

Taylor, C. (1991) 'Shared & Divergent Values', in R. L. Watts & D. M. Brown (eds) *Options for a New Canada*, Toronto: University of Toronto Press, 53–76.

Temko, N. (2006) 'Beckett Rejects Links between Foreign Policy and Terrorism', *The Observer*, 13 August, http://politics.guardian.co.uk/terrorism/story/0,1843687,00.html.

Thomas, C. (2000) *Global Governance, Development and Human Security*, London: Pluto Press.

Thomas, P. A. (2003) 'Emergency and Anti-Terrorist Powers – 9/11: USA and UK', *Fordham International Law Journal*, vol. 26, 1193–233.

Thompson, J. (1998) 'Community Identity and World Citizenship', in D. Archibugi, D. Held & M. Kohler (eds) *Reimagining Political Community: Studies in Cosmopolitan Democracy*, California: Stanford University Press, 120–32.

Timmins, N. (2009) 'Foreword', in D. Utting (ed.) *Contemporary Social Evils*, Bristol: Joseph Rowntree Foundation/The Policy Press, v–vi.

Travis, A. (2009a) 'Commissioner Appointed to Oversee ID Cards', *The Guardian*, 14 September, http://www.guardian.co.uk/commentisfree/libertycentral/2009/sep/14/identity-cards-identity-commissioner.

Travis, A. (2009b) 'Labour's Fickle Defence of Human Rights', *The Guardian*, 29 September, http://www.guardian.co.uk/commentisfree/libertycentral/2009/sep/29/labour-conference-human-rights-act.

Travis, A. (2009c) 'Cameron Pledges Bill to Restore British Freedoms', *The Guardian*, 28 February, http://www.guardian.co.uk/politics/2009/feb/28/conservatives-human-rights.

Tsoukala, A. (2008) 'Defining the Terrorist Threat in the Post-September 11 Era', in D. Bigo & A. Tsoukala (eds) *Terror, Insecurity and Liberty*, London and New York: Routledge, 49–99.

Turner, B. S. (1993) 'Outline of a General Theory of Human Rights', *Sociology*, 27 (3), 489–512.

Turner, B. S. (2006) *Vulnerability and Human Rights*, The Pennsylvania State University Press: Pennsylvania.

Uberoi, V. (2007) 'Social Unity in Britain', *Journal of Ethnic and Migration Studies*, 33 (1), 141–57.

Uberoi, V. (2008) 'Do Policies of Multiculturalism Change National Identities', *The Political Quarterly*, 79 (3), 404–17.

United Nations (2007) *Human Security at the United Nations*, Newsletter, issue 1, http://ochaonline.un.org/humansecurity/HumanSecurityUnit/tabid/2212/Default.aspx.

Unwin, J. (2009) '21st Century Social Evils', *The Friends Quarterly*, Issue 3, 2009, 20–9.

Valverde, M. and Mopas, M. (2004) 'Insecurity and the Dream of Targeted Governance', in W. Larner & W. Walters (eds) *Global Governmentality: Governing International Spaces*, London and New York: Routledge, 233–50.

Van den Brink, B. (2007) 'Imagining Civic Relations in the Moment of their Breakdown: A Crisis of Civic Integrity in the Netherlands', in A. S. Laden & D. Owen (eds) *Multiculturalism and Political Theory*, Cambridge: Cambridge University Press, 350–72.

Van der Ploeg, I. (2005) *The Machine-Readable Body: Essays on Biometrics and the Informatization of the Body*, Maastricht: Shaker.

Van der Ploeg, I. (2006) 'Borderline Identities: The Enrollment of Bodies in the Technological Reconstruction of Borders', in T. Monahan (ed.) *Surveillance & Society: Technological Politics & Power in Everyday Life*, London and New York: Routledge, 177–94.

Van Raalten, J. (2007) Country Studies Series: the Netherlands, Coexistence International at Brandeis University, http://www.brandeis.edu/coexistence/linked%20documents/Judith%20-%20Netherlands%20FINAL.pdf.

Vaughan-Williams, N. (2008) 'Borderwork Beyond Inside/Outside? Frontext, the Citizen-Detective and the War on Terror', *Space & Policy*, 12 (1), 63–79.

Vertovec, S. (2006) *The Emergence of Super-Diversity in Britain*, COMPASS Working Paper 25, http://www.compas.ox.ac.uk/fileadmin/files/pdfs/Steven%20Vertovec%20WP0625.pdf.

Von Tigerstrom, B. (2001) 'Implementing Economic, Social & Cultural Rights: The Role of national Human Rights Institutions', in I. Merali and V. Oosrterveld (eds) *Giving Meaning to Economic, Social and Cultural Rights*, Philadelphia: University of Pennsylvania Press, 139–59.

Waldron, J. (2003) 'Security and Liberty: The Image of Balance', *The Journal of Political Philosophy*, vol. 11 (2), 191–210.

Walters, W. (2002) 'Mapping Schengeland: Denaturalizing the Border', in *Environment and Planning D*, 20, 561–80.

Walters, W. (2004) 'Secure Borders, Safe Haven, Domopolitics', *Citizenship Studies*, vol. 8 (3), 237–60.

Walzer, M. (1995) 'Response', in D. Miller & M. Walzer (eds) *Pluralism, Justice, and Equality*, Oxford: Oxford University Press, 281–98.

Watson, G. (2008a) 'Foreword', in C. Gilmore (ed.) *Making Migration Work for Europe*, Bagehot Publishing: Somerset, 5–7, http://www.alde.eu/fileadmin/files/Download/migration-pamphlet-web.pdf.

Watson, G. (2008b) 'Mitigating Risks, Maximising Benefit: Towards a Progressive Migration Policy in Europe', in C. Gilmore (ed.) *Making Migration Work for Europe*, Bagehot Publishing: Somerset, 72–7, http://www.alde.eu/fileadmin/files/Download/migration-pamphlet-web.pdf.

Wæver, O. (1995) 'Securitization and Desecuritization', in R. Lipshtz (ed.) *On Security* New York: Columbia University Press, 46–86.

Weber, L. (2006) 'The Shifting Frontiers of Migration Control', in S. Pickering & L. Weber (eds) *Borders, Mobility and technologies of Control*, The Netherlands: Springer, 21–44.

Weir, S. (2006) 'Introduction', in S. Weir (ed.) *Unequal Britain: Human Rights as a Route to Social Justice*, London: Politico's, ix–xviii.

Whitehead, T. (2009) 'Home Secretary Abandons Compulsory ID Cards', *The Telegraph*, 1 July, http://www.telegraph.co.uk/news/newstopics/politics/5700798/Home-Secretary-abandons-compulsory-ID-cards.html.

Wildbore, H. (2008) 'Does Britain Need a Bill of Rights? *Politics Review*, 17 (4), http://www.lse.ac.uk/Depts/global/PDFs/Does%20Britain%20need%20a%20Bill%20of%20Rights%20article.doc.

Williams, M. (2007) 'Non-territorial Boundaries of Citizenship', in S. Benhabib, S. Shapiro & D. Petranovic (eds) *Identities, Affiliations & Allegiances*, Cambridge: Cambridge University Press, 226–56.

Williams, R. (1983) *Towards 2000*, Middlesex: Penguin Books.

Wills, M. (2008a) The Constitutional Reform Programme, Leslie Scarman Lecture, http://webarchive.nationalarchives.gov.uk/+/http://www.justice.gov.uk/news/sp120208a.htm.

Wills, M. (2008b) 'Kick-starting a National Debate on a Bill of Rights and Responsibilities', Department of Political Science, University College London, http://www.ucl.ac.uk/constitution-unit/files/events/MichaelWills_Lecture05-03-2008.pdf.

Wintour, P. (2008) 'Cabinet Revolt over Straw's Rights and Responsibilities Plan', *The Guardian*, 4 November, http://www.guardian.co.uk/politics/2008/nov/04/rights-bill-jack-straw.

Wolff, J. (2001) 'Fairness, Respect, and the Egalitarian Ethos', *Philosophy and Public Affairs*, vol. 27 (2), 97–122.

Woowiwiss, A. (2005) *Human Rights*, London and New York: Routledge.

Xenos, D. (2007) 'Asserting the Right to Life (Article 2, ECHR) in the Context of Industry', *German Law Journal*, 8 (3), 1–21.

Young, I. M. (1990) *Justice and the Politics of Difference*, New Jersey: Princeton University Press.

Zedner, L. (2005) 'Securing Liberty in the Face of Terror: Reflections from Criminal Justice', *Journal of Law & Society*, vol. 32 (4), 507–33.

Žižek, S. (2002) *Welcome to the Desert of the Real*, London and New York: Verso.

Index